VALKYRIE
THE NORTH AMERICAN
XB-70

GRAHAM M SIMONS

Pen & Sword
AVIATION

First published in Great Britain in 2011
and again in this format in 2012 by
PEN & SWORD AVIATION
An imprint of
Pen & Sword Books Ltd
47 Church Street
Barnsley
South Yorkshire
S70 2AS

ISBN 978 1 84884 546 6

A CIP catalogue record for this book is
available from the British Library

Printed and bound in England
By CPI Group (UK) Ltd, Croydon, CR0 4YY

Pen & Sword Books Ltd incorporates the Imprints of Pen & Sword Aviation,
Pen & Sword Family History, Pen & Sword Maritime, Pen & Sword Military,
Pen & Sword Discovery, Wharncliffe Local History, Wharncliffe True Crime,
Wharncliffe Transport, Pen & Sword Select, Pen & Sword Military Classics,
Leo Cooper, The Praetorian Press, Remember When,
Seaforth Publishing and Frontline Publishing

For a complete list of Pen & Sword titles please contact
PEN & SWORD BOOKS LIMITED
47 Church Street, Barnsley, South Yorkshire, S70 2AS, England
E-mail: enquiries@pen-and-sword.co.uk
Website: www.pen-and-sword.co.uk

CONTENTS

ACKNOWLEDGEMENTS

A project of this nature could not be undertaken without considerable help from many organizations and individuals. Special thanks must go to Tom Brewer, formerly of the Air Force Museum Foundataion Inc, and later the National Museum of the US Air Force for much help and assistance over the years. Thanks also to the staff of the John F Kennedy Presidential Library, the staff of the Lyndon B Johnson Presidental Library, the staff of the Air Force Historical Studies Office, the staff of the NASA History Office, the History Office of Edwards Air Force Base, North American Aviation, and North American Rockwell.

The author is indebted to many people and organisations for providing photographs for this book, many of which are in the public domain. In some cases it has not been possible to identify the original photographer and so credits are given in the appropriate places to the immediate supplier. If any of the pictures have not been correctly credited, the author apologises.

INTRODUCTION

The first time anyone sees the sole surviving XB-70A Valkyrie it's hard not to be struck dumb by the jaw-droppingly amazing shape of this totally futuristic other-worldly looking aircraft.

Firstly, it's huge. The aircraft is five times heavier and a whole lot larger than the MiG 25 fox bat or SR-71 Blackbird , the design's nearest rivals. Secondly it looks fast. The first time I saw Air Vehicle One was outside the USAF Museum (as it then was) at Wright Field, near Dayton Ohio, in 1980 - it looked as if it was about to go supersonic just parked there! At the time it was playing one of a pair of 'bookends' outside the main building to a later generation Rockwell B-1 'Bone' and the Valkyrie still looked the more advanced!

Thirdly, the aircraft was one very big leap-into-the-future design that pushed the envelope in terms of exotic materials used - such as stainless steel honeycomb, very large amounts of titanium, the use of tool steel for structural components and it would have used the chemical high energy 'zip' fuel if that had not been cancelled.

At one stage - if all the plans and rhetoric had come to fruition - there would have been 250 Valkyries in the air - the pinnacle of General Curtis LeMay's quest for the ultimate strategic bomber operated by his Strategic Air Command.

It has been said that the beginning of the XB-70 story was the search for a nuclear-powered bomber - that started with a highly modified Consolidated B-36 Peacemaker, the design of which came from World War Two when it looked as if the USA would have to fight a two front war from bases only on the mainland. The B-36 was the first interim bomber, replaced almost as soon as it appeared by the Boeing B-52 Stratofortress, itself the second interim design, albeit jet-powered, but it was still subsonic.

The sole surviving XB-70 was retired to the Air Force Museum in February 1969 and spent many years outside in the harsh Ohio climate. *(author)*

The Convair B-58 Hustler came out of the preliminary studies and was supersonic - but at best it could only be called a medium bomber and was too much, too soon. It became a maintenance nightmare, as any crew chief from the time will tell you.

62-0001 was re-painted in the 1980s, and poses here for the obligatory 'Museum Portrait'. (USAF)

What General Curtis LeMay wanted was a machine with the speed of the B-58 and the load-carrying capacity of the B-52 - and without doubt the B-70 looked like it would fulfill his needs. What LeMay got was possibly the biggest fight he ever had experienced - with Robert McNamara and his team of 'Whiz Kids'. This small, elite band of civilians, who had mainly moved over from either the RAND Corporation or the Ford Motor Company and went right to the heart of the John F Kennedy and Lyndon B Johnson presidential administrations. The Whiz Kids invented a world where all decisions could be made based on numbers - an ideal that is still skirted on by many MBA programs and consulting firms. They found power and comfort in assigning values to what could be quantified and deliberately ignored everything else.

The B-70 was cut back to two experimental aircraft - with the possibility of a further machine, as a prototype to the 'Reconnaissance Strike' concept. It was also to be used as a test aircraft in the American ego-driven 'Mach number too far' SuperSonic Transport that was doomed to failure.

Of the two built, one was lost - and two highly experienced test pilots were killed - during what politicians called an illegal flight, despite the same type of event happening many times before.

The revealed story is one of ambition, dreams, spying, and dirty pool politics on Capitol Hill – so nothing unusual there then!

'*Cecil the sea-sick sea serphent*' may have been one of the silliest nicknames ever given to an aircraft, but what an aircraft, what a shape, what a design!

Graham M Simons
Peterborough, England

BACKGROUND

It was the 1950s. Elvis Presley was rocking the world with *Hound Dog,* The Kings of Rythm featuring a guitarist called Ike Turner had already smoked up a storm with *Rocket 88,* Senator Joseph McCarthy saw Reds under every bed and Cadillacs had tail fins that grew larger and longer with every model. It was a time of contrasting optimism, paranoia and consumerism – and the United States of America was aiming at becoming the world's only superpower.

Meanwhile, on the drawing boards of North American Aviation (NAA) in Southern California, a new incredible design was taking shape for a Mach 3 strategic bomber – the B-70 Valkyrie.

The concept of strategic bombing goes back to Harold Lee George. An American aviation pioneer and an outspoken proponent of the industrial web theory, George taught at the Air Corps Tactical School (ACTS) and through his teachings, influenced a significant group of airmen passing through it – ones who were to have powerful influences during and after World War Two. He has been described as the leader of the so-called 'Bomber Mafia', a group of men who advocated an independent military arm composed of heavy bombers.

George studied aeronautics at Princeton University and learned to fly at Love Field, Texas, getting his wings on 29 March 1918. He went to France that September with an initial assignment to the 7th Aviation Instruction Center at Clermont. Two months later he was posted to the Meuse-Argonne front, piloting a bomber with the 163rd Bomb Squadron, 2nd Day Bombardment Group. In the one week that it saw action, the 163rd flew 69 sorties. George observed that massed bombers, flying in formation, swamped enemy defences and so reduced the attacker's casualties.

In France, George met William 'Billy' Mitchell and became convinced that Mitchell's vision of an independent Air Force was the best future direction for the American military.

Lieutenant General Harold Lee George. (19 July 1893 – 24 February 1986) seen during his latter years. George was one of America's first proponents of daylight precision bombing by an independent air arm. *(USAF)*

After the war, George was assigned to the 49th Bombardment Squadron at Kelly Field, Texas, where he was promoted to First Lieutenant in April 1921. He next served with the 14th Bombardment Squadron at Langley Field, Virginia, and with the Aberdeen Proving Ground, Maryland. From 1921 to 1923, George assisted Mitchell in his bombing demonstration against old battleships, and helped develop air-to-ship tactics. In August 1925, George went to Washington as chief of the Bombardment Section in the United States Army Air Corps Operations Division.

In July 1929, George was ordered to Hawaii for two years with the 5th Composite Group at Luke Field, serving Pearl Harbor. In September 1931, he went to Maxwell Field, Alabama, to study at the ACTS, where he helped refine the precision daylight bomber doctrine taught there. Following graduation, George became an instructor at ACTS, teaching air tactics and precision bombing doctrine and became *de facto* leader of the influential 'Bomber Mafia'. With Haywood S Hansell, Laurence S Kuter and Donald Wilson, George researched, debated and finally codified what the men believed would be a war-winning strategy that Wilson had termed as the 'industrial web theory'. This was a military concept which stated that an enemy's industrial power could be attacked at nodes of vulnerability, and thus the enemy's ability to wage a lengthy war could be severely limited and his morale – his will to resist – brought down.

In 1934, George was made director of the Department of Air Tactics and Strategy, and vigorously promoted the doctrine of precision bombing. It was through his directorship of ACTS, that George became known as the unofficial leader of the men in the USAAC who closed ranks and pushed exclusively toward the concept of daylight precision bombing as a strategic, war-winning doctrine using massed air fleets of heavy bombers commanded independently of naval or ground warfare needs. This concept was to influence more than a generation of thinkers within the USAAC, USAAF and even the USAF and, apart from a period when the USAAC adopted the RAF-style area bombing tactics using B-29s over Japan that cumulated in the dropping of the two atomic bombs in August 1945, continued right through to the 1970s and *Linebacker II* missions over Vietnam. It was also to strongly influence the designers and manufacturers of bomber aircraft.

George was promoted to Major in July 1936. He graduated from the Command and General Staff School at Fort Leavenworth, Kansas, the following year and returned to Langley as commanding officer of the General Headquarters (GHQ) Air Corps 96th Bombardment Squadron. George flew to South America as a part of a series of USAAC goodwill flights in February 1938 and November 1939. In 1940, he took command of the 2nd Bombardment Group.

The industrial web theory was put into concrete form by the Air War Plans Division. The plan was submitted for approval to the Joint Army-Navy Board in mid-1941 as AWPD-1, standing for Air War Plans Division, plan number one. A refinement to AWPD-1 came in August 1942 after eight months of direct American involvement in World War Two. The new plan was called AWPD-42 and was submitted to the Combined Chiefs of Staff. Neither AWPD-1 nor AWPD-42 were approved as combat battle plans or strategies – they were simply accepted as guidelines for the production of war materiel necessary to carry out intended or subsequent plans. Finally in 1943, a plan was hammered out in meetings between American and British war planners. The industrial web theory would be put into practical plan form with the Anglo-American Combined Bomber Offensive (CBO).

In the event, the industrial web theory failed to achieve its goals. Various targets were chosen and attacked serially, without evaluating the results in light of their interdependence. American bombing leaders maintained that precision attacks were being carried out, but in early 1944 poor weather over Europe prevented visual sighting, and bombs were dropped indiscriminately by inaccurate radar methods through cloud cover, resulting in general population destruction. By September 1944, all pretence to precision was abandoned when General Dwight D. Eisenhower ordered the area bombing of Berlin. By that time, bombing was not so much strategic as it was tactical, to soften Germany for invasion by

General George Churchill Kenney (6 August 1889 – 9 August 1977), the first Commander of Strategic Air Command. *(USAF)*

ground troops. Thousand-bomber raids were not able to diminish industrial production of war materiel in time to prevent invasion, for when German arms production finally faltered in the third quarter of 1944, only 30% of the total of eventual bomb tonnage had been dropped on the country – this after the French-German border had been reached and the war on the ground had seen its decisive breakthrough.

Germany was conquered by invasion; it did not surrender as a result of bombing; the morale of the enemy was not significantly affected. No population that was bombed in World War Two lost their will to resist. In the Pacific, it was the Emperor, not the people, who decided Japan must surrender.

Despite its failures in practice, the strategic bombing concept of targeting crucial industrial bottlenecks became the first core doctrine of the independent United States Air Force in 1947.

Strategic Air Command

Strategic bombing proponents – in particular General Curtis E LeMay – continued to promote the doctrine into the nuclear age, forming Strategic Air Command (SAC) to carry out a vision modified to fit the needs of the Cold War and the threat of nuclear warfare.

SAC's original headquarters was Bolling Field, the headquarters of the disestablished Continental Air Forces (CAF) in Washington, DC. The headquarters organization of CAF was designated Strategic Air Command. Its first commander was General George C. Kenney. Ten days later, Fifteenth Air Force was assigned to the command as its first Numbered Air Force. In June 1946 Eighth Air Force was assigned. SAC HQ moved to Andrews AFB, MD on 20 October 1946.

General Curtis Emerson LeMay (15 November 1906 – 1 October 1990). LeMay had a stellar career in the Air Force. *(USAF)*

It was created with the stated mission of providing long range bombing capabilities anywhere in the world, but because of multiple factors including the massive post World War Two demobilization and Kenney's unhappiness with being assigned to SAC, for the first two years of its existence, SAC existed mainly on paper. During this period, the United States Air Force itself was established on 18 September 1947. The situation began to change when on 19 October 1948, then-Lieutenant General Curtis LeMay – who was only a lowly 1st Lieutenant ten years earlier, such was his meteoric rise in rank – assumed leadership of the SAC. Soon after taking command, on 9 November, LeMay relocated SAC to Offutt AFB, south of Omaha Nebraska. It was under the leadership of LeMay that SAC developed the technical capabilities, strategic planning and operational readiness to carry out its stated mission of being able to strike anywhere in the world. Specifically, during LeMay's command, SAC embraced and integrated new technological developments in the areas of in-flight refueling, jet engines, and ballistic missiles into its operations.

LeMay had a number of nicknames: 'Boom-Boom LeMay', 'Old Iron Pants', 'Bombs Away LeMay' and probably the most telling,

'Old Iron Balls'. During World War Two he fought in both the European and Pacific Theatres, before returning to Europe in 1948 to head up the American part of the Berlin Airlift.

In 1948, when he returned to the USA to head the SAC, it consisted of little more than a few understaffed B-29 bombardment groups left over from World War Two. Less than half of the available aircraft were operational, and the crews were undertrained. When LeMay ordered a mock bombing exercise on Dayton, Ohio, most bombers missed their targets by at least one mile. *'We didn't have one crew, not one crew, in the entire command who could do a professional job'* noted LeMay.

The main fleets of combat aircraft that went to make up SAC were Convair B-36 Peacemakers, Boeing B-47 Stratojets and Boeing B-52 Stratofortresses.

The massive B-36 Peacemaker was a strategic bomber built by Convair and operated solely by the USAF. The B-36 was the largest mass-produced piston engine aircraft ever made, although its six piston engines were supplemented by four jet engines in two pods. It had the longest wingspan of any combat aircraft ever built, 230 feet, although there have been larger military transports. The B-36 was the first bomber capable of delivering nuclear weapons that fitted inside the bomb bay without aircraft modifications. With a range greater than 6,000 miles and a maximum payload of 72,000 lb, the B-36 was also the first operational bomber with an truly intercontinental range. The B-36, including its GRB-36, RB-36, and XC-99 variants, was in service as part of the SAC from 1948 to 1959.

The Boeing B-47 arose from a informal 1943 requirement for a jet powered reconnaissance bomber, drawn up by the USAAF to prompt manufacturers to start research into jet bombers. Boeing was one a number of companies to respond to this request, with its initial design, the Model 424, basically a scaled-down version of the piston-engined Boeing B-29 Superfortress, but equipped with four jet engines. During the following year, this concept evolved into a formal request-for-proposal to design a new bomber with a specified maximum speed of 550 mph, a cruise speed of 450 mph, a range of 3,500 miles and a service ceiling of 45,000 ft.

Six turning and four burning – Consolidated's enormous B-36 Peacemaker. *(USAF)*

The interior of a previous generation six-engined bomber – the Consolidated B-36, this example being 52-2220 which is preserved at the National Museum of the Air Force in Dayton, Ohio. *(author)*

After the design had passed through numerous stages, the USAAF finally placed an order in April 1946 for two prototypes, to be designated 'XB-47'. Assembly began in June 1947 and the first XB-47 was rolled out on 12 September. The XB-47 prototype made its first flight on 17 December 1947 with the test pilots Robert Robbins and Scott Osler at the controls. SAC was to operate B-47 Stratojets (B-47s, EB-47s, YRB-47s and RB-47s) from 1951 through 1965.

Beginning with the successful contract bid on 5 June 1946, the B-52 Stratofortress design evolved from a straight-wing aircraft powered by six turboprop engines to the final prototype YB-52 with eight turbojet engines. The aircraft first flew on 15 April 1952 with 'Tex' Johnston as pilot. Built to carry nuclear weapons for Cold War-era deterrence missions, the B-52 Stratofortress replaced the Convair B-36. Although a veteran of a number of wars, the Stratofortress has dropped only conventional munitions in combat and carries up to 70,000 pounds of weapons. Its Stratofortress name is rarely used outside on official use; it has been referred to by Air Force personnel as the BUFF – Big Ugly Fat Fucker, and is still in service in the second decade of the 21st century.

Upon receiving his fourth star in 1951 at age 44, LeMay became the youngest four-star General in American history since Ulysses S. Grant and was the youngest four-star General in modern history as well as the longest serving in that rank. In 1956 and 1957 LeMay implemented tests of 24-hour bomber and tanker alerts, keeping some bomber forces ready at all times. LeMay headed SAC until 1957, overseeing its transformation into a modern, efficient, all-jet force. LeMay's tenure was the longest over a military command in close to a hundred years.

The historical record indicates that LeMay advocated justified pre-emptive – or the so-called 'First Strike' – nuclear war. Several documents dating from the period during which he commanded SAC show LeMay advocating pre-

The Boeing B-47
Stratojet. *(USAF)*

emptive attack of the Soviet Union, had it become clear that the Soviets were preparing to attack SAC and/or the United States. In these documents, which were often the transcripts of speeches before groups such as the National War College or events such as the 1955 Joint Secretaries Conference at the Quantico Marine Corps Base, LeMay clearly advocated using SAC as a pre-emptive weapon if and when such was necessary. However, unlike popular belief that has grown up over the years, there is little evidence to suggest that LeMay ever advocated an unauthorized or unjustified nuclear attack on the Soviet Union in the manner of a renegade officer launching a nuclear attack without Presidential permission. To the contrary, a December 1949 letter from LeMay to the Air Force Chief of Staff General Hoyt Vandenberg indicates that LeMay was concerned with having explicit authority from the nation's political leadership to launch a preemptive strike against the Soviet Union. This letter, in LeMay's files at the Library of Congress, shows LeMay being unwilling to operate outside the authority afforded him as a military officer and that he also recognized the constitutional role political leadership played in the decision to initiate war.

LeMay was appointed Vice Chief of Staff of the United States Air Force in July 1957, serving until 1961, when he was made the fifth Chief of Staff of the United States Air Force on the retirement of Gen Thomas White. His belief in the efficacy of strategic air campaigns over tactical strikes and ground support operations became Air Force policy during his tenure as Chief of Staff.

As Chief of Staff, LeMay clashed repeatedly with Secretary of Defense Robert McNamara, Air Force Secretary Eugene Zuckert, and the chairman of the Joint Chiefs of Staff, Army General Maxwell Taylor. At the time, budget constraints and a number of successive nuclear war fighting strategies had left the armed forces in a state of flux. Each of the forces had gradually jettisoned realistic appraisals of future conflicts in favour of developing its own separate nuclear and non-nuclear capabilities. At the height of this struggle, the US Army had even reorganized its combat divisions to fight land wars on irradiated nuclear battlefields, developing short-range atomic cannon and mortars in order to win

The Boeing B-52 Stratofortress. *(USAF)*

appropriations. The United States Navy in turn proposed delivering strategic nuclear weapons from supercarriers intended to sail into range of the Soviet air defense forces. Of all these various schemes, only LeMay's command structure of SAC survived complete reorganization in the changing reality of postwar conflicts.

An apology

It is from this point that the reader is forced to enter the confusing and murky world of military initialisms, jargon and acronyms that was so popular in the 1950s and 60s. The US defence establishment – both civilian and military – seems to have loved reducing names, departments and organisations down to a confusing set of letters during this time. There appears to have been no universal agreement on the precise definition of the various terms, nor in their written usage. It seems that they used individual letters or parts of words to create new, shortened 'words' that have been listed in a glossary elsewhere; most are mercifully short. We should be thankful that the B-70 was for the US Air Force, otherwise this book might include ADCOMSUBORDCOMPHIBSPAC, which was a United States Navy term that supposedly stands for 'Administrative Command, Amphibious Forces, Pacific Fleet Subordinate Command'!

Finding a B-52 replacement – the first competition.

It was during his nine-year tenure with SAC that LeMay helped shape the development of America's strategic all-jet bomber force. LeMay's vision was focused on the future – the 1965 to 1975 time period, when the jet bombers currently in service would need to be supplemented and ultimately replaced by newer types due to their obsolescence.

LeMay began to plan requirements for a new jet- powered bomber weapon system, one with the range and pay load of the B-52 and the speed of the B-58, the world's first supersonic bomber, capable of Mach 2 dash speed. He was convinced that such a bomber was technically feasible and he pursued its creation.

The Convair B-58
Hustler. *(USAF)*

Although Convair's B-58 was more advanced and faster than Boeing's B-52, it was ordered into production as a supplement rather than a replacement and was also regarded as being obsolete in the time period of 1965-75.

SAC – and LeMay in particular – sent Headquarters USAF a series of requirement letters, calling for the development of a manned intercontinental heavy strategic bomber weapon system to follow the B-52. It was presumed that the proposed bomber would be a 'split mission' aircraft that would fly subsonically like the B-52 to the enemy early warning line, then 'dash' supersonically like the B-58 to the target. It would then withdraw from the target area subsonically.

On 14 October 1954, HQ USAF published General Operational Requirement (GOR) No. 38 for a Piloted Intercontinental Strategic Bombardment Weapon System. As GOR 38 stipulated, the advanced bomber was to be all-chemical-fueled, was to fully replace the B-52, and was to be active in SAC inventory in the 1965-75 timeframe. The Air Force, the National Advisory Committee on Aeronautics (NACA – now the National Aeronautics and Space Administration (NASA)), and six selected airframe contractors had studied this proposed weapon system for at least two years under Secret Project MX-2145 before GOR 38 was published under the formal Study Requirement (SR) number 22 by the Air Force Air Research and Development Command (ARDC).

GOR 38 identified WS (Weapon System) number 110A and established 1963 as the target date for the first wing of 30 operational WS-110A bombers. SR 22 called for 0.9 Mach cruise speed and 'maximum possible' dash speed during a 1,000 nautical mile penetration as specific performance objectives. It stipulated that high-speed flight was not as important as penetration altitude and radius. It further demanded that the proposed bomber would use existing SAC base runways and maintenance facilities. Finally, the WS-110A would have to carry a 25,000-pound payload 6,000 nautical miles.

On 22 March 1955, a second GOR, GOR 82, for the WS-110A bomber, superseding GOR 38, was issued by HQ USAF. Then, on 15 April, a revised requirement was issued by HQ ARDC to supersede the original SR 22 as SR 22 (Revised). The speed objective was modified slightly: '...*aircraft cruise speed should not be less than .9 Mach unless a significant increase in maximum radius of action or time in a combat zone may be obtained. Maximum possible supersonic dash speed in a combat zone is desired."*

On 6 April, the Weapon System Project Office (WSPO) for WS-110A was established as part of the Bomber Aircraft Division, Directorate of Systems Management, Detachment No. 1, HQ ARDC at Wright-Patterson AFB, Dayton, Ohio. During the period from 6 May through 12 July, the WS-110A WSPO presented a briefing to HQ AMC, HQ ARDC, HQ SAC, Air Force Air Staff, Air Force Air Council, and the Department of Defense (DoD), outlining its proposed programme to develop and deliver the WS-110A bomber at Wing strength by 1963. It was proposed that the operational air vehicles be preceded by one static test article and 20 flight/service test aircraft. On 21 June, the Deputy Chief of Staff for Development directed that WS-110A development be initiated as soon as possible with a multiple, competitive Phase One programme.

Prior to this, in early 1955, HQ USAF issued GOR 96 for an intercontinental strategic reconnaissance system that had similar objectives to WS-110A. Then on 1 July HQ ARDC issued a study requirement in support of GOR 96 which established a reconnaissance version of the WS-110A, identified at the time as WS-110L (confusingly the 'L' meant reconnaissance). The bomber and reconnaissance weapon system programs were later combined, and the project was then identified as WS-110A/L.

A few days later, on 13 July, a joint AMC/ARDC Source Selection Board put forward a list of six airframe contractors — Boeing, Convair, Douglas, Lockheed,

Boeing's answer to the WS-110A study. The Model 724-13 used a pair of Model 724-1001 'floating' wings to carry extra fuel, that were later discarded as the mission progressed. *(USAF)*

North American
Aviation's original
WS-110A design
proposal.

The outer 'wings'
complete with tanks
were used during the
subsonic part of the
mission, then jettisoned.

The 'broad arrow' canard
was thought to restrict
aircrew visibility too
much, especially during
take-off and landing.
(USAF)

Martin, and North American – all of whom were eligible for consideration for the development of the WS-110A/L aircraft. Of these six, only the Boeing Aircraft Company and North American Aircraft, Inc. chose to submit proposals.

Boeing and North American each received Phase One WS-110 engineering contracts as prime WS-110A/L contractors on 8 November 1955. A month earlier, on 11 October, HQ ARDC issued Amendment No. 1 to SR 22 (Revised), which changed the target date for the first operational thirty aircraft WS-110 wing from 1963 to July 1964. The schedule was now for full-scale engineering mockup inspection to take place in November 1957, first flight in March 1960, and equipage of the first SAC Wing, with the first operational production aircraft, by December 1963.

Four months after the award of contracts in April 1956, both airframe contractors submitted their respective WS-110A/L preliminary design proposals. For undisclosed reasons, due to a secret re-evaluation of GOR 96 by HQ ARDC on 27 April 1956, work on the WS-110A/L reconnaissance system was ordered to be held in abeyance and was not subsequently revived. The reason for this was not revealed for many years: it was the two 'black' projects for the highly secret Lockheed Skunk Works, the U-2 spy plane and later A-12/SR-71 aircraft.

The WS-110A studies from Boeing and North American – along with the USAF evaluation – were put together into a presentation given to the commanders of the AMC, ARDC, SAC, and HQ USAF over a period 26 May through to 13 June

1956. A briefing at HQ USAF on 13 June was attended by Generals Curtis E. LeMay, Donald L. Putt, Edwin W. Rawlings, and Clarence 'Bill' Irvine. This was followed in July by teams conducting on-site evaluations at Boeing and North American who reported their findings to the second Source Selection Board on 10 August.

On 18 October 1956, due to the reviews of WS-110A, HQ USAF ordered that Phase One development be discontinued but that Boeing and North American were permitted to continue their studies on a reduced research and development schedule. The programme was effectively cancelled at this time as a direct result of the Air Force's disappointment in both Boeing's and North American's studies. Neither company had produced a satisfactory design – both designs were colossal, incredibly complex and very overweight. To satisfy range and payload requirements, both companies suggested that the air vehicle might weigh 750,000 pounds or more, and that it would require giant disposable outer wing panels, termed 'floating wingtips' to supply fuel for the outgoing trip that weighed some 190,000 pounds each. Their respective top speeds after discarding their wingtips – the so-called 'dash' speeds – was projected at 2.3 Mach. General LeMay in particular was upset. He reportedly exploded at one meeting: *'Back to the drawing boards. These aren't airplanes—they're three-ship formations!'*

Boeing's initial WS-110A design, its Model B-724, featured a basic aircraft comprising a fuselage, bicycle landing gear similar to that of the B-47 and B-52, wing, vertical tail, four turbojet engines, canard foreplane, and floating wing panels. The floating wing extensions attached to the basic airplane's own wingtips and featured large bullet-shaped fuel pods, each about the length, diameter, and weight of a B-47's fuselage, their own vertical and horizontal tails for stability, and expendable takeoff landing gear.

North American's first WS-110A proposal, its Model NA-239, also showed the floating wing panel configuration. However, the NA-239 featured twin vertical tails, six turbojet engines, and a large arrowhead-like canard foreplane that would have reduced forward and downward vision by some 50%.

As split-mission bombers – subsonic cruise-supersonic dash – both designs were to take off in their three-part mode, top off their fuel supplies via inflight refueling, cruise at Mach 0.9 and 60,000 feet toward their pre-planned target,

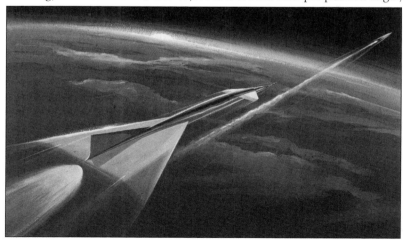

Artist's impressions during the late 1950s and early 1960s were always very 'spacey' showing dark skies, curvature of the earth and rocket exhausts. Here a North American artist depicts a single-tailed aircraft with a single either chemical or atomic engine – but clearly it is one with many B-70 influences. *(NAA Rockwell)*

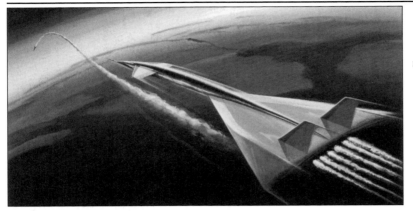

The curved horizon suggests near space as this Valkyrie in full afterburner launches a missile from its weapons bay. *(NAA Rockwell.)*

jettison their spent wing panel fuel pods, dash supersonically at 2.3 Mach to and away from their target, reduce speed to 0.9 Mach, and return home to the nearest friendly airbase.

It was suggested that there were a number of techniques that could be used to increase range – the use of High Energy Fuels (HEF), the use of a Boundary Layer Control (BLC), the use of advanced aerodynamics, and the use of high-cycle engines possibly with a re-design the aircraft to take on board the Area Rule Theory.

'Area Rule' , sometimes termed the 'Whitcomb area rule' or the transonic area rule, is a design technique used to reduce an aircraft's drag at transonic and supersonic speeds, particularly between Mach 0.75 and 1.2. The area rule was discovered by Otto Frenzl when comparing a swept wing with a w-wing with extreme high wave drag while working on a transonic wind tunnel at Junkers works in Germany between 1943 and 1945. He wrote a description on 17 December 1943, with the title 'Arrangement of Displacement Bodies in High-Speed Flight'; this was used in a patent filed in 1944.

The results of this research were presented to a wide circle in March 1944 by Theodor Zobel at the Deutsche Akademie der Luftfahrtforschung (German Academy of Aeronautics Research) in the lecture 'Fundamentally new ways to increase performance of high speed aircraft'. The design concept was applied to German wartime aircraft, including a rather odd Messerschmitt project, but their

An artist's impression of the re-designed NAA WS-110A project that is clearly B-70. *(North American Rockwell.)*

More B-70 artwork – this time showing the non-blended forward fuselage to main body design that the mock-up also exhibited along with no sign of the folding wing-tips. Note also the SAC sash wrapping around the fuselage just aft of the canards. *(The Aeroplane and Astronautics)*

complex double-boom design was never built even to the extent of a model. Several other researchers came close to developing a similar theory, notably Dietrich Küchemann, who designed a tapered fighter that was dubbed the 'Küchemann Coke Bottle' when it was discovered by U.S. forces in 1946. In this case Küchemann arrived at the solution by studying airflow, notably span wise flow, over a swept wing. The swept wing is already an application of the area rule.

In the USA Wallace D. Hayes, a pioneer of supersonic flight, developed the supersonic area rule in publications beginning in 1947 with his Ph.D. thesis at the California Institute of Technology.

Richard T Whitcomb, after whom the rule is named, independently discovered this rule in 1952 while working at NACA. While using the new Eight-Foot High-Speed Tunnel at NACA's Langley Research Center, he was surprised by the increase in drag due to shock wave formation. Several days later Whitcomb had a 'Eureka' moment. The reason for the high drag was that the 'pipes' of air were interfering with each other in three dimensions. He realised that it was not possible to simply consider the air flowing over a two-dimensional cross-section of the aircraft as others could in the past; now they also had to consider the air to the 'sides' of the aircraft which would also interact with these stream pipes. Whitcomb realized that the Sears-Haack shaping – that is an aerodynamic body shape with the lowest theoretical wave drag – had to apply to the aircraft as a whole, rather than just to the fuselage. That meant that the extra cross-sectional area of the wings and tail had to be accounted for in the overall shaping, and that the fuselage should actually be narrowed where they meet to more closely match the ideal.

Another competition

A second WS-110A competition followed. Both companies went back to their drawing boards and slide rules before on 1 July 1957 they submitted further reports before attending another round of briefings to HQ USAF, HQ AMC, HQ ARDC, and HQ SAC. Both contractors concluded that with HEF, specifically, a high-energy chemical fuel called boron in the engine afterburner section, the proposed WS-110A could be an all-supersonic-cruise air vehicle.

North American, had added a further refinement to its project that dealt with advanced aerodynamics. It was called compression lift. In aerodynamics, compression lift refers to an aircraft that uses shock waves generated by its own supersonic flight to generate lift. This can lead to dramatic improvements in lift for supersonic/hypersonic aircraft, which often fly at high altitudes and thus suffer from decreased lift due to the thin air. Clarence A. Syvertson and Alfred J. Eggers, two NACA aerodynamicists, discovered this phenomenon in 1956 as they analyzed abnormalities at the re-entry of nuclear warheads.

The basic concept of compression lift is now well known; 'planing' boats reduce drag by 'surfing' on their own bow wake in exactly the same fashion. Using this effect in aircraft is more difficult, however, because the 'wake' in air takes the form of shock waves that are generated at supersonic speeds, and these could be employed to produce additional lift, but only if they are highly angled. Aircraft have to be carefully shaped to take full advantage of this effect. In addition the angle of the shock waves varies greatly with speed, making it even more difficult to design a craft that gains significant lift over a wide range of speeds.

Neither Boeing nor North American knew of this aerodynamic discovery in the first competition, but a later search through NASA's scientific periodicals by three North American aerodynamicists – Ed Wendt, Art Ley, and Dave Beck – brought the concept to light – and into use.

Both organisations had overhauled their respective WS-110A designs and could now claim a continuous 3.0 Mach – or 2,000 mph – cruise at 70,000 feet or more altitude, a double payload of 50,000 pounds, and an un-refuelled range of 7,600 nautical miles.

Boeing's new WS-110A Chemically Powered Bomber (CPB) appeared as its Model B-804, a 200-foot-long delta-wing design with variable geometry (VG) canard foreplanes. Boeing's rejuvenated studies of aircraft configurations, exotic fuels, aerodynamics, metallurgy, and power plants prescribed the use of six podded, underwing General Electric X-279E turbojet engines rated to 4.0 Mach. Maximum takeoff weight had dropped to an acceptable 500,000 pounds.

General Thomas Sarsfield Power (1905–1970) *(USAF)*

To take full advantage of NASA's compression lift, North American likewise reconfigured, their WS-110A CPB, Model NA-259, now featured large delta wings with VG wingtips that were folded down for increased stability and lift at high supersonic speeds. It retained its canard foreplane, but this was relocated to the area aft of the cockpit windows, thus eliminating interference with pilot vision. It still sported twin vertical tails and its engines – also six General Electric turbojets – were located side-by-side in a huge boxlike structure below but integral with the aft fuselage section and wing junction. It was also fitted with a two-position VG windscreen—down for low-speed and up for high-speed operations.

On 30 August 1957, HQ USAF started a forty-five day competitive design period that peaked with on-site inspections of the contractor's facilities by a Source Selection Board evaluation group. Since both companies had failed to satisfy the Air Force with their initial three-part designs, a

Phase One, Part Two contest for the WS-110A CPB was agreed to.

On 1 July 1957 General Thomas S. Power, who had been LeMay's Vice Commander in SAC from 1948 to 1954, now became SAC'S new Commander in Chief. Since 1954, General Power had headed the ARDC. LeMay became U.S. Air Force Chief of Staff. Power had in-depth knowledge of bomber aircraft and was well informed about the WS-110A CPB programme. He was also knowledgeable about the Intercontinental Ballistic Missile (ICBM) programmes, which were becoming more and more 'popular' as a relatively low cost and more simplistic option in targetting the enemy – especially with the politicians. Power's job was to create a mixed bomber and missile force for SAC – two legs of America's tripod of manned bombers and land-based ICBMs, the US Navy's submarines creating the third leg.

The Source Selection Board evaluation group – sixty officers and men from SAC, AMC, and ARDC – descended on North American to review its new WS-110A CPB proposal during the last week of October. A Boeing review was conducted the following week. On 27 November, the team captains representing the trio of Air Force commands reported their findings in a briefing presided over by Gen.

An Atlas ICBM of SAC is maintained 'combat ready' at Vandenburg AFB in California. Its hydrogen bomb warhead is attached, and sits ready to be fired at fifteen minutes notice. It was this kind of missile that the B-70 was up against in the decision stakes. *(USAF)*

This looks like a photograph, but it is in fact more B-70 artwork. Again there is the SAC sash wrapping around the fuselage just aft of the canards and now the hint of a line denoting the folding wing tips. The date is November 1960. *(The Aeroplane and Astronautics)*

LeMay to the three commanders of SAC, AMC, and ARDC at Wright-Patterson AFB. Recommendations from the three commanders — Gen. Thomas S. Power, General Edwin W Rawlings, and General John W Sessums Jr were then submitted in sealed envelopes to the Secretary of the Air Council.

When the envelopes were opened, the North American proposal had been judged to be superior by a considerable margin. Gen. Irvine stated before the Air Council that the WS-110A CPB source selection exercise had been the most thorough and the most effective competition ever conducted by the United States Air Force.

On 23 December 1957, the long-awaited decision came down. HQ USAF announced that North American Aircraft had been selected as WS-110A CPB prime contractor. Simultaneously, AMC and ARDC were directed to determine the degree to which the programme could be accelerated in an effort to equip the first SAC bomb wing with WS-110As at the earliest possible date.

Boeing, seen by themselves as the undisputed leader in bomber aircraft design and production since at least 1940 with its B-17, B-29, B-50, B-47, and B-52 aircraft, could not believe or accept the decision. As with the KC-X refuelling tanker saga of recent years, Boeing immediately called for and got a congressional inquiry in an effort to have the decision overturned. However, it was determined that NAA's design had a far better lift over drag (L/D) ratio, and it was this which had convinced the Air Force.

Boeing had been advised to investigate NASA's Compression Lift Theory, which it did in a somewhat half-hearted manner. They remained highly sceptical and did not think NAAs revised L/D figure was valid, or that their design would reach its stated performance goal.

The AMC and ARDC, along with North American, investigated the programme acceleration problem and found that an 18-month acceleration to the current schedule was possible. A briefing given to Generals LeMay, Anderson, Putt, and Irvine on 4 January 1958 recommended procurement of the entire weapon system, with the exception of the power plant, through NAA under Category I. It was also recommended that the engine be procured from the General Electric Company at Evendale, Ohio, under Category II. These two recommendations were approved by HQ USAF, and a letter contract (AF33-600-36599) was signed on 24 January 1958. This action officially established NAA as the weapon system contractor and General Electric as the power plant contractor.

DEVELOPMENT, POLITICS AND 'THE WHIZZ KIDS'

Now the contracts were issued, both NAA and GE had much to do – especially as the WS-110A CPB programme had been moved up eighteen months to meet the Air Force's new projected Initial Operational Capability (IOC). At the time, the Air Force and SAC intended to procure a fleet of 250 WS-110A CPB bombers at an estimated cost of $6 billion. General Electric would have to produce at least 1,500 engines for these aircraft, plus spares.

The Defense Department issued a more standard B-for-Bomber classification to the WS-110A CPB, so it became the B-70 CPB on 6 February 1958. SAC and ARDC attended one of the B-70 CPB Weapon System Evaluation Conferences at North American during the week of 14 April to revise the design concept of the proposed air vehicle, to increase its design gross take off weight so as to fully utilize its onboard load and volume capabilities and to reduce the probability of retrofits being required in the future. This doubled the aircraft's payload to 50,000 pounds and gave the machine another mission of Missile Platform Bomber (MPB), similar to the upcoming Boeing B-52G and B-52H MPB aircraft. The conference also incorporated the use of decoy missiles into its defensive subsystems.

NAA initiated its subcontracting project for the B-70 in May 1958; thousands of companies in nearly every state of the Union were to share in the B-70 CPB effort. For example, the aircraft's AN/ASQ-28(V) bombing and navigation and missile guidance subsystem would be built by International Business Machines (IBM); Beech would make the Alert Pod subsystem; Boeing, the wing; Westinghouse, the defensive subsystem; North American's Columbus, Ohio, facility, the lower fuselage; Lockheed, the upper fuselage; Sperry, the auxiliary gyro platform; Motorola, the AN/ASQ-43 Mission and Traffic Control (M&TC) subsystem; Autonetics, the automatic flight control subsystem; Zenith, the nose radome; Chance-Vought, the canard foreplanes and vertical tails; Sundstrand, the secondary power generating subsystem; John Oster, power plant instrumentation; Cleveland Pneumatic, the landing gear assemblies; Hamilton Standard, the air induction control and the environmental control subsystems; Solar, the engine extraction air ducting; AiResearch, the central air data subsystem; and BF Goodrich, the brakes, wheels, and tires for the landing gear assemblies. Many hundreds of other subcontractors around the country were also involved.

What's in a name?

The company started to look around for a name for the new design and decided that through the SAC publicity office a 'name-the-plane' contest would be held. From the 20,235 entries the name 'Valkyrie' was officially approved on 27 June 1958; and was announced publicly on 3 July jointly by the Air Force, SAC, and North American. The winner of the contest. Air Force T/Sgt Francis W. Seller, was one of 13 entrants to submit the name in the six-week contest, but Seller's entry had the earliest postmark – 3 April. In Norse mythology, a valkyrie – taken from

Old Norse *valkyrja* the 'chooser of the slain' – is one of a host of female figures who decide who will die in battle. The valkyries – attested in the Poetic Edda, -bring their chosen to the afterlife hall of the slain, Valhalla, ruled over by the god Odin, where the deceased warriors become einherjar. There, when the einherjar are not preparing for the events of Ragnarök, the valkyries bear them Mead, a beer-like drink. Valkyries also appear as lovers of heroes and other mortals, and are sometimes described as the daughters of royalty, sometimes accompanied by ravens, and sometimes connected with swans.

The first of the B-70 CPB Weapon System Development Engineering Inspections (DEI) took place at North American from 2 March through 11 March 1959. During this DEI, 761 Request For Alterations (RFAs) were written by the 159 attending USAF participants representing all commands. After a review of all RFAs by a team of Air Force and North American personnel, only 381 RFAs were considered Category 1-type changes, or those to be accomplished as part of the current contractual requirements.

The Weapon System mockup review took place from 30 March through 4 April 1959. The full-scale engineering mockup review differed from the DEI in that it was styled to present the operational characteristics and suitability of the configuration and the general arrangement of the operational article presented, rather than detailed system analysis and theory. A total of 50 RFAs were written by the 47 Air Force personnel in attendance.

High energy fuels and the B-70

As already mentioned, after preliminary investigations by several companies, the use of high energy fuels in air-breathing turbojets had seemed a likely possibility of increasing the power-output of aircraft engines, with numerous special fuels being considered. Metal slurries – in particular magnesium – and liquid hydrogen received some attention, especially from Lockheed, who spent a considerable time on the development of a hydrogen powered aircraft – called the CL-400 and twice the size of a B-52 – under their own Project *Sun Tan*.

Research suggested that alkylborane fuels

Two differing views of how North American Aviation 'marketed' the B-70. Above is a very dramatic painting of a valkyrie on her steed, complete with Strategic Air Command crest on her shield.

Below a Californian valkyrie meets the B-70 Valkyrie in scale model form. *(both North American Aviation)*

offered the greatest promise. Weighing approximately the same as conventional fuels and occupying about the same volume, the boron-based fuels were expected to produce 40% more energy than standard JP-4, (Jet Petroleum) which was jet fuel blended from 50% kerosene and 50% gasoline. The eventual boron-based high energy fuels included: HEF-1, ethyldiborane; HEF-2, propylpentaborane; HEF-3, ethyldecaborane; HEF-4, methyldecaborane; HEF-5, ethyl-acetylenedecaborane.

After investigation, it seemed that alkylborane products could serve as the only propellant or as additives to standard fuels. Their use could also be limited to only the afterburner – thought to be the easiest immediate implementation – or they could be used in the primary combustor, although this approach would take a complete re-evaluation of the hot-section of the engine. High energy fuels promised a 16% range improvement over an all JP-4 mission when the new fuels were used only in the afterburners. Research suggested that engines using boron fuels in the primary combustor and afterburner would have a 30% range improvement.

The Power Plant Laboratory had conducted some experiments using boron fuels in representative afterburners, but a lack of sufficient quantities of the fuels for useful testing led the laboratory to abandonment of the trials. Only General Electric gave any indication of serious interest in high energy fuel afterburner development; Pratt & Whitney stated that it had no interest in alkylborane fuels until more of the problem areas were defined and resolved.

The confusing definition of the WS-110A systems led to a strong requirement for some sort of range extension, and boron fuels seemed to offer a relatively easy solution. Although they would require a largely new infrastructure, including a dedicated tanker fleet, they would allow the new bombers to conduct their final refueling well outside Soviet airspace, and require fewer tankers per mission.

However, during the early 1950s, nobody had the capability to produce the alkylborane fuels in large quantity. A small pilot plant was constructed that produced 0.8 tons per day by mid-1957, with production rising to 25 tons per day over the next two years. Facilities needed $8 million in Fiscal Year (FY) 56, with an additional $12 million required for each of the three succeeding years.

The military interest in boron fuels spurred development of a relatively unknown field, since boron chemistry was very complex and differed considerably from other fields. General Electric was one of the first companies to conduct an investigation of boron compounds as special fuels, beginning in the mid-1940s. About the same time, the Navy Bureau of Aeronautics also began studying boron hydrides. It was not until 1952 that the Bureau of Aeronautics launched a boron fuel programme – Project *ZIP* conducted by the Callery Chemical Corporation and the Olin Mathieson Chemical Corporation. This led to HEF becoming known as 'zip fuels' in most later literature. Callery began producing small amounts of a alkylborane – called ethyldecaborane – in November 1953. Meanwhile, GE was continuing its research as a subcontractor to Olin Mathieson.

The Air Force awarded a $178,000 contract to General Electric for a small-scale fuel evaluation known as Project *DASH* to determine the thermodynamic characteristics of boron oxide exhaust products. Although General Electric's early research was somewhat hampered by a lack of fuel, by the end of 1957 they had concluded that the use of high energy fuel in the afterburner of an engine was feasible. This early work accomplished considerable advances in useful materials, definition of design problem areas, fuel properties, and new data on exhaust products and thermodynamics.

The tactical and strategic values of the new fuels were apparent, but this had to be balanced against such serious problems as the production of fuels, predicted handling difficulties, and high production costs impeded their utilization. Basic research revealed that one of the most critical problems in burning boron fuels was the formation of boron oxide deposits that proved to be an excellent flux for certain metal oxides, limiting the construction materials that could be used. Boron oxide was a viscous liquid, melting at about 900° F, and fluid to temperatures over 3,000° F. The solid and liquid exhaust products, however, could be quite harmful to the working components of high performance engines and could greatly reduce operating efficiency and longevity.

In March 1957 the Air Force Headquarters received a high energy fuel evaluation programme report. This plan emphasized the development of a turbojet with an afterburner that used the new fuel. It was oriented around requirements to support WS-110A. The report stated that a qualified afterburner was expected in 1962 and a main combustor in 1963.

Soon after North American became the weapon system contractor in late 1957, the B-70 Project Office reiterated its belief that HEF-3 was the most economical method to achieve the desired 15% range increase over an all JP-4 mission. GOR 82 was revised on 7 March 1958 to include a study of all methods of range extension to achieve an un-refueled range of 11,000 nautical miles. The range augmentation effected through the use of HEF-burning in the J-93 afterburner was on the order of 10% while the range increase through the use of one in-flight refueling via a Boeing KC-135 was about 20%. Somewhat surprisingly, high energy fuel was never a specific requirement for the B-70 programme, although the use of HEF-3 in the afterburner and the resultant dual-fuel capability to handle JP-4 and HEF-3 did become an integral part of the early B-70 design.

The development of new alloys or resistant coatings was imperative. Numerous meetings were held in 1958 to solve this fundamental problem. The results of these consultations indicated that an alloy could probably be developed for unstressed engine components operating at temperatures up to 2,300° F, and a silicon bearing or silicate refractory coating for temperatures over this figure.

These inquiries established that most metallic materials had little effect upon HEF-3, although some lead and copper alloys could catalyze fuel decomposition. Even more disturbing though was that HEF-3 was ten times more toxic than cyanide, necessitating the development of special handling and storage techniques. This toxicity also raised questions regarding the fuel's use by operational military units, but it was expected that methods could be found to mitigate the hazard. The low spontaneous ignition temperature required a nitrogen atmosphere in all areas of the fuel tanks, as well as a nitrogen purge of all empty fuel tanks and lines.

The HEF-3 fuel also had the nasty habit of tending to solidify after a time at high temperatures, and the presence of moisture and oxygen accelerated this decomposition; however, it was thought that bulk fuel in airframe tanks would probably not reach temperatures high enough for thermal decomposition to become a problem. Little additional thermal decomposition would occur when the fuel passed through high temperature zones in the fuel system, but residual fuel that remained in tanks or stood idle in fuel systems could easily reach solidification temperature in a short time. In-flight flushing with JP-4 was a possible answer, but that required that the two fuels were compatible.

While petroleum fuels required relatively simple refining operations, crude boron mixtures had to be manufactured from basic chemicals before they could be refined. These extra steps imposed a substantial cost penalty on production of high energy fuels, and the additional electric power required further increased costs. One estimate held that a 10 tons-per-day production facility to support one B-70 Wing with HEF-3 would cost $35 million to build.

By the time the B-70 became operational, high energy fuel production costs per pound could be reduced to $1.50 or so, still very much higher than JP-4 at $0.02 per pound (about ten cents a gallon in 1964 dollars). However, in terms of performance gains, the new fuels use – and costs – could be justified.

On 12 February 1959 Richard E Homer, Assistant Secretary of the Air Force for Research and Development, called for a change in special-fuel priorities, suggesting that there was an 'apparent need' to study further the application of high energy fuel to the B-70, and recommending a delay in the construction of additional fuel production facilities.

SAC's reaction to this recommendation was emphatic. General Power urged on 25 March 1959 that no action be taken to divert high energy fuel priorities pending the completion of studies his command was making on the subject. He stated that it would be unwise to interrupt the programme at the very time it was gaining momentum from developmental successes. General Power also stated that the use of high energy or JP-4 in the B-70 engine afterburner had always been part of the basic design.

General Samuel E Andersen, Commander of the Air Materiel Command, seconded this position on 1 May 1959, when he called upon the Air Force Chief of Staff for a firm commitment regarding the use of high energy fuels over the next seven years. General Anderson pointed out that a five tons-per-day production facility would be operative by July 1959, but this plant could not supply the needs of operational B-70 bombers. He anticipated that production costs could drop to $1 per pound for full-scale production and he called for an immediate decision on firm high energy fuel requirements to provide '...*maximum flexibility and overall economy*'.

In contrast to Secretary Homer's recommendation, the B-70 Project Office on 24 February 1959 urged SAC to make a 'realistic evaluation' of the B-70's operational advantages with high energy fuel, since the Air Force programme would soon come to the point where further direction was necessary. The Project Office reminded SAC that budgeting for high energy fuel production facilities had to be accomplished no later than FY60 so that engineering and construction could begin by January 1961. The Project Office underscored the inter-relationship of

General Samuel E Andersen, (1906 – 12 September 1982) commander of the Air Material Command, Wright-Patterson Air Force Base, Ohio from 10 March 1959 to 1 April 1961. *(USAF)*

timely fuel production and a successful high energy fuel engine programme, noting that the latter was, in February 1958, ahead of schedule.

Delays in making high-level decisions on the fuel programme led the Air Materiel Command at the end of April 1959 to notify North American of a six month slippage in the J93-GE-5 engine programme. By this time North American had already converted the second weapons bay into extra fuel tankage to enable the early B-70s to meet their range requirement using the new JP-6 fuel then being produced.

After studying feasibility and cost data, in late May SAC recommended that first allocations of high energy fuel should aim at qualification of the J93-GE-5 engine, that the first B-70 operational Wing should have the -5 (rather than the -3) engine to avoid costly future modifications, and that high energy fuel – though its cost was competitive – should not exclude other means of range extension. Noting that the B-70 should exceed minimum range requirements even with the new JP-6, SAC emphasized that the new fuel would allow greater target coverage, heavier payloads, better penetration routes, a choice of recovery bases, and more adequate landing reserves.

On 8 July 1959 the ARDC, AMC, and SAC made a joint presentation on high energy fuels to the Air Force Weapons Board. The board chairman. Colonel J C Jennison, recommended a continued authorization of J93-GE-5 engine development, inclusion in the FY61 budget round of funds for the first 10-tons-per-day fuel facility, an allocation of $3.75 million for an all-HEF engine development feasibility study in FY60, and the provision of $27.6 million in FY60 for fuel purchases to support the current engine developmental programme. There were no recommendations, however, to commit the B-70 to high energy fuels.

On 16 July 1959 HQ USAF authorized purchases of the new fuels in FY60, but on 10 August the Pentagon drastically reduced the overall scope of the high energy fuel and cancelled the J93-GE-5 engine programme. The motives were vague, but cited a general lack of interest, fiscal constraints, and environmental concerns. Cancellation of the -5 engine limited B-70 planning to an engine using only JP-type fuels, and this restriction in turn forced North American to embark upon a redesign of the B-70's fuel system.

This action was interpreted by the media and the public as a preliminary move that foretold the total cancellation of the B-70 CPB Weapon System. It was not generally known, nor was it clarified for the benefit of the public, that the YJ93-GE-3 model engine being produced under contract for the XF-108 LRI, was similar in thrust output and slated for use in the bomber. In fact, the first air vehicle was scheduled to be equipped with the -3 model engine even before the -5 model engine was axed.

As designed, the -3 model engine would burn JP-6, and did not incorporate HEF-burning in its afterburner section. As the result of design improvements coming from continuous wind tunnel testing, the calculated range of the B-70 had reached a point where HEF was no longer required to meet the minimum range requirement. The HEF programme cancellation, as it related to the B-70 programme, was almost a blessing in disguise, for it resulted in the removal of considerable fuel system complexity, and reduced the projected operational cost tremendously.

Cancellation and the rise of ICBMs

On 3 December 1959, America's air arm, reaching toward the 1965-75 time period, was severed at the wrist. Maurice H. Stans, budget director for the Eisenhower Administration, who extolled the virtues of ICBMs, was frantically searching for a way to balance the budget during President Elsenhower's final year in office. He seized upon the task force study that had indicated that a long-term reassessment of the manned bomber airplane programme was in order. The Air Force subsequently announced the cancellation of the B-70 Weapon System and directed North American and the B-70 WSPO in Dayton to take steps to re-orient the programme toward the development of a single XB-70 prototype only.

Subsystems were canceled and sub-contracts were either terminated or redirected to other aircraft programmes. Only the XB-70 prototype, YJ93 engine, bombing and navigation and missile guidance system, landing gear, secondary power generating system, air induction control system, engine extraction air dualing system, environmental control system, and central air data system continued to be developed. Moreover, the lone XB-70 prototype was re-scheduled to first fly in January 1963, with continued flight testing through the year 1967.

In the 1950s and early 1960s ICBMs emerged as a reliable weapon system option that cost a fraction of their manned counterparts. Their lower initial cost, coupled with the fact that they needed no human crew, strongly enticed military planners. As the consequence, the missile-versus-bomber debates were born.

Pro-missile supporters argued that the lower cost, near-pinpoint accuracy, intercontinental range, and quick strike ICBMs were far superior to manned bomber aircraft. Those in the pro-bomber camp countered with the fact that manned bomber aircraft could be recalled after launch; they submitted that once an ICBM was launched, it was committed to strike its programmed target, that it cannot change its robot mind. Furthermore, they justified that since an ICBM required only a mere 30 minutes or so to reach its target, there would not be adequate time for any war-saving negotiations, that an all-out nuclear confrontation could ensue. These arguments grew heated and persisted for many years.

General Twining, a former Air Force chief of staff, argued that the Air Force needed the B-70 to penetrate the Soviet Union to search out and destroy mobile ICBMs on railroad tracks. '*If they* [the Air Force] *think this, they are crazy*' replied Eisenhower. '*We are not going to be searching out mobile bases for ICBMs; we are going to be hitting the big industrial and control centers*'.

A series of persuasive arguments – in particular those made by USAF Chief of Staff Thomas D White and USAF Deputy Chief of Development Roscoe C Wilson – led to the reallotment of monies by Congress for the B-70 programme.

General White presented the Air Force's case for the B-70. The nation could not rely wholly on missiles, none of which had ever been fired in combat. Missiles could not be recalled, as aircraft

Maurice Hubert Stans (22 March 1908 – 14 April 1998) was an American accountant, high-ranking civil servant, Cabinet member, and political organizer. He was a political servant for a number of American Presidents and was a peripheral figure in the ensuing Watergate Scandal. He was also the person that killed off the B-70 as a weapons system.

could. Bombers could stand off and remain airborne while awaiting orders, thus giving the President a range of options in a crisis. Bombers would complicate the enemy's problem, forcing it to defend against several different kinds of attack. Finally, the B-70 bombers would act as a demonstration of military might and have a powerful psychological effect on friend and foe alike.

By 1960 it was oft-quoted that one-third of the SAC bomber force could be airborne within fifteen minutes of the word being given; this was the warning period expected for an ICBM attack. SAC were also planning for an airborne alert force; in other words, a proportion of SAC bombers would always be airborne so that they could not possibly be caught on the ground.

Under the SAC 'positive control' system, the B-70 bombers were to take-off when an attack warning was received and head for enemy targets. They could be recalled at any time if the warning was a false alarm, but would turn round at a 'positive control' point unless they received specially coded orders, the so-called 'go code', to continue. Nuclear weapons were not armed until the bomber was ordered to attack; co-ordinated effort by several crew members was needed to arm the weapons.

General Dwight David 'Ike' Eisenhower, 34th President of the USA (14 October 1890 – 28 March 1969)

It was claimed that neither bombers nor ICBMs could be launched on an attack without Presidential authority. This meant that ICBMs could not be fired until after enemy weapons had landed, because the missiles could not be recalled in the same way as could the bombers.

Many people were worried that a nuclear war might be triggered off accidentally by, say, a new satellite or meteorite which was interpreted as an ICBM aimed at the US. In the thinking of the time, one journalist reported that '... *it is very reassuring to be told, as I was last year at SAC headquarters and this year in the Pentagon, that American military authorities accept the possibility of several nuclear warheads hitting the US without triggering off an automatic massive retaliation'.* I do not think he was being ironic!

Another study showed that if major U.S. cities were attacked by 250 megatons of nuclear weapons, less than half their population would be casualties. Coldly, the number-crunchers said that the total death-toll might be 20 million people, which need not necessarily be crippling to a nation of 180 million.

The report went on to state that *'Fall-out is not considered to be as dangerous as often thought. If a country were subjected to a massive nuclear attack, much of its population could survive merely by staying indoors for several days; and the fall-out effect on the rest of the World would not be serious. Nuclear war is considered possible without ending life on the Earth.*

In fact, attacks on cities and populations are now considered to be an unsophisticated way of using nuclear weapons, even in retaliation. Target discrimination is needed, and it is considered pointless to indulge in a population-killing contest. The counter-force argument is based on attacking an enemy's military forces and ability; cities will only be attacked when they happen to contain military targets such as headquarters'.

On 31 July 1960, Congress approved an additional $75 million, thereby increasing total FY61 appropriations to $365 million. This amount made it possible

General Thomas Dresser White (6 August 1901–22 December 1965) the fourth Chief of Staff of the United States Air Force.

for NAA to complete the XB-70 prototype, build one static test article, reinstate all subcontractor programmes, and produce 12 fully operational B-70s.

With ICBMs such as Convair's Atlas, Martin's Titan, and Boeing's Minuteman under development in concert with Boeing's B-52G/H MPBs and North American's B-70, the mixed force concept was set to become a reality. Clearly the politicians had decided that both types of weapon systems were needed.

Eisenhower respected General White, both for his leadership in World War Two and for his wide-ranging intellect. But the President also knew that White was pressing him as the official representative of a large bureaucratic Institution with its own vested interests at stake. The President did not accept White's military rationale for the B-70. He told the Air Force chief of staff that the bomber role was served adequately by the B-52, and by the time the B-70 was ready its role would be filled by missiles.

A change of ideology, a clash of culture

With his election as the 35th President of the United States, it was not long before John F Kennedy issued a controversial announcement on the B-70 programme from the White House.

On 2 November 1960 as Senator Kennedy, he gave a speech at the Horton Plaza, San Diego, during which he said: '*... This year, as a result of the efforts by Senator Engle and others, the Congress of the United States appropriated $300 million for the B-70's. I endorse wholeheartedly the B-70 manned aircraft. We could not get the administration to release the funds until this week. That is progress*'.

Four months later after his election, Kennedy effectively sounded the B-70's death knell as an operational bomber when, following the direction of his Secretary of Defense, Robert S McNamara, the President released an official statement in March 1961, which said in part that America's forthcoming ICBM capabilities '*...makes unnecessary and economically unjustifiable the development of the B-70 as a full weapon system*'.

The 35th President of the USA, John Fitzgerald 'Jack' Kennedy (29 May 1917 – 22 November 1963)

The President further recommended that the B-70 programme '*...be carried forward, essentially to explore the problems of flying at three times the speed of sound with an airframe potentially useful as a bomber, through the development of a small number of prototype aircraft and related bombing and navigation systems*'.

Defense Secretary McNamara stopped NAA's B-70 production go-ahead in April 1961, and only authorized the construction of the three air vehicles, which were to be completed not as bomber prototypes, but as high-speed aerodynamic research machines. On 10 April, NAA received a revised contract to build three XB-70 aircraft; the YB-70 service test version was canceled. On 31 July, the $365 million already appropriated by Congress for FY 61 was trimmed to $75 million and the first flight date for the first aircraft, already set back, was set back again, this time to December 1963.

Robert McNamara was born in San Francisco, California and was an American business executive and the eighth Secretary of Defense, who was to serve under Presidents John F. Kennedy and Lyndon B. Johnson from 1961 to 1968. McNamara graduated from Piedmont High School in Piedmont, California in 1933. He graduated in 1937 from the University of California, Berkeley, with a Bachelor of Arts in economics with minors in mathematics and philosophy. He then earned an MBA from the Harvard Business School in 1939.

McNamara worked a year for the accounting firm Price Waterhouse in San Francisco. In August 1940 he returned to Harvard to teach accounting in the Business School and became the highest paid and youngest Assistant Professor at that time. Following his involvement there in a programme to teach analytical approaches used in business to officers of the Army Air Forces, he entered the Armed Forces as a Captain in early 1943, serving most of the war with the AAF's Office of Statistical Control. One major responsibility was the analysis of U.S. bombers' efficiency and effectiveness, especially the B-29 forces commanded by Major General Curtis LeMay in China and the Mariana Islands. He left active duty in 1946 with the rank of Lieutenant Colonel and with a Legion of Merit.

Secretary of Defense
Robert Strange
McNamara (9 June 1916
– 6 July 2009)

In 1946 McNamara joined Ford Motor Company, owing to the influence of Charles 'Tex' Thornton, a Colonel for whom he had worked while in the military. Thornton had read an article in *Life* magazine which reported that the company was in dire need of reform.

McNamara was one of ten former World War Two officers known within Ford as the 'Whiz Kids', who helped the company to stop its losses and administrative chaos by implementing modern planning, organization and management control systems. Starting as manager of planning and financial analysis, he advanced rapidly through a series of top-level management positions. Opponents argued that McNamara's embrace of rationalism – his seeming fetish for numbers and charts – impeded rather than enhanced his ability to comprehend reality.

After his election in 1960, President-elect John F. Kennedy first offered the post of Secretary of Defense to former secretary Robert A. Lovett; he declined but recommended McNamara. Kennedy then sent Sargent Shriver to approach him regarding either the Treasury or the Defense cabinet post less than five weeks after McNamara had become President at Ford. McNamara immediately rejected the Treasury position but accepted Kennedy's invitation to serve as Secretary of Defense as long as the President gave assurances that McNamara had complete control of the Department of Defense, subject only to the higher authority of the President as commander in chief.

McNamara was known to have no fondness of the military in general, or the Air Force in particular – he also had a low opinion of his former boss, General LeMay. He frowned upon LeMay's statistical accounting methods and easily 'found fault' with the weapons systems favoured by LeMay.

This immediately put them in direct confrontation over the B-70 project.

McNamara thought that too much money was being spent on such weapons systems and greatly preferred to neatness and apparent economy of the ICBM with it's attendant theory of Mutually Assured Destruction.

Although not especially knowledgeable about defense matters, McNamara immersed himself in the subject, learned quickly, and soon began to apply an 'active role' management philosophy, in his own words *'providing aggressive leadership questioning, suggesting alternatives, proposing objectives and stimulating progress'.* He rejected radical organizational changes, such as those proposed by a group Kennedy had appointed, headed by Sen. W. Stuart Symington, which would have abolished the military departments, replaced the Joint Chiefs of Staff (JCS) with a single chief of staff, and established three functional unified commands. McNamara accepted the need for separate services but was determined to overhaul the DoD, arguing that *'...at the end we must have one defense policy, not three conflicting defense policies. And it is the job of the Secretary and his staff to make sure that this is the case'.*

Like a latter-day svengali, Robert McNamara surrounded himself with a group of 'experts' from the Rand Corporation that inherited the somewhat disparaging nickname of 'The Whiz Kids' that travelled over with McNamara from the Ford Motor Company in order to turn around the management of the United States Department of Defense (DoD). The purpose was to shape a modern defence strategy in the nuclear age by bringing in economic analysis, operations research, game theory, computing, as well as implementing modern management systems to coordinate the huge dimension of operations of the DoD with methods such as the Planning, Programming, and Budgeting System (PPBS). The group included (among others): Harold Brown, Alain Enthoven, Patrick Gross, William Kaufmann, Jan Lodal, Frank Nicolai, Merton Joseph Peck, Charles O. Rossotti, Henry Rowen, Ivan Selin, Pierre Sprey and Adam Yarmolinsky.

The Whiz Kids invented a world where all decisions could be made based on numbers – an ideal that is still touched on by many Masters of Business Administration (MBA) programmes and consulting firms today. They found power and comfort in

President John Kennedy with Secretary of Defense Robert McNamara on 8 July 1961, in Hyannis Port. McNamara was one of the few members of the Administration who socialised with the Kennedy family.

assigning values to what could be quantified and deliberately ignored everything else.

Perhaps it's a hyperbole to say that they saved and then almost destroyed the USA. But the Kids' approach would ultimately cause the drop in quality and innovativeness of American cars, opening the door to the foreign invasion from which American automobile manufacturing has yet to recover. The Whiz Kids' doctrine is also arguably responsible for America's continued involvement in the Vietnam War after 1965, which led to the vast majority of the war's 58,209 US casualties and the millions of Vietnamese military and civilian deaths. They had many of the right ideas. They brought analytical discipline to the military and American business that desperately needed it, but they inadvertently swung the pendulum too far.

The Rand Corporation (Research ANd Development) was set up in 1946 by the United States Army Air Forces as Project RAND, under contract to the Douglas Aircraft Company, and in May 1946 they released the preliminary design of an experimental world-circling spaceship. In May 1948, Project RAND was separated from Douglas and became an independent non-profit organization. Initial capital for the split came from the Ford Foundation. Since the 1950s, RAND has been instrumental in defining US military strategy. Their most visible contribution is the doctrine of nuclear deterrence by Mutually Assured Destruction (MAD), developed under the guidance of then Defense Secretary Robert McNamara and based upon their work with game theory.

This was – and is – a branch of applied mathematics that is used in the social sciences, most notably in economics, as well as in biology, engineering, political science, international relations, computer science, and philosophy. Game theory attempts to mathematically capture behaviour in strategic situations, or games, in which an individual's success in making choices depends on the choices of others. While initially developed to analyze competitions in which one individual does better at another's expense (zero sum games), it has been expanded to treat a wide class of interactions, which are classified according to several criteria.

Chief strategist Herman Kahn's major contributions were the several strategies he developed during the Cold War to contemplate 'the unthinkable', namely, nuclear warfare, by using applications of game theory – he is often cited as the father of scenario planning. Kahn considered Eisenhower administration's prevailing nuclear strategy of massive retaliation, as being untenable because it was crude and potentially destabilizing. Arguably, the 'New Look' invited nuclear attack by providing the Soviets with an incentive to precede any conventional, localized military action worldwide such as in Korea or Africa, with a nuclear attack on U.S. bomber bases, thereby eliminating the Americans' nuclear threat immediately and forcing the U.S. into the land war it sought to avoid.

Chief strategist, a proponent of the winnable nuclear war, Herman Kahn (15 February 1922 – 7 July 1983)

In 1960 Kahn published *On Thermonuclear War,* in which he rested his theory upon two premises, one obvious, one highly controversial. First, nuclear war was obviously feasible, since the United States and the Soviet Union currently had massive nuclear arsenals aimed at each other. Second, like any other war, it was winnable. This led to claims that Kahn was one of the models for the titular character of Stanley Kubrick's film

Dr. Strangelove or: How I Learned to Stop Worrying and Love the Bomb.

Two of McNamara's whizz-kids would play a part in the B-70 much later on. Harold Brown was initially Director of Defense Research and Engineering and later became Secretary of the Air Force. A forceful advocate of US nuclear testing, physicist Brown was Secretary McNamara's principal technical advisor. One Air Force officer who tangled with him over the derailed RS-70 bomber programme said of him *"He's awfully cocky and sure of himself."* A Columbia PhD at 21, Brown worked throughout the 1950s with the University of California's Radiation Laboratory, where he did research in the design and application of nuclear explosives, the detection of nuclear blasts, and the controlled release of thermonuclear energy.

Henry S Rowen was Deputy Assistant Secretary of Defense for policy planning and national security affairs, and also came to Defense through the Rand Corporation after graduating from MIT and studying at Oxford. Planner Rowen concentrated on strategic questions for the future rather than day-to-day defence programmes. Articulate and wide-ranging in his interests—which could have been NATO or guerrilla warfare—Rowen worked at Rand on a broad study of overseas bases that turned into a full-dress comparative review of US vs Soviet strategic airpower. *'As soon as he touches a sensitive nerve,"* said an Air Force planner, *"..the military begin to yell. But he always knows what he's talking about."*

Secretary of the Air Force Harold Brown. He worked under Robert McNamara as Director of Defense Research and Engineering from 1961 to 1965, and then as Secretary of the Air Force from October 1965 to February 1969.

McNamara's approach to defense policy emphasized systems analysis. He averred that while the country could afford any level of expense demanded by national security, it should examine all expenses and ensure that taxpayer money was wisely spent. Numerical analysis favoured breaking things down to the lowest common denominator and options were considered critically.

McNamara's institution of systems analysis as a basis for making key decisions on force requirements, weapon systems, and other matters occasioned much debate. Two of its main practitioners during the McNamara era, Alain C. Enthoven and K. Wayne Smith, described the concept: *'First, the word 'systems' indicates*

that every decision should be considered in as broad a context as necessary… The word 'analysis' emphasizes the need to reduce a complex problem to its component parts for better understanding. Systems analysis takes a complex problem and sorts out the tangle of significant factors so that each can be studied by the method most appropriate to it'.

Enthoven and Smith said they used mainly civilians as systems analysts because they could apply independent points of view to force planning. McNamara demonstrated a tendency to take military advice less into account than had previous Secretaries and to override military opinions. This contributed to his unpopularity with service leaders. It was also generally thought that systems analysis, rather than being objective, was in fact subjective being 'customised' by the civilians surrounding the Secretary of Defense to both justify and support decisions that McNamara had already made. Accordingly McNamara applied these concepts to the XB-70 programme – and to General Curtiss LeMay.

According to Special Counsel Ted Sorensen, Kennedy

regarded McNamara as the '*...star of his team, calling upon him for advice on a wide range of issues beyond national security, including business and economic matters*'.

Initially, the basic policies outlined by President Kennedy in a message to Congress on March 28, 1961, guided McNamara in the reorientation of the defence programme. Kennedy rejected the concept of first-strike attack and emphasized the need for adequate strategic arms and defence to deter nuclear attack on the United States and its allies. US arms, he maintained, must constantly be under civilian command and control, and the nation's defence posture had to be '*...designed to reduce the danger of irrational or unpremeditated general war*'. The primary mission of US overseas forces, in cooperation with allies, was '*...to prevent the steady erosion of the Free World through limited wars*'. Kennedy and McNamara rejected massive retaliation for a posture of flexible response. The United States wanted choices in an emergency other than '*...inglorious retreat or unlimited retaliation*', as the President put it. Out of a major review of the military challenges confronting the United States initiated by McNamara in 1961 came a decision to increase the nation's 'limited warfare' capabilities. These moves were significant because McNamara was abandoning President Dwight D Eisenhower's policy of massive retaliation in favour of a flexible response strategy that relied on increased US capacity to conduct limited, non-nuclear warfare.

Another of the 'new regime' was economist Alain Enthoven. He was a Deputy Assistant Secretary of Defense from 1961 to 1965, and from 1965 to 1969 he was the Assistant Secretary of Defense for Systems Analysis.

Following the guidance of his rationalist brethren at the RAND Corp., the famed think tank brimming with mathematicians and game theorists, McNamara found an alternative in the doctrine of counterforce, whereby the United States would try to limit a nuclear exchange by initially targeting only enemy military forces. The idea was to hold Soviet cities hostage to a follow-on strike in an attempt to control escalation and prevent retaliation.

On 30 June 1961, President Kennedy swore in General Curtis LeMay as Chief of Staff, US Air Force. He said in his speech: '*I want to express our great pleasure at the assumption of this responsibility by General LeMay. He was one of the most distinguished combat commanders in World War II. He played a most instrumental role in developing SAC into its present high peak as the great shield of the United States in the free world.*

He brings to the responsibilities of the Chief of Staff long experience in the Air Force, and also a wide recognition of the challenges and responsibilities and opportunities which face the United States in meeting our commitments around the globe.

It's a source of satisfaction to me personally as President, to be able to rely on his counsel as a member of a group of distinguished Americans, the Joint Chiefs of Staff; and I think the fact that so many Members of the Congress are here from both parties indicates the wide respect which he has in the country.

So, General, we want to say that, speaking personally, and also as President, that it's a great pleasure to welcome you as the new Chief of Staff of the United States Air Force and member of the Joint Chiefs of Staff'.

As Air Force chief of staff, LeMay clashed repeatedly with McNamara, Air Force Secretary Eugene Zuckert, and the chairman of the Joint Chiefs of Staff, Army

General Maxwell Taylor. At the time, budget constraints and successive nuclear war fighting strategies had left the armed forces in a state of flux. Each of the armed forces had gradually jettisoned realistic appraisals of future conflicts in favour of developing its own separate nuclear and non-nuclear capabilities. At the height of this struggle, the US Army had even reorganized its combat divisions to fight land wars on irradiated nuclear battlefields, developing short-range atomic cannon and mortars in order to win appropriations. The United States Navy in turn proposed delivering strategic nuclear weapons from super-carriers intended to sail into range of the Soviet air defence forces. Of all these various schemes, only LeMay's command structure of SAC survived complete reorganization in the changing reality of postwar conflicts.

General LeMay shared White's contempt for the whizz kids and for McNamara. He believed the civilians had usurped the proper role and expertise of the military. In LeMay's analogy, McNamara was a reckless amateur who ran the Defense Department like '...*a hospital administrator who tried to practice brain surgery*'. Exasperated by McNamara's iron grip on Air Force programmes, LeMay would ask friends: '...*would things be much worse if Khrushchev were Secretary of Defense?*'

More seriously, LeMay's evaluation of Secretary McNamara as having a '...*bombastic confidence*' in the ability of the United States to retaliate effectively with ICBMs. McNamara had a growing reputation for his reliance on statistics and little else. If there existed a concept, or even a piece of hardware, that he could not reduce to numbers or a chart, there was a good chance that he would question its value. The B-70 was a complex aircraft and the programme for its development was likewise complex and expensive.

McNamara disliked the B-70 programme because of this. Despite his later claims to the contrary, there is solid evidence that he would not accept any testimony about the aircraft's potential as a long-range bomber. He even claimed that the B-70 could not be used to drop conventional bombs but could only launch short-range attack or cruise missiles. This supposed lack of conventional bombing potential of the

General LeMay reached the summit of his Air Force career on June 30, 1961, when he was sworn in as Chief of Staff by Secretary of the Air Force Eugene M Zuckert. Observing the ceremony in the rose garden of the White House are the late President John F Kennedy and the then Vice President, Lyndon B Johnson.

President John F
Kennedy visiting Atomic
Energy Commission-
supported Lawrence
Radiation Laboratory
(LRL) on March 23, 1963.
Picture taken in front of
Building 70A at LRL in
Berkeley, California. Left
to right: Dr Norris
Bradbury, Dr John S.
Foster, Dr Edwin M.
McMillan, Glenn T
Seaborg, President John F
Kennedy, Dr Edward
Teller, Robert McNamara
(Secretary of Defense),
and Dr Harold Brown
(Director of Defense
Research and
Engineering). *(The Los
Alamos National
Laboratory)*

aircraft was used as one of his reasons to discredit the B-70 programme.

Yet McNamara wanted to have the Air Force put the bombers on 24-hour alert, even to the extent of having some of them in the air 24 hours a day, just in case there would be an enemy strike that would put the bombers in jeopardy.

Air Force officers could not match the whizz kids at using their analytic techniques. When Alain Enthoven testified before Congress, he overwhelmed the generals with charts and graphs showing that '*...the B-70 would add minimal extra firepower at huge cost*'. Still, the military rejected the notion that a computer- generated 'truth' provided better answers than the judgment and experience of men who had actually fought a war.

General White, who had just retired as Air Force chief of staff, commenting about those who had set about savaging the B-70, programme said: '*I am profoundly apprehensive of the pipe-smoking, tree-full-of-owls type of so-called professional defense intellectuals. I don't believe a lot of these often over-confident, sometimes arrogant young professors, mathematicians, and other theorists have sufficient worldliness or motivation to stand up to the kind of enemy we face*'.

The TFX project

There was another reason for slashing the B-70 project. In the 1960s, defence contractors were also competing for an aircraft contract under the TFX (Tactical Fighter 'X'), or F-111 programme. This was a joint Navy and Air Force project to develop a fighter that could be used by both services, ostensibly to preserve the idea of economy through commonality between them. The fact that the Navy really didn't want the TFX made no difference. In November 1962, the Department of Defense – that is McNamara – decided that the TFX looked incredibly cost effective on paper and that it would be produced by General Dynamics, Fort Worth, Texas,

The heart of Strategic Air Command, SAC's command and control system located deep beneath their Headquarters. Senior operations personnel were in continuous contact with all SAC missile and bomber bases and with national civil and military centers. The SAC commander in chief could be contacted within seconds. SAC's famous 'red telephone' was located on the communications panel, centre. Graphic and pictorial information was shown via projectors on the large screens at left. *(USAF)*

of course, was – not so coincidentally – the home state of Vice President Lyndon Johnson. The go-ahead for the F-111 program, and selection of General Dynamics as the contractor, would be a political plus for the Kennedy administration, and would be the ideal payback to the Vice President for his ultimate support of Kennedy's election to the presidency – another good reason for it to be supported by the President. The selection of General Dynamics as the TFX prime contractor was announced at a rally and a breakfast that was given at the Texas Hotel, on the morning of the day that Kennedy would be assassinated in Dallas.

Money for the F-111 had to come from somewhere, and what better place to begin looking for it than to cut a programme the administration did not like in the first place? So McNamara cut the B-70 bomber programme back to three experimental research XB-70s and laid down the law governing budgets and bombers. He would have his way with the military and his way, he believed, would dissuade any aggressor from mounting a first strike against the United States.

A change in requirements – the Reconnaissance-Strike B-70 .

The mission requirements for manned bomber aircraft were starting to change at this time — and, for good reason. Russia, after shooting down Francis Gary Powers' Lockheed U-2 on 5 May 1960, had effectively proved that it could 'hit a fly in the sky', as the Soviet Premier Nikita Khrushchev had boasted. What is more, the Soviet Union was creating the MiG 25, a high-altitude Mach 3 interceptor, specifically to shoot down the B-70.

So, for the most part, high-speed, high-altitude bombers were becoming obsolete. This prompted the USAF to take a closer look at its upcoming stand-off capability with its B-52G/H MPB aircraft, and look toward the creation of a totally new manned bomber type of aircraft, specifying low 'treetop' level altitude and high subsonic speed penetration characteristics instead—specifically, an advanced manned bomber, but with similar B-52G/H type mission profiles. Subsequently, in 1961, the Air Force initiated its SLAB (Subsonic Low Altitude Bomber) study.

In its effort to revive the Valkyrie programme, the USAF created the Reconnaissance-Strike B-70 Weapon System Programme. To do this, the Air Force altered the B-70 mission classification from B-for-Bomber to RS-for-Reconnaissance Strike, and thereby created the proposed RSB-70 Valkyrie. The USAF proposed to field a fleet of 60 RSB-70 aircraft by 1969, with another 150 aircraft to be delivered by 1971 – one XRSB-70, 210 production RSB-70s. As projected, the first 10 production aircraft would be used as RDT&E (research, test, development and evaluation) aircraft, then absorbed later by user bomb wings.

Initially three aircraft would be built. American referred to these machines as AV – standing for Air Vehicle – 1,2, and 3, or AV 1, AV 2 and AV 3. The YB-70 service test example, or AV 3, was to be completed with the installation of the full B-70 weapon system and was to have provisions for the intended operational four-man crew.

The Air Force issued serial number 62-0001 to AV 1 (XB-70-1), 62-0207 to AV 2 (XB-70-2), and 62-0208 to AV 3 (YB-70). Overall programme cost had risen to $1.3 billion.

The general arrangement of the XB-70. *(NAA Rockwell)*

Somewhere down the line the aircraft designation changed. Certainly in

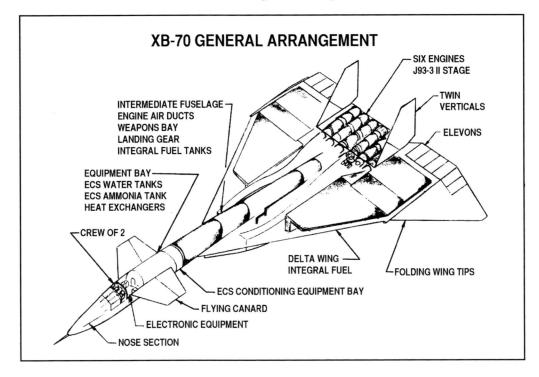

XB-70 GENERAL ARRANGEMENT

SIX ENGINES
J93-3 II STAGE

TWIN VERTICALS

ELEVONS

INTERMEDIATE FUSELAGE
ENGINE AIR DUCTS
WEAPONS BAY
LANDING GEAR
INTEGRAL FUEL TANKS

EQUIPMENT BAY
ECS WATER TANKS
ECS AMMONIA TANK
HEAT EXCHANGERS

CREW OF 2

DELTA WING
INTEGRAL FUEL

FOLDING WING TIPS

ECS CONDITIONING EQUIPMENT BAY

FLYING CANARD

ELECTRONIC EQUIPMENT

NOSE SECTION

September 1964 edition of *Skywriter,* a North American Employee Report, they were still calling 62-0001 as the 'XB-70' as the headline, but on in the text, they refer to the same aircraft as the XB-70A. A month earlier in August, the USAF issued an Interim Flight Manual which also called the aircraft the XB-70A, which is the designation I will use from here on when talking about the two completed air vehicles.

Some sources suggest that the third aircraft – 62-0208 – was to be designated as the XB-70B, others called it the YB-70A, which is probably more likely given that it was closer to the actual operational design.

It was not until after the entire project closed and the sole survivor was retired to a museum – in April 1972 – that North American revealed the differences with the three aircraft. According to NAA ...*At the time of program redirection to three XB-70 air vehicles (3-31-61), it was planned that AV's 1 and 2 would be identical in design to demonstrate the technical feasibility of B-70 type aircraft design and AV 3 would include provisions to demonstrate the functional operation of a prototype bombing-navigation system'.*

Subsequent to this redirection, systems development and manufacturing considerations led to further significant differences between AV's 1 and 2, as follows:

1. *AV 1 had zero degree wing dihedral versus 5 degree on AV 2. This change was issued to correct lateral dynamic stability problems at intermediate supersonic speed and became evident too late in the manufacturing process to be incorporated on AV 1 which utilized a bob weight to provide the capability for pilot compensation.*

2. *A manual air induction control system was utilized on AV 1 versus an*

The general arrangement of the proposed RS-70. *(NAA Rockwell)*

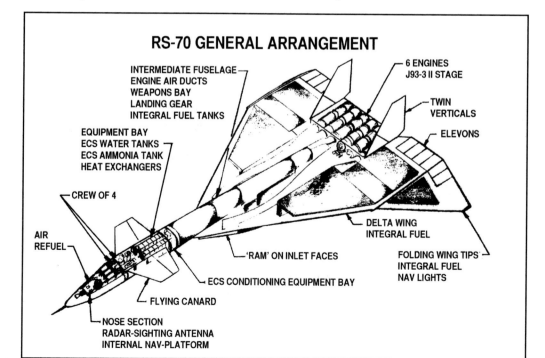

RS-70 GENERAL ARRANGEMENT

INTERMEDIATE FUSELAGE
ENGINE AIR DUCTS
WEAPONS BAY
LANDING GEAR
INTEGRAL FUEL TANKS

EQUIPMENT BAY
ECS WATER TANKS
ECS AMMONIA TANK
HEAT EXCHANGERS

CREW OF 4

AIR
REFUEL

6 ENGINES
J93-3 II STAGE

TWIN
VERTICALS

ELEVONS

DELTA WING
INTEGRAL FUEL

'RAM' ON INLET FACES

FOLDING WING TIPS
INTEGRAL FUEL
NAV LIGHTS

ECS CONDITIONING EQUIPMENT BAY

FLYING CANARD

NOSE SECTION
RADAR-SIGHTING ANTENNA
INTERNAL NAV-PLATFORM

automatic system on AV 2. An interim manual system with limited automatic features was flown on AV 1 due to development schedules associated with the automatic system.

3. *The wing-to-fuselage joint design differed between AV's 1 and 2. Due to wing-to-fuselage mismatch problems encountered on AV 1, the joining transition area was redesigned to facilitate assembly.*

4. *AV 2 had a 2800 gallon greater fuel capacity than AV 1. This fuel capacity difference was primarily attributable to Tank No. 5 being blocked off on AV 1 due to problems experienced in sealing.*

It was planned that AV 3 would be similar in structure as AV 2 but that modification would be made to include provisions for the bombing-navigation system as follows:

1. *Four-man crew on AV 3 versus two-man crew on AV's 1 and 2. An observer and system operator position were required in support of bombing-navigation missions and systems operations.*

2. *AV 3 required major modifications in the environmental control system. Double versus single air cooling loops were required to support the additional crewmen and electronic equipment on AV 3. In addition, a greater cooling capacity and added liquid cooling loops were required.*

3. *Equipment bay variances Major electronic equipment additions were required in support of the bombing-navigation system which resulted in rearrangement of the electronic and ECS equipment bays plus the blocking off of the No. 1 fuel tank for ECS water/ice tank.*

4. *Nose cavity additions. The AV 3 bombing-navigation required the addition of an inertial navigation platform and radar antenna equipment with associated cooling loops in the nose section.*

5. *Secondary power system additions. An additional generator on engine No. 5, line contactor, stepdown transformer, secondary bus and the associated controls*

STANDARD DISPLAYS

A pair of artist's impressions of the cockpit of the proposed B-70, the first showing the use of what were then 'conventional' instruments...

were required in support of the added electronic equipment on AV 3'.

In July 1963, the House Armed Services Committee, headed by Carl Vinson, requested $491 million for the completion of two XB-70s and one XRSB-70 – the latter being AV 3, formerly the YB-70, but modified to the RSB-70 configuration. Congress only allocated $52.9 million, totalling $275.9 million, far short of the required amount. As proposed for the RSB-70 programme, AV 1 would continue in development unaffected and would proceed with its planned fabrication and flight test programme.

AV 2 would be modified to incorporate a dry in-flight refueling receptacle and its associated hydraulic fluid power actuation equipment within the nose section forward of the VG windscreen on the aircraft's centreline. This machine would be retrofitted with a new 51° swept back leading edge on the canard foreplane instead of the 31° to evaluate the performance and flying qualities of the revised surface during flight. After its initial flight test programme, a fixed missile launcher capable of launching two powered strike missiles, together with a missile cooling system, would be incorporated within AV 2's aft weapons bay. Equipment to power-open/close the aft segment of the weapons bay door was also to be incorporated. This would allow the evaluation of launch and separation characteristics of the proposed strike missile.

AV 3 – which would be the XRSB-70 prototype and formerly the YB-70 service test air vehicle, would retain the basic structure of AV 1 and AV 2 with the modification to employ the new higher sweep angle canard foreplane tested on AV 2. A revised left-hand vertical stabilizer would be incorporated, with an isolation strip to house the proposed AN/ARC-90 UHF (ultra high frequency) Command Communication system antenna.

Provisions for the proposed four-man crew and a pressurized and cooled electronic equipment bay were to be provided, as had been planned for the YB-70. A power-operated weapons bay door was to be provided for the aft weapons

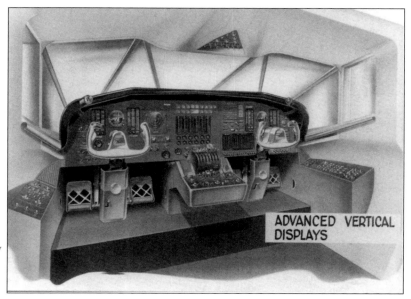

...compared to the vertical 'tape' instruments used particularly for the engine displays. In reality aspects of both were used on AV.1 and AV 2 *(both NAA Rockwell)*

ADVANCED VERTICAL DISPLAYS

bay. In addition, the structure in the lower portion of the #1 forward fuselage fuel tank was to be modified to permit the installation of an 8-foot-long phased array antenna on either side of the air vehicle. As planned, the first production RSB-70 was to fly in early 1965, and AV 13, or RSB-70 number 10, in early 1967.

The proposed RSB-70 differed from the B-70 in that multiple – up to 20 – guided air-launched missiles and associated reconnaissance equipment would be incorporated into the weapon system as a primary capability rather than as an alternate means of target destruction. Each segment of the two-part weapons bay would be able to carry ten 900-pound strike missiles on a powered rotary-type launcher.

SOR 82, which was revised on 28 February 1961, called for the procurement of RSB-70 aircraft and specified that it be capable of performing missile strikes against heavily defended enemy strategic and military targets, strategic bombardment (both nuclear and conventional), and strategic reconnaissance. The USAF/SAC Operational Plan (OP) for the RSB-70, of 15 April 1961, stated that the aircraft would be capable of carrying diversified weapon loads of guided and free-fall ordnance and that RSB-70 squadrons would operate from both primary operating and maintenance bases and also from a large number of dispersed bases to reduce vulnerability and reaction time. It went on to say that the RSB-70 must have the 'flexibility to respond effectively throughout the whole spectrum of possible conflict'. But the RSB-70 programme did not go forth.

During the construction of the third Valkyrie, the Air Force project managers were fighting to save the programme. They had devised seven alternate plans,

An artist's impression of the defensive station at it would have appeared on the production B-70. It has been oft-stated that the aircraft would carry a state-of-the-art suite – unfortunately no one seems to know what it would have looked like!
(NAA Rockwell)

each one trying to save something of AV 3, or for that matter, trying to salvage everything possible of the entire programme. All the alternatives were based on a minimalist proposal – building three air vehicles and flying two of them. The flight test programme was to be just extensive enough to prove the range of the envelope, including flight work at Mach 3.

Supporters hoped the programmes would provide a wealth of information on high-performance vehicles, including data on speed, payload, altitude, and duration of flights at high speed. The SST programme testing, with funding from NASA, was a big selling point for NASA, the Air Force, and congressional interests.

Air Vehicle 3 – allocated tail number 62-0208 – was to be the evaluation aircraft for much of what was planned for the RSB-70. The design for AV 3 was completed on 31 October 1963. Many of the technical problems had already been worked out on the first two aircraft, including much progress on the complicated brazing techniques, the redesign of the honeycomb panels for fabrication, and the elimination of assembly problems.

The procurement process for the raw materials was completed. The aircraft required 24,452 square feet of honeycomb core PHI 5-7, sheet metal quoted at 157,846 pounds, and 26,403 feet of linear extrusions. Fabrication processes on the subsystems and the subcontracted structure were all on schedule. The honeycomb panel design was complete, with the fabrication of the honeycomb panels was still underway. By 24 January 1964, the Bombing and Navigation systems developed by IBM — and the Doppler radar — had passed acceptance tests. Radar sighting equipment had passed acceptance tests at General Electric

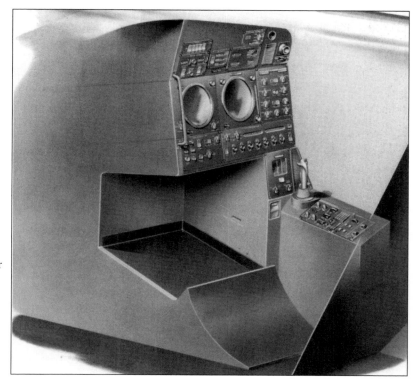

The offensive avionics suite was further advanced, with IBM completing the ASQ-28 bomb-nav system for Air Vehicles 2 and 3. The IBM system had been tested in a fragmentary manner on a variety of surrogate aircraft, but never as a complete package.
(NAA Rockwell)

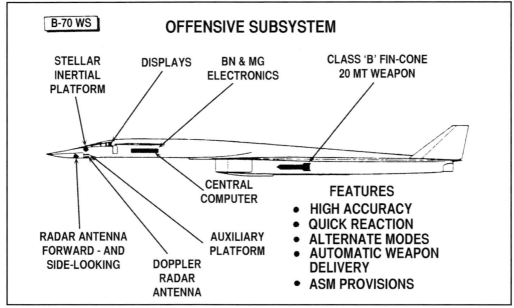

The proposed offensive systems of the B-70. This shows a single 20 megaton nuclear bomb on board – however the aircraft could carry a variety of other nuclear and conventional bombs as well as missiles. *(NAA Rockwell)*

and was delivered on time. Integration tests at IBM were all on schedule. The digital computer had completed its functional test with the Doppler radar.

AV 3 was to carry a four-man crew, two pilots and two observers, in what later would have been Bomb/Nav Officer and Defensive Systems Officer. The radome was able to support 130 cubic feet of equipment for 1,000 pounds as star trackers, antennas, and so on. New requirements for the equipment bay brought changes increasing in size from 300 cubic feet to accommodate 12,000 pounds of new equipment. The weapons bay was enlarged to 1,200 cubic feet and could hold 25,000 pounds of ordnance. The structural difference in the AV 3 was the lower fuselage, which was changed to accommodate a new environmental control system and the associated ducting and plumbing needed for a four-man crew compartment and for cooling the electronic equipment.

There was another interesting fact concerning the third Valkyrie. Because of the shape of the engine inlet ducts, the Valkyrie was considered to be a prime candidate for evaluating the performance of RAM (radar absorbent material) coatings placed within the ducts. With the long endurance and high-speed cruise capacity of the XB-70, designers felt that it was particularly well suited for RAM endurance and radar-suppression test flights. Tests were needed to measure the detectability of the XB-70 and other large high-performance aircraft by radars and infrared seekers, both with and without suppression aids. Radar suppression would have been tested by placing the RAM material in the air inlet ducts to diminish the reflected radar energy. Infrared suppression was to be tested by coating the XB-70 skin with material that could suppress infrared energy at tactically pivotal wave lengths.

Ground radar was used in trying to determine the radar cross-section (RCS) differences in several radar frequency ranges. The information gathered at different air intake duct ramp configurations determined the effect of duct shape on the RCS. From this, researchers determined the effectiveness and the durability of the RAM coating. The effect of this coating on skin temperature and structural integrity would be measured by onboard instrumentation.

RCS was one of the tough selling points of the XB-70; on radar it looked like a barn door coming over the horizon. After Gary Powers was shot down in his U-2 in May 1960, RCS became even more important, with every effort made to make the XB-70 look smaller on radar screens.

In desperation, find other uses!

One task description written for Valkyrie AV 3 cited plans for it to be used as a high-altitude astro-observatory. That aircraft would be equipped with astronomical equipment and would fly to the best possible locations for observing and recording astronomical events such as solar eclipses. The justification explained that the greater the flying observatory's velocity, the longer an eclipse could be viewed. At Mach 3.0, eight minutes were available for viewing compared to four minutes at Mach 1.0. In addition to longer viewing times, the higher a flying observatory went, the less atmospheric absorption there was, and cloud cover was no longer an issue. The XB-70 was the only high-performance vehicle that was stable enough and could carry the necessary payload to support such a project.

Despite the merits of the project, it was not taken up. The USA pursued larger observatories on the ground. It was not until the launch of the Hubble Space Telescope several decades later that the USA finally gained a high-altitude platform from which to view the stars.

Another idea was to use the B-70 as a recoverable booster system to launch things into low earth orbit. Likely candidates included a proposed satellite-interceptor and the Aerospace Plane. The DynaSoar program, the first effort by the United States to use a manned boost-glider to fly in near orbital space and return, was also considered in this context in November 1959. The B-70 was to carry the 10,000-pound DynaSoar glider and a 40,000-pound liquid rocket booster to 70,000

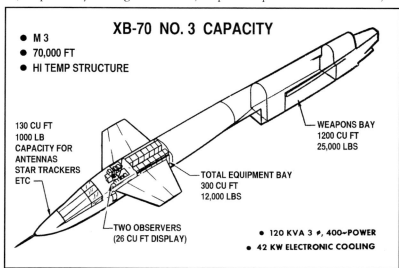

XB-70 NO. 3 CAPACITY

- M 3
- 70,000 FT
- HI TEMP STRUCTURE

130 CU FT
1000 LB
CAPACITY FOR
ANTENNAS
STAR TRACKERS
ETC

WEAPONS BAY
1200 CU FT
25,000 LBS

TOTAL EQUIPMENT BAY
300 CU FT
12,000 LBS

TWO OBSERVERS
(26 CU FT DISPLAY)

- 120 KVA 3 ⚡, 400~POWER
- 42 KW ELECTRONIC COOLING

The capacity of AV 3 if it had been completed, showing the weapons bay, the equipment bay and the nose bay for radar, star-trackers etc. *(NAA Rockwell)*

feet and release them while traveling at Mach 3. The booster could then push the glider into its final 300-mile orbit.

There were technical problems to overcome. A weight issue had to be wrestled with, since the B-70 would have been overweight in order to accomplish the launch. It was the first time that the Air Force tried to merge missile, space, and aeronautical sciences into one package, so many issues of communication and compatibility had to be addressed.

Had the system been completed, it would have had the capability to carry its payload anywhere for launch and positioning—a useful feature when bad weather threatened a conventional launch schedule. With the space shuttle system, a launch must be delayed if the weather over the launch pad or in an emergency recovery area is not favourable, resulting in the loss of hours or days.

There was also a scheme to use the B-70 as a satellite killer to both inspect and intercept enemy satellites in orbit. The B-70 would carry missiles or drones to the upper atmosphere for launch against orbiting targets.

In the late 1950s the B-70 was a unique airframe, which presented an opportunity to explore static and fatigue problems and extremely complex loading of the aircraft. It was hoped that these tests would lead to design answers concerning the Advanced Manned Penetrating Strategic System (AMPSS) and the SST as is described in detail in a later chapter. Static and fatigue testing would have scrutinized the forward fuselage, wing panels, horizontal stabilizer, and the landing gear.

Testing would also evaluate the closed-loop engine inlet shock wave controls to monitor unstart conditions. The aim was to limit the violent buffeting of the aircraft that resulted from the loss of shock wave positioning in the engine inlet.

The proposed propulsion testing and in-flight 'space simulation' package for the third valkyrie.
(USAF)

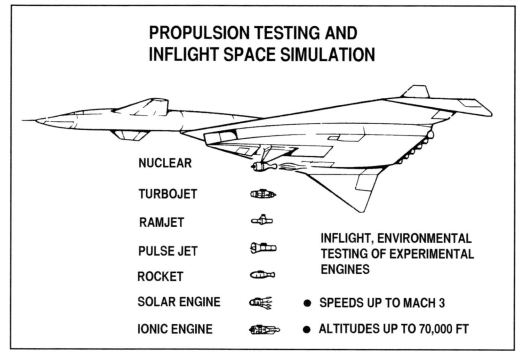

PROPULSION TESTING AND INFLIGHT SPACE SIMULATION

NUCLEAR

TURBOJET

RAMJET

PULSE JET   INFLIGHT, ENVIRONMENTAL
                             TESTING OF EXPERIMENTAL
ROCKET   ENGINES

SOLAR ENGINE   ● SPEEDS UP TO MACH 3

IONIC ENGINE   ● ALTITUDES UP TO 70,000 FT

Plans were also made for a recoverable booster system that would permit air launches from the best possible position to attain low-earth orbit. *(USAF)*

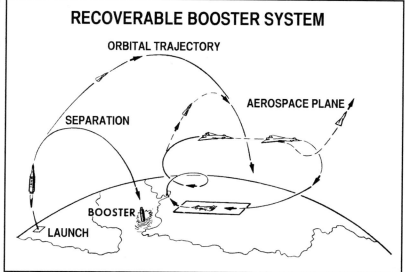

RECOVERABLE BOOSTER SYSTEM

ORBITAL TRAJECTORY

SEPARATION

AEROSPACE PLANE

BOOSTER

LAUNCH

This test would allow evaluation of inlet control signals that could provide the information needed to record inlet air currents. Ambitious as it sounded, the information from this test would develop the SST and AMPSS inlet control and propulsion system and help limit the effects of jet wash or turbulence caused by one supersonic aircraft passing another.

The danger from SAMs to high-flying aircraft was demonstrated by the U-2 incident involving Francis Gary Powers – this also had implications for the B-70. When an Air Force General suggested to the head of North American Aviation, James H 'Dutch' Kindelberger, that the B-70s high-altitude mission was too dangerous due to the SAM threat, he decided to investigate low-altitude penetration. The purpose of the investigation was to see if the pilot and the aircraft could respond to the environment of near-supersonic speed at low altitude in enemy territory. Test pilots were to fly the B-70 at Mach .95 at sea level and evaluate the effect of speed and clearance attitudes, predict the ability to avoid terrain, and detect ground defence sites. The justification for it all was to recommend low-level capability for a B-70 type of design. Ultimately, similar high-speed missions were flown years later by the Rockwell B-1B Lancer.

Another programme was to help estimate the defence of the United States and to provide information for the improvement of air defence systems. With new antennas and other countermeasure systems installed in the bomb bay, the military was to test and evaluate US defence systems against threats, including manned enemy penetrators. The large payload capacity of the B-70 was to allow for many different types of countermeasure systems to be tested from subsonic to Mach 3 at high altitudes. It was hoped that one aircraft would be able to simulate each of the different manned penetrators that were considered to be potential threats.

Performance of communications equipment when working at high altitude and high speed was also considered for study. The tests would use the XB-70s AN/ARC-50 UHF set and the AN/ARN-65 TACAN (with the addition of a power amplifier) to show the increased communication range afforded by the high altitude. The tests would aid SST as well as military research. Testing would also encompass evaluation of supersonic static discharge — a critical factor in communications noise reduction. The tests were to be done in two phases: Part I to measure and record field strengths and discharge currents, and Part II to determine the static discharge device's field life.

Aircraft panel response to flutter and dynamic pressures from outside disturbances was an aeronautical issue at any speed. In the world of high-speed flight and the threat of unstarts, it was of grave concern. Instrumentation was to be provided to measure the effects that occurred from acoustical forces. Noise-measuring instruments, including microphones, transducers, and even thermocouples, were to be mounted in high-noise-level areas such as the aft fuselage and the engine inlets. This test would not require any excess flight time and was to be done during normal flight procedures.

A crew protection and environment study was to evaluate the crew under various circumstances and tolerance levels to determine the type of protection required. Environment was the heading under which temperature, pressure, air composition, and workload were measured. Radiation levels in the upper atmosphere were also a concern.

High-speed and altitude operation, fuselage flexibility, air vehicle size, landing attitude and speed, and extended temperature and pressure environments were all issues needing exploration. Adaptive control systems were beneficial to the evaluation of the AMPSS and SST, the automatic landing systems, and the emergency descent capsule used for in-flight emergencies.

Weapons and components testing research was to aid in the design of new ordnance, missiles, and components for use in supersonic aircraft. Environmental data would be gained for the effects of aerodynamic heating, vibration, acoustics, and G load. Instrumentation would provide for weapon ejection shock, safe separation, and trajectory. The tests would also provide information pertaining to in-flight platform alignment of inertial-guided missiles, missile delivery accuracy, and ballistic determination of supersonic gravity-dropped ordnance. Since the

Exhibit 20 in the
B-70 Final Report – the
Over-Nose Vision
Mockup.
(NAA Rockwell)

The B-70 mock-up seen from a different angle that shows at this time there was a distinct 'join' line between the front fuselage and the main body that was blended away by the time the aircraft was actually built. *(NAA Rockwell)*

XB-70 was the only aircraft capable of performing in this high-speed, high-altitude theatre, its navigation system was unique in that it could provide weapons release data for advanced weapons systems.

The B-70 was to be used to study the effects of high altitude and high speed on navigation performance, including Stellar-Doppler inertial, Doppler inertial, pure Doppler, and pure inertial radars. The ability of a Doppler radar to lock on to a usable ground return signal at high speed and high altitudes needed to be determined. The designers also planned to evaluate the stellar monitor which, if it were to be used in any high-speed, high-altitude regime, needed to function properly. The XB-70 could create a shock wave severe enough to affect refraction of light going to the stellar monitor. The XB-70 was the only aircraft that could fly this regime that was already equipped with Stellar-Doppler inertial navigation system.

Supersonic refueling was to precipitate the need for refueling high-speed aircraft. The study would determine the feasibility and develop the technique for fuel transfer at supersonic speed. Test vehicle modifications were to be based on the results of wind tunnel, flight simulator, and flight tests and would consist of a 'dry hookup' between the XB-70 and another supersonic aircraft (perhaps another B-70), simulating a tanker.

Another possibility under consideration was to turn the B-70 into a nuclear-powered aircraft. Under a USAF contract North American made a special design study of a possible nuclear-powered version that would give a bomber with almost unlimited range and endurance. It could maintain a long-duration standing patrol carrying Air-Launched Ballistic Missiles (ALBMs), could approach, an enemy target from any direction without aerial refuelling and could launch an attack at any speed from Mach 0.9 at sea level to Mach 3 at altitude.

Possible roles, in addition to strategic bombing, would have been anti-submarine patrol and attack; early detection of hostile aircraft; interception of attacking forces at great distances from the US; ballistic missile early warning and use as a launching platform for anti-ICBM missiles; airborne mobile command post; and use for rapid deployment overseas for action in limited wars.

It was thought that several features of the B-70 made it suitable for operation with nuclear power. Its large size was considered an advantage, because of the weight of the reactor and crew shielding. The long distance between the crew

The proposed B-70 RBS (Recoverable Boost System) with a Dyna-Soar style space vehicle enclosed in a bulged belly. *(NAA Rockwell)*

and the power plant would help minimize radiation. It also appeared that much of the aircraft's basic structure could be retained without significant changes.

Other Views – Other Implications

In an in-depth interview given on 9 May 1964, Director of Defence and Research Engineering Harold Brown revealed much about the XB-70 programme, along with a great number of insights into how one of McNamara's 'whizz-kid' disciples saw the Air Force's lobbying and the RSB-70:

'The Air Force has been the glamour service, and I think this has impressed many congressmen. But this is outside of my field. I am just expressing a non-expert opinion. I think the Air Force has devoted a good deal of effort to gaining this support. It has a long history of doing it. It has always been more willing to go over the heads of its legally constituted superiors to the Congress. I think that probably comes from the fact that the Air Force is a less restrained service. It is younger as a service. The people in it, senior people in it have seen it emerge to a position of equality or dominance for a period there, from being part of another service, from being part of the Army. In the period of the '30s and '40s they fought hard to give it autonomy, subsequently to give it independence, and after that to give it dominance, and they succeeded.

Of course, the pendulum has swung back a ways now, but this history of increasing prominence and success, and less tradition, or younger tradition, I think has made senior Air Force officers more willing to, or less willing to be bound by decisions of civilian superiors.

It is going on right now. It has been going on for years. General LeMay , when the decision went against the B-70, or when the Secretary of Defense declined to approve $50 million in the 1965 budget for advanced manned penetrating system development, didn't hesitate to send people up to the Hill, Air Force people up to Capitol Hill, to lobby against those decisions, and got Congress at one point to direct money to be spent on the so-called RS-70 system. He was doing what he thought was right, and I think there is just no question *that he is legally entitled to do so.*

The B-70 was a program which had had its ups and downs. It had more or less been decided against in 1959, and again in 1960 it had been cut way back. In fact, it had been effectively reduced to component development. Then in the fall of 1960, during the presidential campaign, a tentative decision was made and announced to reinstitute a program, but without making a decision for deployment. The decision was announced to go back to a substantial development program.

The money for that was never released, so in January and February of 1961, the new administration – this was before I arrived – was faced with a decision as to what to do. The decision that was made at that time was to have a three aircraft prototype program with no deployment, no production. It was believed three aircraft prototype program could be carried out with a total cost of $1.3 billion.

This is the XB-70. XB means experimental bomber. That X means just an experimental aircraft, not a production item. Most of that $1.3 billion had already been spent, but of that five or six hundred million dollars remained. This was the way things went along until – well, this was the decision. Things went along that way until the following spring for the revised Kennedy-Eisenhower budget.

That fall the corresponding budget was put in for the XB-70, but in October of 1961, the Air Force based on some suggestions that people in my own office had made to them, started to look at what they called the reconnaissance strike concept, but we asked them to think about what an aircraft could do that a missile could not do, and come up with some answers to that question. They did think about it, and they came up with a briefing in October of 1961, on what they then called the RS-70, which was different in idea from the B-70. The B-70 had just been a conventional bomber with one or two or three great big bombs in it which would be carried over to a predetermined target and dropped on it.

The idea of the RS-70 was to put in many smaller bombs, missile launched, actually, so as to give one better effectiveness for the system. It doesn't really take a 50 megaton bomb to put most military targets out of commission. This would allow you to attack many targets. It also added such concepts as a side-looking radar to give you good resolution, good bombing accuracy, so that you might

Another proposal was to use a B-70 as a launch vehicle for something like an X-15, with a docking bay fitted onto the B-70's spine to get the small craft aloft.
(NAA Rockwell)

be able to get by with very small yield, very small nuclear yield, and also some other concepts which were really just ideas.

After impact, you could see whether the crater that you had left included the target. I think that had a certain – to a degree that probably is true.

There was this enormous collection of claims for the aircraft, supportable, dubious, and ridiculous, which gradually evolved between the time the first presentation was made to the Secretary of Defense in October, and the time at which it was presented to Congress, actually to the House Armed Services Committee, on the House Armed Services committee's request, after someone in the Air Force had informed them that there was such a briefing.

They went up and they presented this. The committee decided that this presentation was worth $300 million, and put that money in the bill. They put it in originally directing it be spent, which did lead to a fairly nasty executive-legislative conflict of 'can the legislative direct that money be spent for something even if the executive does not want to spend it for that?'

Even though this was research and development money, and if I remember correctly there was no authorization for research and development required at that time, the House Armed Services Committee put into the authorization bill the money and the direction that it be used. The Senate went along and the bill passed, although the Senate did change the wording from directing Secretary of the Air Force to spend the money, to language which removed the attack on executive prerogative. But then the money had to be appropriated after having been authorized. That is when I spent my time with the House Defense Appropriations Subcommittee. They appropriated only $52 million of the three hundred and some odd million which was authorized, on the basis that the instrumentation required had not been developed. There was no proof that it could be developed. This money was to help develop it.

Interesting enough, after the money had been appropriated for this, the Air Force, since it was clear there was not going to be a big RS-70 program, got very much less interested in the question of whether any of the things which they had said they could do and would do as far as the RS-70 were feasible, and so I think although that money has been used, it has been incorporated into the XB-70 program to try to get the airplane to fly, and very little of it in the end has been used for developing side-looking radar of this resolution.

Brown was asked if the XB-70 programme had been continued all the time -

'That is right. It has stayed the Defense Department-Administrative program. It has required in the end $200 million of additional funding, and the program has been reduced to two aircraft, from three. The first aircraft is a year and a half late. It was supposed to fly in December of 1962. It will probably fly this summer. But the big question was never really about the aerodynamic capabilities—that is to say, whether you can fly a Mach 3 aircraft. It was whether the crew of a manned aircraft, whether the avionics, the side-looking radar, the bombing system, the navigation system, the air launched missiles could be accurate enough, resolution good enough, and the crew quick enough at assimilating the information and trying to find unknown targets to make a system a success.

The questions are still unanswered, because as I say, when it became clear

Another plan for the third Valkyrie was for an high-altitude observatory which would provide better access to astronomic phenomena than a ground based observatory. Air Vehicle 3 would be able to 'chase' a solar eclipse for example along it's path across the earth rather than rely on a single ground based observation. *(USAF)*

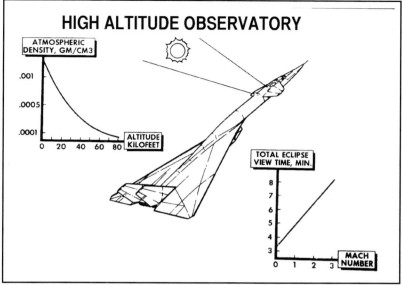

there was not going to be a $10 billion RS-70 program, the Air Force suddenly got very much less interested in answering the questions. I think that they are going to come up again in connection with the advanced manned penetration system. But the whole question of technical feasibility, the human capability is still an unanswered one. There is an antecedent unanswered one which McNamara insists on having answered first, and which is really the very first question, and that is, what is that you are going to do with this that you can't do better or as well or cheaper in other ways? There is the damage assessment mission. There is the precise attack which is a very accurate attack mission. There is the mission of finding targets you did not know about. There is the mission of finding mobile targets.

One has to weigh all of these against the following criteria: can they be done at all? Can you do them in other ways? How expensive is it to do them in other ways? How important is it to do them? Until those questions are answered, any such program is unlikely to be approved for very large expenditures.

The interviewer then questioned Brown if it was his office that had pushed the Air Force into generating the concept, but that he – Brown – had never been satisfied with their defence of...

I think that is accurate as an appraisal of the situation. We were the ones that said to them, 'You have to find something that the aircraft can do – the only justification for manned bombers, aside from diversity of the force, which is some justification, but not much, is to find things that it can do that missiles can't do'. They took off from that point to try to come up with the answers. I don't think they have come up with acceptable answers yet, but I think that they should keep trying.

The interviewer then asked Brown had he explicitly decided against their dropping big bombs?

'No, I think that is a separate question. I think that they decided if dropping big bombs on predesignated targets was the game, that airplanes were not

necessarily the best way to do that'. Clearly, this was a simple expression of preference to ICBMs.

The interviewer asked what was the President's role in these considerations, in particular about what became known as the Rose Garden incident – this was the infamous deal between Senator Carl Vinson, then head of the House Armed Services Committee, and a B-70 supporter, and President Kennedy, made in the White House Rose Garden.

McNamara had refused to spend funds assigned to the B-70 programme by using an obscure power created in a 1958 change in the National Security Act. So much was Kennedy enamoured of his Secretary of Defense that he worked out a deal with Vinson so that Congress would let McNamara have his way. It was known that McNamara did not have the political savvy to work out a situation in the normal Washington style, so the President, using his political skills with Vinson, had helped. Brown explained:

'Well, there was the famous Rose Garden session with Carl Vinson in which President Kennedy is alleged to agreed with Mr. Vinson that he would spend of the order of $50 million on the program, thus saving one sixth of Mr. Vinson's face, and Vinson had put in $300 million dollars, I guess. In return, Vinson agreed to withdraw or to recede from the language which he had put into his bill, which directed the administration to spend the money.

The Senate took out the language in their version of the authorization bill, and it went to conference. The Senate included the money in the authorization but with different language.

It seems that McNamara reacted to events like an on-off switch. It was all or nothing. That kind of attitude didn't cut it with Congress, the epitome of compromise. Figures didn't lie, McNamara believed; but he also knew that figures could be manipulated to prove anything. He had, at least, learned the basics. The interviewer then turned to the sniping that had being going on on Capitol Hill..

Oh, there are a lot of congressmen who are still mad that the B-70 – well, there are very few congressmen who will stand up for the B-70, but for the wrong reason, because it has not flown, and the program is obviously a lemon. That is not really quite fair. The issue is the same as it was. What good is the manned aircraft, and the issue never was can a manned Mach 3 aircraft fly, although as it turns out now, that is not the best platform to use. The Air Force in thinking about new manned bombers now is not thinking of Mach 3 high-flying aircraft. They are thinking of probably a variable sweep aircraft that can fly low and be less vulnerable that way.

But the real issue is as it has been. One of the things that a manned aircraft can do better than a ballistic missile system launched from the U.S. or from a submarine, is it feasible to do these technically? How much does it cost and is it worth it? Those remain the issues, but as I say most congressmen have become disillusioned with the B-70 but they are still for manned aircraft, and to that extent the argument persists and will come up again next year. It did come up again this year in connection with advanced manned penetrating system, and will come up again next year when the Air Force asks for quite a lot of money to do this, as I assume they will.

I think it has left quite a bit of bad feeling between some congressmen and

It is not surprising that due to the radical nature of the design, models of the B-70 spent a great deal of time in various wind tunnels, like this one at NASA. *(NASA)*

civilian officials of the Defense Department, probably the more so because these congressmen, many of them recognize that the outcome of the B-70 program has made them look bad, even though if you penetrate one layer deeper it is clear that the arguments they have made—while they may be wrong, they are not proven wrong by the fact that the B-70 fabrication of the aircraft has been unsuccessful.

The contractor really underestimated the fabrication problem, which shows that programs can go off the track, badly for non-fundamental reasons, but that pushes them off the track just as badly.

The Congress, as I say, contains many people who are very unhappy still, principally members of the Armed Services Committee of the House, and to a lesser extent some of the members of the Armed Services Committee of the Senate. But I think the senators, well, Senator Russell [Richard B. Russell, Jr.] and Senator Symington, Senator Saltonstall [Leverett Saltonstall] don't feel nearly so strong about that. I think they recognize that there are some fundamental questions here that the Air Force has not answered.

The Appropriations Committees, particularly the House Appropriations Committee, although they feel as many people feel that it is a mistake to rely entirely on missiles, has not adopted personal attitude. They do not feel that their personal honor is involved. Inevitably I have become the focus of some of the congressional feeling on some of these, since I have been the one that has often been used to defend the Secretary of Defense's position in this matter, which I think is a completely defensible position.

Brown was then asked to be specific as to who was doing the attacking...

Oh, I guess people like — not Mr. Vinson, himself. He has always been very gentlemanly about this. But F Edward Hébert, Porter Hardy, Jr, Mr Rivers to some degree, William G Bray, Leslie C Arends. The issue always presented is one of me versus General LeMay. The outcome is a peculiar one. I think General LeMay and I agreed on many of the questions. I don't think we — and many of the factors, and I think we disagree on the conclusions. But by and large I would be willing to spend more money on this than I think the Secretary of Defense is willing to spend, although far less than General LeMay wants to spend. So General LeMay does not regard me as his opponent here. If anything he regards me as, if not an ally, at least someone who is sympathetic.

The interviewer asked Brown his views on contractor performance...

I don't think there is a general statement that one can make. I think that there are a few good contractors, and that even the good ones fall down fairly often, and that most contractors find it hard being responsible. They don't like to take responsibility. In this I don't think they are very different from government officials or military men or anyone else. But I think that the Bell Telephone Laboratories performance on the Nike Zeus was outstanding. There is no question about it. They performed about that they said and about the time they said for about the price they said. I think that the North American performance on the B-70 has been singularly poor. They didn't think about it enough before they made their promises, and then they didn't take strong enough action and they got into trouble.

It is too early to tell how well it will succeed, but I think quite a lot of work has been done in incentive contracting in research and development. I don't think it has produced the result it should because the research and development contract is only a small part of the total and a contractor can still buy in on the research and development contract, that is, underbid, even if he knows it is going to lead to a penalty, even if he knows it is going to lead to a zero fee, and expect to recoup on the production. But I do believe that such things as project definition, which force the contractor and the service to think out in detail what the problems are going to be of the development, how long the development should take, how much it should cost, force them to prove out the component technologies before they go into a big engineering or operating systems development, or showing some success.

This leads to the question of did McNamara and his whizz kids really understand the technology behind the B-70 and the demands it was placing on those trying to develop it? After all, they were numbers men. They saw things in black and white terms of statistical analysis. The interviewer asked Brown if contractor performance evaluation was an innovation of McNamara's?

It has happened in the last three years, yes. I think we were the ones in this office who pushed it. Before you commit to a full scale development, you first go through a period of some months in which you detail the development in terms of cost, time, milestones, and so on, and assure yourself that the technologies have developed to the point where they can be put together in a system. You arrive at a schedule and cost and performance figures which can be made the basis of an incentive contract. This way the Secretary of Defense knows when he makes a decision what he is making a decision about, that is, it avoids putting him in a position of deciding to go ahead with this $500 million project which then turns out to cost $1.5 billion, and had he but known, he would not have approved it.

The design had been fully worked over, the money allocated. It was time to put politics aside and cut metal.

CONSTRUCTION

With its unique configuration, size, and power, the XB-70 was still an incredible thing to see on the ground, let alone in flight. From the forward canards to the massive vertical twin tails, it looked like a cobra just waiting to strike. Its appearance was kinetic: people who saw it parked on the flight line felt as if it was already moving.

The B-70 was basically a delta wing aircraft with canards; these aided in counteracting the trim changes that were intrinsic to flight at transonic speeds. They increased stability at high angles of attack and allowed for changes to be made without affecting the performance of the delta wing.

The canard trailing edges could be lowered up to 25 degrees, which would force the nose up. To compensate, the elevons moved down, causing all the surfaces to lift with nothing being lost from the basic wing lift. This permitted the B-70 to land at a conventional speed equivalent to commercial jet aircraft. Although canards were a mainstay of the B-70, in certain configurations they created unstable airflow around the entrances to the engine inlets.

Compression lift was designed into the B-70 with the wedge-shaped engine box positioned under the wing of the aircraft. This caused positive static pressure behind the main shock wave to react on the large underwing surface. Since there is no effect on the air flowing over the top of the wing to cancel out the resulting lift, at least a 30% improvement in lift was available without any increased drag on the aircraft.

The folding wingtips – if given their size they could be called 'tips' – of the B-70 were another design innovation. They pivoted in flight so they could be folded down for supersonic cruise. This configuration reduced supersonic directional stability problems, allowed the vertical stabilizers to be smaller than they might

Looking like something other worldly, the fuselage of AV 1 starts to come together. *(NAA/USAF)*

2 February 1962, and the
titanium cockpit of AV 1
comes together. The
four escape hatches are
clearly visible.
(NAA/USAF)

otherwise have been, and decreased trim drag at high Mach numbers. There were
three positions for the wingtips:

    1. Up at subsonic speed.

    2. 25 degrees down for low-altitude supersonic flight.

    3. 65 degrees down for high-altitude Mach 3 flight.

The XB-70 design had a long, graceful nose that supported a movable nose
ramp that formed one of two windshields. The moveable windshield and ramp
assembly consisted of five full-tempered glass panels in a framework structure
hinged at the forward end and guided by four frame-mounted roller assemblies.
In the full-up position, the slope of the ramp and wind-shield formed a nose
section contour that provided minimal drag. In the full-down position, a 24-degree
slope provided increased visibility for low-speed operations. Intermediate
positions could be selected as necessary.

The moveable windshield and ramp assembly was hydraulically operated and
electrically controlled. An emergency system was provided that allowed the ramp
to be fully lowered if the primary system failed. A windshield anti-ice and rain
removal system directed 600° F high-temperature engine extraction air through
two nozzles on the leading edge of the movable windshield. The inner fixed
windshield consisted of five glass panels in a 78-inch wide, 200 pound 7Al-4Mo
titanium forging. A defogging system was provided for the inner surface of both
the moveable and fixed windscreens.

The canard served mainly as a trimming device, but could be used in
conjunction with the elevons for additional pitch control. The entire canard could
be deflected from zero to six degrees for trim control, and the trailing edge could
be lowered 20 degrees to function as a flap. Leading edge sweep was 31.7 degrees

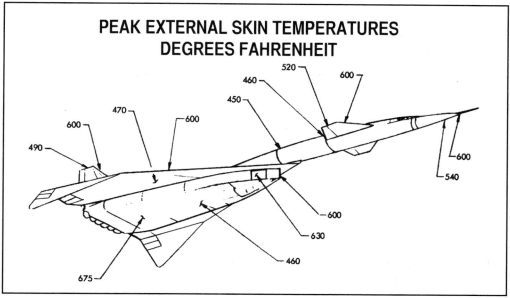

PEAK EXTERNAL SKIN TEMPERATURES
DEGREES FAHRENHEIT

The projected external skin temperatures on the XB-70.
(North American Rockwell)

with a total area of 265.28 square feet (415.59 square feet including the fuselage portion). The canard was constructed from a torsion box made of corrugated titanium spars and skin panels. Its leading edges were made from stainless steel honeycomb sandwich, and the trailing edge flaps were titanium.

High temperatures encountered when flying at Mach 2 to 3 made it necessary to build the XB-70 out of something other than standard aircraft aluminium.

That 'something' was stainless steel honeycomb. The XB-70 was not the first aircraft to be designed with stainless steel honeycomb sandwich panels; the B-58 Hustler had used it in several places earlier on. However, the XB-70 airframe consisted of at least 69% honeycomb material. Powerful as the aircraft was, weight was an important constraint. Since the honeycomb material lent itself to light weight, strength, smoothness, fatigue resistance, low heat transfer, and reliability at high temperature, it was considered the prime candidate for the B-70.

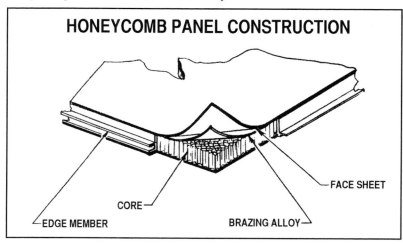

HONEYCOMB PANEL CONSTRUCTION

FACE SHEET

CORE

EDGE MEMBER

BRAZING ALLOY

The makeup of the stainless steel honeycomb panel construction used over large areas of the XB-70.
(North American Rockwell)

North American engineers designed the XB-70's skin so that instead of a single layer, it was a 'three-thickness skin', incorporating a two-inch layer of honeycomb foil between two thin sheets of stainless steel.

The stainless steel honeycomb was expensive to produce in such large quantities as would be required by the XB-70. Special autoclaves had to be built so that the sheets could be heat-treated in larger sizes than had ever been done before. The sheets had to be rolled so thin, down to almost two-thousandths of an inch, to compensate for any additional weight gain. Brazing the sheets together brought with it problems so critical that workers had to wear gloves to prevent oil from their fingertips from interfering with the metals as they were joined together. After cooling, the sheets were inspected by a sonar beam to detect any flaws.

This honeycomb material was used in the wings, engine box, mid-fuselage, and vertical stabilizers. The stainless steel used was PHI 5-7 Mo. (molybdenum steel). Titanium was about 8% of the total dry weight of 150,000 pounds, used mainly in the forward fuselage. There were actually three typess of titanium used. The first was Titanium 6Al-4V, which was heat-treated and used in thicknesses of 0.030 inches to 0.070 inches for the forward fuselage skin and 60-foot skin and stringers. The second was 4Al-3Mo-lV, heat-treated to 170,000 pounds/square inch. The third type of titanium, 7Al-4Mo, was used and also heat-treated to 170,000 pounds/square inch. In all, a total of 22,000 titanium parts were used in the XB-70 with 12,000 in the forward fuselage alone. Titanium was also used in the canard's main box, flaps, and vertical stabilizers.

As Wayne A Reinsche of NAA explained at the time the background to the

The major sub-assemblies of the forward fuselage. (North American Rockwell)

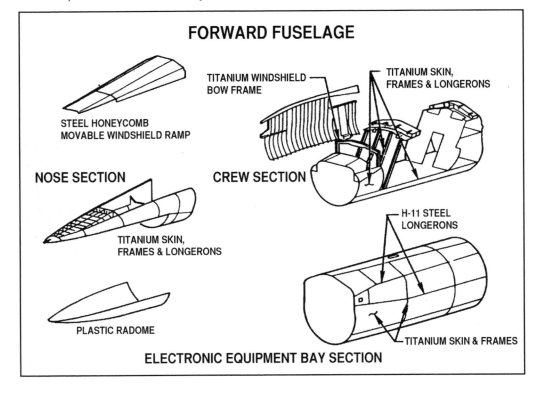

FORWARD FUSELAGE

STEEL HONEYCOMB
MOVABLE WINDSHIELD RAMP

TITANIUM WINDSHIELD
BOW FRAME

TITANIUM SKIN,
FRAMES & LONGERONS

NOSE SECTION

CREW SECTION

TITANIUM SKIN,
FRAMES & LONGERONS

H-11 STEEL
LONGERONS

PLASTIC RADOME

TITANIUM SKIN & FRAMES

ELECTRONIC EQUIPMENT BAY SECTION

A low-light time exposure seems to somehow make this picture of fitting the extreme nose section look all the more dramatic....

material and how it became used in the B-70:

'*Titanium provided us with an unusual opportunity to observe, and to participate in the development of, a structural metal from its initial halting steps of technical development to its position today as a mature material with a solid record of accomplishment, and the promise of an ever brighter future.*

A number of false starts and innumerable detail problems inevitably arose. They ran the spectrum from poor surface condition, lack of flatness, and poor thickness control, to alloy segregation, hydrogen contamination, and the welding of the material to cutting tool edges.

Attesting to the satisfactory solution to these problems is the outstanding service record achieved by titanium alloys over years of military and commercial applications in airframes and engines.

...a few days later, on 6 February, the cockpit section was mated with the other forward fuselage components. *(Both NAA/USAF)*

The developments in titanium technology in the past 10 or 15 years probably exceed the progress made in aluminium or steel technology for any comparable time span. This point has been emphasized repeatedly when we have used aluminium and steel to make comparisons with our titanium data, only to find

The first stage of AVCO Aerospace Structures process for fabricating the stainless steel honeycomb structure was to create a master model in a similar manner to how De Havilland's of England made their DH Mosquito back in 1940. This master model was then used to create the complex shapes. *(ACVO Corp)*

that similar data have never been obtained in these more prosaic materials.

In 1955 a daring concept of an aircraft with the ability to carry a payload intercontinental distances was viewed by many knowing technical people as not feasible. A further study of the concept imbedded this conviction more deeply in the minds of many, and kindled the spark of inspiration in the minds of a few who had the vision and faith to proceed.

The XB-70 was characterized by a long forward fuselage – often referred to in documents as the 'neck' – with a canard located just aft of the flight deck. At touchdown, the pilot was 30 feet above the ground and 110 feet ahead of the main landing gear.

The fuselage was a semi-monocoque structure of basically circular section, changing to a flat-top section in the crew compartment area. The forward fuselage was made of riveted titanium frames and skin over longerons of H-11 steel commonly called 'tool steel' by engineers.

The main crew entrance was on the left side of the aircraft, forward of the canard. This entrance was seventeen feet above ground level, requiring special access stands for entry and exit. Care had to be taken to ensure the access stand did not touch the fuselage, since rubbing could result in minor surface damage that would be aggravated by Mach 3 flight. There were four separate hatches in the upper fuselage, corresponding

The intermediate forward fuselage section – under construction by AVCO Aerospace Structures of Nashville TN. After fabrication and inspection, the panels were joined together by fusion welding. *(ACVO Corp)*

to the positions of the expected four-person crew in any future production version. In the XB-70As, the two forward hatches were removed by explosives in the event of crew ejection; the two aft hatches could be ballistically or manually removed for aircrew escape during ground emergencies.

In theory the XB-70As provided a 'shirt sleeve' environment, but in fact every flight over 50,000 feet was conducted with the crew in pressure suits. The crew compartment temperature could be regulated between 42°F and 105°F, according to crew preferences. A constant pressure altitude of 8,000 feet was maintained under normal circumstances, and an emergency ram air system could maintain a pressure altitude of 40,000 feet (requiring oxygen, but not pressure suits) in the event of a primary system failure.

Wayne A Reinsche continues to explain the construction details: *The airframe of the XB-70 contained 12,000 pounds of efficient titanium alloy structure comprising 23,000 detail parts. The structure also contained 22,000 square feet of stainless steel brazed honeycomb paneling; 22,000 pounds of high- strength H-11 steel; and lesser amounts of René 41, Inconel 718 and other alloys.*

The selection of the proper materials for various sections of the airframe was a painstaking engineering process, in which tentative target properties were first established for titanium alloys, steels, and aluminium alloys. Then, with the combined efforts of materials suppliers and North American engineers, specific alloys and types of construction were selected.

The airplane performance requirements dictated that aerodynamic heating

The assembly was then inverted, and fitted with stainless steel frames and bulkheads. The entire unit was then shipped from Nashville to Palmdale. *(ACVO Corp)*

would produce temperatures ranging from 450° F to 630° F over most of the aircraft, with higher temperatures in the engine areas. The requirement for extreme range meant that the structure would contain large volumes of kerosene-like fuel. Previously used concepts for fuel containment had to be abandoned. Fuel bladders would have been prohibitively heavy. Temperature fluctuations would make groove sealing inadequate. The concept of fuel-containing structure employing welding and brazing was, therefore adopted. For purposes of reviewing the materials selection and the structural configuration, we can consider two categories: fuel-containing and non-fuel-containing. In both categories, the high temperatures eliminated aluminium alloys as candidates, and the choice lay between titanium alloys and high-strength stainless steels.

The forward fuselage of AV 1 arrives outside the final assembly building on 31 March 1962. The lower cut-out in the extreme nose for the attack radars is very noticeable. These radars were never installed in the two aircraft that were completed. *(NAA/USAF)*

From a strength-to-weight ratio, titanium alloys were the better choice; however, in the fuel-containing areas, insulation became a controlling factor. It was necessary to keep the fuel below 300° F, and this could be accomplished by the use of honeycomb sandwich construction, with no additional insulation or refrigeration.

Brazed titanium honeycomb sandwich was very seriously considered for these areas, but was abandoned because little was known about the brazing of titanium. The final choice was brazed stainless steel honeycomb for most of the fueled areas.

In the forward 60 feet of fuselage, the design conditions were different. Here, honeycomb, even with insulation, would be inadequate to provide a habitable environment for the crew and for the electronic equipment, and refrigeration

The centre fuselage arrived at the final assembly building on 1 April...
(NAA/USAF)

would be necessary. Trade-off studies showed that, being committed to refrigeration in this area, titanium skin and frame construction would be more efficient than steel honeycomb.

With the wealth of successful experience as a background, the titanium applications for the XB-70 were approached with confidence. One of the main design parameters was that the aircraft sustain a life of 5000 flight hours. This is a relatively short life requirement in comparison to the requirement of 40,000 or 50,000 hours for a commercial supersonic transport, and it meant that the fatigue life of the structure would be determining factors.

... and was soon lifted into position on the assembly jigs.

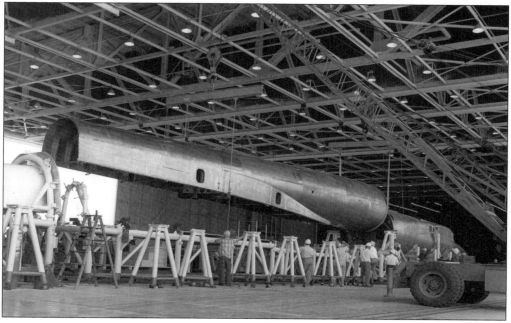

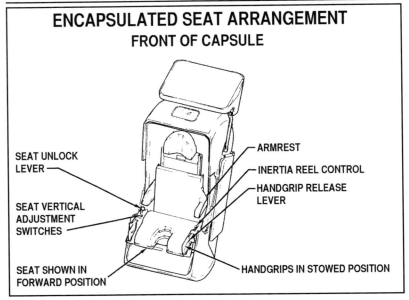

ENCAPSULATED SEAT ARRANGEMENT
FRONT OF CAPSULE

SEAT UNLOCK
LEVER

SEAT VERTICAL
ADJUSTMENT
SWITCHES

SEAT SHOWN IN
FORWARD POSITION

ARMREST

INERTIA REEL CONTROL

HANDGRIP RELEASE
LEVER

HANDGRIPS IN STOWED POSITION

Details of the
encapsulated seat as
fitted to the B-70.
*(North American
Rockwell)*

Crew Capsules

The pilot and co-pilot sat side-by-side in individual escape capsules. On AV 3 and operational aircraft there would have been offensive and defensive systems operators sitting behind the two pilots. Each escape capsule had a self-contained oxygen and pressurization system, affording complete crew protection during and following ejection. The capsules could also be closed, if necessary, for crew protection during an in-flight emergency, particularly one that involved the decompression of the crew compartment. Limited control of the aircraft and engines (throttle down only) was possible from inside the closed capsules, which had a window on the front edge so the occupant could see the instrument panel.

When the capsules were closed the crew microphones were constantly 'on' to

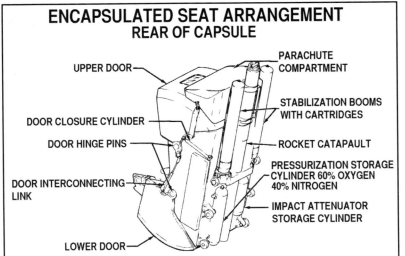

ENCAPSULATED SEAT ARRANGEMENT
REAR OF CAPSULE

UPPER DOOR

DOOR CLOSURE CYLINDER

DOOR HINGE PINS

DOOR INTERCONNECTING
LINK

LOWER DOOR

PARACHUTE
COMPARTMENT

STABILIZATION BOOMS
WITH CARTRIDGES

ROCKET CATAPAULT

PRESSURIZATION STORAGE
CYLINDER 60% OXYGEN
40% NITROGEN

IMPACT ATTENUATOR
STORAGE CYLINDER

The B-70 Final Study
Report as drawn up by
North American
Rockwell provided much
additional information
about the general
arrangement of the
encapsulated seats.
*(North American
Rockwell)*

provide continuous communication. The capsules provided a meaningful method of escape from the B-70 from an altitude of zero to 80,000 feet and at speeds from 100 to 2,000 mph.

The encapsulation and ejection process was controlled by handgrips within the capsules. Raising the handgrips automatically encapsulated the crewman, while squeezing a trigger within the handgrip jettisoned the escape hatch in the roof and ejected the capsule. A rocket catapult mechanism propelled the capsule from the aircraft and clear of the vertical stabilizers, while stabilization booms deployed to prevent the capsule from tumbling. As the capsule descended, barometrically-controlled actuators deployed the recovery parachute and impact attenuator. The extended stabilization booms provided the capsule with a self-righting characteristic in the event of water landing, and the capsule was water tight and could float for prolonged periods.

From the drawing board to reality – the open and closed 'escape capsule' as fitted to the B-70. *(NAA/USAF)*

Indeed, an Air Force volunteer survived 72 hours afloat in a B-70 capsule in January 1960 during tests. Survival equipment consisting of cold weather clothing, a life raft, sustenance gear, signaling equipment, first aid kit, and rations was provided in four separate kits in each capsule, mounted on the upper left and right walls and under the capsule floor.

The encapsulation seat system was heavily evaluated at the Joint Parachute Test Facility at El Centro, CA, undergoing 52 rate of descent and structural integrity tests from April to November 1959. This was followed by five capsule drops at 130 knots

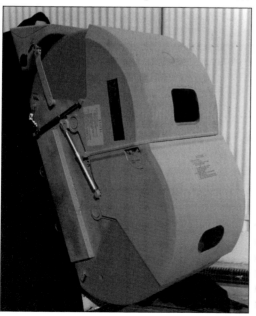

from a C-130 and twelve ejections at 200 to 280 knots at an altitude of 40,000 feet from a B-47. A further two ejection tests were also performed at speeds between Mach 0.8 and Mach 1.6 at 38,000ft using a B-58. Rocket sled tests were accomplished at Hurricane Mesa, Utah test facility and Edwards AFB.

In the laboratory pressure chamber, the capsule underwent tests to a maximum 'altitude' of 100,000 feet using dummy, simian and human occupants. Out of doors, the capsule was dropped from a crane seventeen times over land and water with either a dummy or human on board.

The B-70 instrument panels were a mixture of traditional round instruments and the unique vertical 'tape' instruments that found brief favour during the 1960s. The instruments were colour-coded and illuminated by white light, as the traditional red cockpit lighting washes out colour. Critical flight instruments were visible from inside the capsules when the doors were closed.

AV 1 with the moveable
windshield ramp
installed. The twin
rudders are also in place
and one of the wing
panels is being moved
into position for
trimming to contour...

Folding Wings

The wing had an aspect ratio of 1.751:1, with a mean chord of 117.75 feet at the root and 2.25 feet at the tip. The leading edge was swept back at 65.56 degrees and the total area was 6,297.15 square feet. The entire upper and lower wing surface was covered with brazed stainless steel honeycomb sandwich panels welded together. Leading edges were attached directly to the front spar. The spars were of the sine-wave webbed type. AV 1 had no anhedral, but the second aircraft featured 5 degrees of dihedral. Both aircraft had a slight aerodynamic twist on the outer panel leading edge. The wing-to-fuselage joint was 80 feet

...which was done using a
special rig with 'skates'
running on tracks as
seen here to complete
the final trim.
(NAA/USAF)

The trimming rig is in place to cut the final fitting of the wing hinge. A large number of the wing panels are yet to be installed.

The wing-to-fuselage joins were different between AV 1 and AV 2, as shown in these detail sketches.
(North American Rockwell)

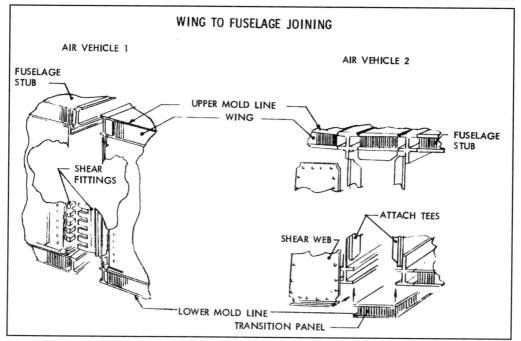

WING TO FUSELAGE JOINING

AIR VEHICLE 1

AIR VEHICLE 2

FUSELAGE STUB

UPPER MOLD LINE
WING

FUSELAGE STUB

SHEAR FITTINGS

ATTACH TEES

SHEAR WEB

LOWER MOLD LINE
TRANSITION PANEL

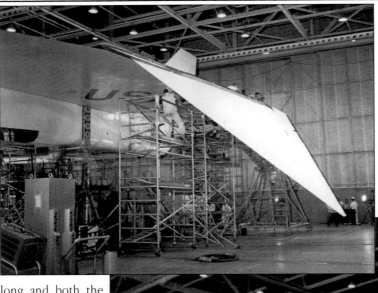

Two views of the front and rear of AV 1 with the wingtip in fully 'down' position. The aircraft had to be put on very tall jacks to prevent the wingtip hitting the floor. *(North American Rockwell)*

long and both the inner and outer honeycomb face sheets of the upper and lower wing surfaces had to be welded together. The first step welded the inner edge of the honeycomb using a tungsten electrode inserted through a 0.125 inch gap between the outer face sheets, which were then joined with a filler strip welded with an electron-beam gun to minimize shrinkage. In all, there were over six miles of welding during component assembly and two and a half miles of welding during final assembly; several of these miles involved the edges of fuel tanks.

The outer 40% span of each wing could be folded downward to increase directional stability during high-speed flight. Each tip occupied about 500 square feet of area and was driven by six Curtiss-Wright 32,000:1 motor hinges housed under a black magnesium-thorium fairing. On production aircraft the leading edge of the fairing would have housed an infrared sensor for the defensive avionics. The wing tips could be set to three positions: UP, HALF (25 degrees down on AV 1 and 30 degrees on AV 2), and DOWN (64.5 degrees on AV 1 and 69.5 degrees on AV 2). The UP position was used or landing, take-off, and subsonic flight, the HALF position was used for supersonic flight, while the DOWN position was used at very high speeds (Mach 2.5 and up). Use of the folding wing tips eliminated the increased drag that would have resulted if larger vertical stabilizers had been used instead. When the tips were fully down, the shock wave they generated impinged on the bottom surface of the wing, adding about 5% more lift to the compression lift already being generated.

Weight-on-wheels sensors prevented the wings from being folded on the ground since the tips would impact the ground in the full down position. An emergency up system was provided in the event the two primary systems failed to return the wings to the up position during flight.

At first the design folded the outer 20% of each wing – however, wind tunnel models soon indicated that additional surface area was required for directional stability, so the fold line was moved inboard to between the fourth and fifth elevon. This led to complications since the outer two elevon sections would be located on the folding part of each wing tip. A wing fold disengage system was incorporated that automatically locked the outer two elevon sections on each wing at the neutral position and disengaged them from further movement until the wings were unfolded.

Elevons at the wing trailing edge were segmented into six sections per side to reduce air load bending effects. Two hydraulic actuators powered each elevon segment, which could move 30% up or down from the centre line. Symmetrical movement of the elevons provided basic pitch control; differential movement provided roll control.

Above: A close-up of the wing hinge mechanism before the aerodynamic fairing covered it.

Right: The date is 6 June 1964, and AV 1 undergoes wing fold tests with the wingtip in the mid position.
(Both North American Rockwell)

The XB-70As had a flight augmentation control system that used electrical signals in parallel with mechanical linkages between the control columns and hydraulically-actuated flight controls. The actual deflection of the flight control panels was primarily by the mechanical linkage; the electrical control provided a small degree of deflection for trim purposes. The augmentation system also provided auto-damping about all three axes.

The vertical stabilizers had a leading edge sweep of 51.76 degrees and 234 square feet of area. Interestingly, if North American had not opted for the folding wingtips, the vertical stabilizers would have needed 468 square feet to provide equivalent directional stability. Only the forward lower edge (about a third of the area) was fixed; the rest of the surface was used as a rudder driven by dual hydraulic actuators. The hinge line was located at 45 degrees from the vertical. The rudders could deflect 12 degrees either side of centre.

The fixed supporting base was a multi-spar design with honeycomb skin panels and was attached to the wing root junction by mechanical fasteners. The movable rudders were also multi-spar with brazed honeycomb skin panels. Leading and trailing edges were full-depth honeycomb wedges.

The aft fuselage was a hybrid structure consisting of a variety of different construction techniques and materials. During high speed flight the external skin temperatures of some areas could reach 600° F, while the internal temperatures could exceed 900° F in the aft fuselage due to engine heat.

Since the engines occupied most of the last 26 feet of the lower fuselage and the air intakes and weapons bay occupied most of the forward section, North American could not use full-depth transverse framing. In order to carry the wing bending loads across the fuselage, NAA used multiple shallow-depth crossbeams to form the upper part of the box. The side and lower transverse frames supported the engine access doors and were used to complete the box. The spars were machined from H-11 and used titanium webs. At the side of the fuselage, the honeycomb sandwich wing stub was joined to the H-11 frames with high-strength mechanical fasteners. The skin covering the top and sides of the lower fuselage was 6A1-4V titanium alloy riveted in place. The engine compartment doors used 6A1-4V titanium alloy skins over 4Al-3Mo-IV titanium frames.

Part of the aft fuselage was a complex piece of engineering design. It had to mount the six J93 engines, be stiff enough to absorb the massive aerodynamic loads of the wings flexing in flight and also provide space for large doors to give access to the engines. *(NAA/USAF)*

The original B-70 design included two weapons bays. When it became clear that the high energy fuel programme would not materialize and the new bomber would have to rely on less-efficient JP6, the aft weapons bay was converted into additional fuel storage. As built, the 29-foot long weapons bay on the XB-70As extended from fuselage station YF1356 to YF1704. The opening of the bay was seven feet above ground level and was covered by two sets of doors operating on a single set of tracks, the length of which permitted only one set of doors to be opened at a time. Moving both doors aft opened the forward fourteen feet of the bay; moving only the aft door opened the rear fourteen feet of the bay. The centre one foot was unusable since the doors never cleared the area. This also meant that weapons longer than about thirteen feet could not be carried by the B-70.

In the closed position the leading edge of the forward door was held tight against the step fairing of the fuselage by two interconnected hooks that engaged the fuselage structure. The aft door was locked to the forward door in an identical manner. It should be noted that the weapons bay doors on AV 1 and AV 2 were not powered and could not be opened in flight. AV 3 would have had powered doors, as well as suspension and release equipment in the rear portion of the weapons bay for a single type of weapon for demonstration purposes.

Wayne Reinsche talks again about the B-70 structure – particular care had to be taken with how they were handled and treated: *'The search for the alloys with maximum strength, adequate fracture toughness, and maximum stiffness led to the selection of a number of highly specialised materials in sheet, bar forging and extruded form. These alloys were used in the solution treated and aged condition (STA) for nearly all applications.*

For skins where high strength combined with high fracture toughness was needed, the 6A1-4V(STA) material was used. Where high strength coupled with maximum formability was needed, such as in frames, the UAl-3Mo-lV (STA) material was used.

The fabrication processes used for the titanium areas of the XB-70 included

A J93 engine is given a trial installation as a functional check on 26 July 1962. The size of the 'six pack' as the engine area became known is very evident here. From the photograph it is possible to see that one vertical fin has been installed, along with a temporary strut. *(NAA/USAF)*

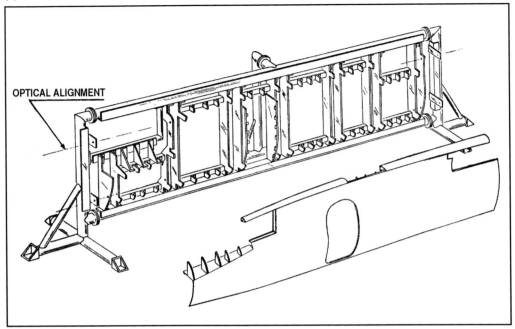

OPTICAL ALIGNMENT

many new developments, a number of established practices, and some modifications of existing processes to accommodate the solution treating and aging sequences and the attendant high strengths. Of particular interest were thermal processing, forming, welding, chemical milling, and machining.

The thermal processing of titanium alloys could be used to strengthen, to soften, to relieve forming or welding stresses, to recover compressive yield strength lost by forming, or to impart special corrosion-resistant properties. Thermal processing can produce undesirable characteristics in the alloys, as well. Foremost among these are surface contamination by oxygen and nitrogen, and distortion.

Both contaminated surfaces and distortion from quenching were considered serious problems if this operation were to be performed at North American. Another choice was the purchasing of material in the solution treated (ST) or solution treated and aged condition (STA) from the mill. The latter choice would require that the contaminated surface problem and quenching distortion would be taken care of at the supplier's mill.

It had the obvious advantages that material with contaminated surfaces from the mill would have predictable thickness tolerances and, if chemical processing were used to remove the contaminated surfaces, the hydrogen content, which might be increased by pickling, could be determined prior to shipment. A penalty for this choice would be reduced formability.

It developed that the suppliers were able to remove contamination by belt grinding and pickling, and keep the hydrogen levels within acceptable limits. By stretcher leveling and roller leveling, a flatness of 3% or less could be met. This was measured by dividing the depth of a wave or buckle by one-half the length of the wave, measured crown-to-crown. It was decided that the reduced formability of ST material compared to that of A material was acceptable, and

The 26 feet long by 9 feet tall major assembly fixture for the crew compartment side panel that used optical alignment to check accuracy of build. All the major sub-units were built in this manner and then assembled into larger and larger units. *(North American Rockwell)*

the sheet material for STA parts was procured as ST or STA.

Just as Lockheed were pushing against the boundaries of what was known with the construction of their highly secret RS/SR-71 Blackbird, so North American were coming up against similar obstacles. The forming of titanium and its alloys was once considered unpredictable and difficult by the aircraft industry. Prior to and during the XB-70 programme, working this metal broke new ground and developed into a series of procedures capable of producing close-tolerance parts with high structural integrity at an acceptable cost. The higher cost of titanium alloys was one of the reasons for the development of precision forming methods, since the scrap rates acceptable in the industry for aluminium alloy parts were intolerable for similar titanium alloy parts. To bring the rejection rates to an acceptable level, a systematic approach was made to categorize the alloy characteristics which affected forming to identify the material defects and variations which could cause rejected parts, and to establish exacting forming procedures and limits.

Wayne Reinsche: *Titanium alloys are somewhat notch-sensitive, requiring careful attention to removal of burrs, edge notches, and surface scratches before being formed. Marks left by belt grinding of sheet surfaces have, at times, been a problem and have required polishing prior to forming.*

Two specific types of contamination can be detrimental to forming operations and service performance. One is formation of a brittle surface layer produced by heating above about 900° F in the presence of air. This contamination can be removed by blasting, pickling, or chemical milling. The

From the B-70 Aircraft Study comes these details of the construction of the rear fuselage *(North American Rockwell)*

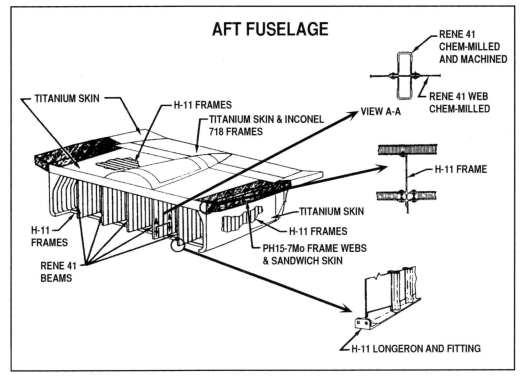

AFT FUSELAGE

TITANIUM SKIN

H-11 FRAMES

TITANIUM SKIN & INCONEL 718 FRAMES

VIEW A-A

RENE 41 CHEM-MILLED AND MACHINED

RENE 41 WEB CHEM-MILLED

H-11 FRAME

TITANIUM SKIN

H-11 FRAMES

PH15-7Mo FRAME WEBS & SANDWICH SKIN

H-11 FRAMES

RENE 41 BEAMS

H-11 LONGERON AND FITTING

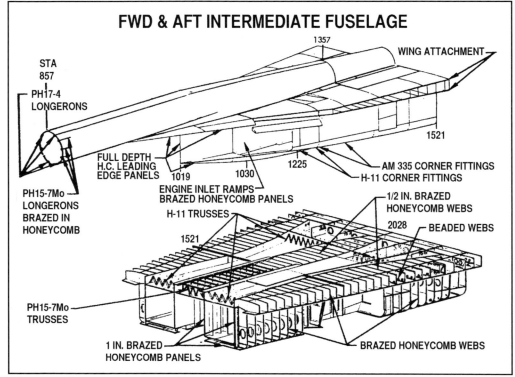

FWD & AFT INTERMEDIATE FUSELAGE

The intermediate fuselage was divided into fore and aft sections and contained a number of fuel tanks and air ducting for the engines. *(North American Rockwell)*

other type of contamination results in cracking during heating and is caused by such things as fingerprints which contain chlorine, other halogen-containing materials, and iron oxide. This problem is avoided by using clean tools and carefully cleaning parts before they are subjected to heat.

All standard sheet metal practices were used in forming XB-70 titanium parts, but with special care. These basic forming operations were performed at room or elevated temperatures depending on configuration, and a part with compound curvatures may have required drop-hammer forming because of its unique shape. Since forming of titanium is best accomplished at a slow rate, but drop hammering is a rapid operation, elevated temperature forming was mandatory. Heating for drop-hammer forming was accomplished by quartz lamp, by electrical resistance methods, and by heating in conventional recirculating air furnaces with a quick transfer to the forming die.

Simple frames were formed on a rubber pad hydro-press with a slow deformation rate. This was performed at room temperature, resulting in a partially completed shape. It was followed by hot-sizing. The soak time was usually about 10 minutes, with the die being the same steel tool as is used for hydropress preform operations, additionally augmented with matched side members.

Power-brake forming was used to produce angles, Z-sections, hat sections, and channels on standard brake tools. These shapes usually were formed at room temperature where an inherent springback of approximately 30 degrees in the included angle occurred.

NAA eventually reached the point with the XB-70 where rejection rates in forming and working titanium was at negligible levels and the company was able to produce parts to close tolerances that permitted efficient assembly sequences which included fusion and resistance welding, riveting and bolting.

The Valkyrie's nose radome was constructed of a product called Vibran; it was laminated to ensure protection of all the electronics it carried. All these different metal types, the comprehensive stress analysis, elastic analysis, load factors, and the myriad of other tests that were done during the initial design phase, comprised one of the most ambitious programmes in the construction of an airframe. Mach 3 did not come easy for the Valkyrie, but it would come.

Bringing the parts together

Major airframe mating commenced with the joining operation of the fuselage aft and forward centre sections on May 18, 1962 and progressed to a completion of fuselage joining on July 18. Subsequently, major problems in structure repair, wing to fuselage mismatch and fuel tank sealing were encountered. These problems delayed completion of wing joining on AV 1 from 14 January 1963 until 24 April 1964.

The sealing of the fuel tanks to essentially a zero leakage level was required not only to prevent fuel leaks but primarily to prevent dissipation of the gaseous nitrogen which was used as an inerting agent in the fuel tanks. The basic fuel tank sealing was accomplished by a metal-to-metal seal provided by welding or brazing in the process of joining individual panels. The criterion for sealing required that a tank hold air at a pressure of 10 pounds per square inch with so-called 'zero leakage'. Since the accuracy of the measurement of leakage was not absolutely precise, an indicated leakage of less than 10 cubic inches per minute was considered acceptable. This is equivalent to allowing one hole the diameter of a human hair in a 3,000 square foot surface.

To locate the leaks, the tanks were either vacuum or pressure checked utilizing various methods of leak detection. Detecting leaks was a repetitive operation, with lesser leaks showing up as larger leaks were eliminated. Leaks

The part-assembled Air Vehicle One on its own landing gear is wheeled to the next stage of the build. It appears that the machine has been fitted with some kind of temporary fairing enclosing the nose equipment bay and covers up the cockpit glazing. Some accounts suggest that this was a coating of 'Spraylat' peelable paint, applied to protect the completed area. *(NAA/USAF)*

which were approximately .050 to .060 inches in diameter were located by application of a soap solution over the suspect area with incoming air creating bubbles at the point of leakage. Another method utilized for detecting sizable leaks was to locate the point by an ultrasonic device which detected the passage of air through an orifice. A staining dye activated by ammonia drawn through the holes was used to outline smaller or pinpoint holes, while almost invisible holes were located by means of a helium gas sniffer.

Another view of the part-completed machine, presumably taken at the same time, but this time from the rear, showing the upper surface of the main wing box is incomplete, but the rear already contains the vertical fin 'stubs' to which will later be fitted the rudders. *(NAA/USAF)*

Prior to the end of 1962 a seal brazing technique was used on the aforementioned pinhole leaks or if a doubler type repair was required. This technique utilized a braze alloy that melted at a temperature of about 1,160° F, applied by a hand-held torch. This process was very critical and time consuming, since no sealing was accomplished if the temperature was too low and secondary damage to the thin honeycomb panel face sheets occurred if the temperature was too high. Damage of this nature to various fuel tank sections caused a heavy workload at the end of 1962. Approximately 3000 of these areas had to be inspected and repaired where damage was found.

Another process which contributed to delay was the portable nickel plating utilized in structural repairs. As this process was used, it was found that if a small fissure or defect existed in the panel, the plating solution could seep through into the panel and cause core corrosion. Repairing this damage necessitated the removal and replacement of complete steel honeycomb panels, which in turn further delayed tank completions and sealing.

It also became apparent during the XB-70 structural assembly, that thin-faced honeycomb panels were prone to handling damage. The repair and associated sealing of the damaged panels presented special processing problems not previously anticipated. The use of brazing and welding methods of sealing the thin gauged structure proved very difficult and resulted in formation of structurally unacceptable wrinkles and buckles. With precise process control, the sealing procedures were used successfully; however, when the brazing and welding procedures were used in areas of limited access or under adverse conditions, panel damage occurred. This unacceptable condition initiated investigations to find a sealing method compatible with the thin gauged structure under the adverse working conditions usually experienced in tank sealing.

A new method of sealing small pinhole leaks was developed in the early months of 1963. This process consisted of plasma-spraying aluminium over a leaking area and then applying six coats of DuPont Viton-B sealant cured at 375°F. This sealing method did result in some secondary heat damage to the structure but considerably less than that experienced with earlier processes. Viton sealing was constrained at times during the mating operations due to the flammability potential when welding was taking place in adjacent areas.

A series of tools were originally programmed to assure the close tolerances required to mate the wing to the wing stubs. However, in order to conserve funds, most of the wing joining tools were eliminated in the programme redirection of April 1961 and only contour support tools were provided. This necessitated matching the wing joint by optical methods, involving the fit of four contoured surfaces along an 80 foot distance to an accuracy of .008 inches or less. When this was initially attempted in late 1962, it was found that the support surfaces along the length of the wing would move and that ambient temperature differentials would also move the two surfaces of the wing and wing stub apart. After several attempts, matching by this technique was abandoned and a fitting was designed to attach to the wing stub to compensate for the inaccuracies in the joint alignment permitted by the simplified tooling. These match operations were constrained by the fuel tank sealing required in the wing root stub tanks. Fusion and electron beam welding were employed in wing joining; fusion on the inner weld and electron beam on the outer. Subsequent to inner weld completion and prior to starting the outer weld, the

Plywood protection sheets cover most of the upper wing surfaces to prevent damage by people walking on the stainless steel honeycomb. One of the two doors covering the brake chute compartment has been fitted, as are the jury struts holding the rudders in place. This is AV/2 and the date is 20 January 1965.
(NAA/USAF)

wing joint was x-ray inspected and the tanks were pressurized for leak detection. Extensive preparations were required in support of the external electron beam welding. These preparations consisted of cleaning the weld joint, applying RTV 77 sealant, and then placing a smooth plate over the sealant to hold the vacuum box and electron beam gun.

The first step of the wing mate was to bring the wing up to the wing stub and complete the final trim on the areas to be welded. Shear ties – 49 to each wing – were then located and welded to the wing and stub frames. Subsequent to this a few cross ship installations were completed after which the actual joining commenced.

Fueling the beast

The fuel system of each XB-70A was equipped with eleven tanks, although this itself does need some explanation. There were eleven physical tanks, although most of the NAA documentation states that there were eight – because the two adjacent wing tanks were considered as one unit since they were controlled together in order to control the centre of gravity. Also, since tank No. 3 was over the centre of gravity, it was used as a sump tank and not for fuel storage. Five of the tanks were located in the aft part of the fuselage neck, and three integral tanks were in the main part of each wing. On AV 1, tank No. 5 was inoperative due to the unresolved leakage problems.

The wing tanks were emptied first. From the main tanks, fuel was fed to the No. 3 sump tank as dictated by engine requirements and center of gravity concerns. At cruise power, fuel flowed from tank No. 3 to the engines at 785 pounds per minute. Fueling and de-fueling were accomplished through a single-point receptacle at a rate of 600 gallons per minute. An adjacent control panel allowed ground crew to select which tanks were to be filled or drained. A fuel

This view gives a good idea of the size of the forward avionics bay and the empty upper hatches.
(North American Rockwell)

tank sequence panel on the copilot's instrument panel presented a graphic display of tank sequencing. Dual-coloured tapes (white and black) were used to indicate the fuel level in each tank – white indicated fuel; black indicated no fuel. When the display was completely black, the tank was empty. The inter-tank transfer of fuel was automated on AV 2, but was accomplished manually by the copilot in AV 1.

Following studies, it was planned that the third prototype and production aircraft would have included an aerial refueling receptacle on the upper surface of the nose forward of the articulating windshield. At one stage studies were planned to determine the feasibility for supersonic refueling. AV 3 would be used to make a series of 'dry hook-ups' between itself and another supersonic aircraft, possibly another B-70.

Fuel was used for cooling various systems through a series of heat exchangers supplied from the sump (No. 3) fuel tank. At Mach 3 the fuel could absorb over 30,000 BTUs per minute from the hydraulic, engine oil, and environmental control systems. However, towards the end of the mission or during periods when the fuel flow was low (such as during in-flight refueling when the engines were throttled back) a secondary cooling method used 4,000 pounds of water that acted as a substitute heat sink. The water was vapourised at a rate of 28 pounds per minute in a boiler by the latent heat from the systems normally cooled by the fuel.

Gaseous nitrogen was used for fuel tank pressurization and inerting. Two liquid nitrogen storage vessels each holding 350 pounds of LN2 under 83 psi pressure. A vaporiser circuit converted liquid nitrogen into gaseous nitrogen which was then supplied to the various fuel tanks and lines under pressure. At the end of a high-speed flight, a fuel-to-water heat exchanger assured that the fuel delivered to the engines did not exceed 260° F.

Oxygen in the JP-6 was considered detrimental both to the stability of the fuel

and also to aircraft safety. To help eliminate the oxygen, the fueling process for the XB-70A was somewhat elaborate. A tanker full of JP6 began by pumping the fuel into a second, empty tanker. At the same time, the second tanker was being pressurized with high-pressure dry nitrogen which was bubbled through the JP-6 as it was pumped in. The dry nitrogen drove out any oxygen in the fuel, and the 'clean' JP-6 was then pumped into the XB-70 already partially pressurized with nitrogen.

Many of the other systems of the XB-70 were also revolutionary and while the wing mate and tank seal problems were being solved, other parts of the aircraft were being worked on.

AV 1 takes another trip outside, this time under the glare of a pair of huge floodlights. Unlike the RS/SR-71 being built in great secrecy at the Lockheed Skunk works, NAA were proud of what they were building and never missed a chance for more photographs. (NAA/USAF)

A comfortable environment

The 'shirt sleeve' environment for pilots was a concept unheard of at the flight speed and altitude that was marked for the XB-70. The shirt sleeve environment was accomplished mainly by use of a high-pressure bleed air system, supported by Freon refrigeration units. This twofold system maintained the cabin pressure at 8,000 feet. If a rapid decompression occurred due to mechanical or some other failure, the

The twin verticals are installed on AV-1. (NAA/USAF)

AV 2 comes together in the assembly hangar at Palmdale. The aircraft sits on jacks ready to test the wing-fold mechanism. *(North American Rockwell)*

pilots could encapsulate and fly the XB-70 from within clamshell capsules. The refrigeration system relied on two Freon units that helped cool the crew cabin and the equipment bays. These units used high-pressure bleed air to run the Freon compressor turbines. The air entered at 850° F, but by the time the additional bleed air for the fuselage pressurization left the Freon exchangers, the temperature was reduced to 45°F. Any area that was to be cooled actually had tiny holes perforating the walls. Air was then circulated into a glass-lined plenum cell at the end of the porous wall and ducted back to the heat exchangers after passing through a water vaporizer. There was even a provision for a liquid ammonia tank so that the ammonia could be used as a powerful, short-term evaporative coolant as a backup for when the water tank was empty at the end of a long flight. Through all of this, the crew cabin was left at a comfortable temperature.

Engine breathing

All engineers designing supersonic aircraft have to find a way to slow down the engine intake air to subsonic velocities. In the XB-70A, two separate and independent inlet duct systems were provided, each delivering air to three engines. Each intake was about seven feet high at the splitter. From there the air was ducted approximately 80 feet back to a plenum chamber just ahead of the engines. The plenum chamber was the size of a small bedroom. The rectangular-section intake was manufactured from brazed stainless steel honeycomb sandwich panels except for H-11 tool steel sections around the front of the engines. The primary function of the Hamilton Standard inlet control system was to position the shock waves created at supersonic speeds so that the air entering the engines was subsonic. Each duct system incorporated a rectangular variable-geometry inlet, a variable area bypass, a boundary layer bleed air control, and an air inlet control system (AICS). Varying the inlet geometry was accomplished by a movable panel system in each inlet duct. Each inlet had three fixed ramps, three movable panels, plenum divider panels that

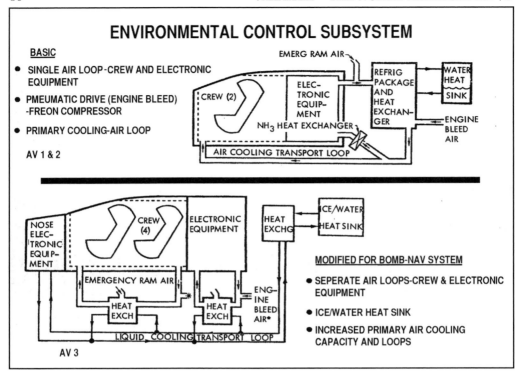

ENVIRONMENTAL CONTROL SUBSYSTEM

BASIC

- **SINGLE AIR LOOP-CREW AND ELECTRONIC EQUIPMENT**
- **PMEUMATIC DRIVE (ENGINE BLEED) -FREON COMPRESSOR**
- **PRIMARY COOLING-AIR LOOP**

AV 1 & 2

EMERG RAM AIR

CREW (2)

ELEC-TRONIC EQUIP-MENT

NH₃ HEAT EXCHANGER

AIR COOLING TRANSPORT LOOP

REFRIG PACKAGE AND HEAT EXCHAN-GER

WATER HEAT SINK

ENGINE BLEED AIR

NOSE ELEC-TRONIC EQUIP-MENT

CREW (4)

ELECTRONIC EQUIPMENT

HEAT EXCHG

ICE/WATER HEAT SINK

EMERGENCY RAM AIR

HEAT EXCH

HEAT EXCH

ENG-INE BLEED AIR*

LIQUID COOLING TRANSPORT LOOP

AV 3

MODIFIED FOR BOMB-NAV SYSTEM

- **SEPERATE AIR LOOPS-CREW & ELECTRONIC EQUIPMENT**
- **ICE/WATER HEAT SINK**
- **INCREASED PRIMARY AIR COOLING CAPACITY AND LOOPS**

isolated four compartments just inboard of the inlet, and hydraulic actuators to position the panels. These ramps and panels served three primary functions: they formed the inlet duct wall, set up a shock wave pattern during supersonic flight, and provided a means of bleeding the boundary layer air.

Approximately 90% of the air compression was performed in the inlet, not in the engine. The inlet was designed to reduce the free-stream air velocity from Mach 3 to less than Mach 1 by a series of shock waves, beginning with the primary shock wave created by the leading edge of the splitter duct and ending aft of the minimum throat area. Ideally, the terminal shock wave would have been at the minimum throat area. But factors such as gust disturbances could 'pop' the shock outside the inlet, resulting in an 'unstart' and possible engine flameout. Engineers decided to accept a small performance penalty and move the shock wave further aft in an attempt to prevent this.

Two secondary shock waves prior to the duct entrance were caused by breaks in the sweep of the splitter duct. The air followed a circular route in the duct, which caused another series of shock waves. The terminal shock to subsonic velocity was the last to occur. Three movable panels, positioned by two hydraulic actuators, opened or closed the throat area to meet engine air requirements; the maximum opening was 48 inches wide while the minimum was 19 inches. A three-position switch in the cockpit allowed the pilots to choose how far back the terminal shock wave would be positioned. For maximum range and most efficient air recovery, the shock wave was positioned forward. However, if the aircraft was flying through turbulent air or manoeuvring, the shock would be positioned

The cockpit environmental system varied between AV 1 and AV 2 and 3 as seen in this schematic shown in the B-70 Study. (North American Rockwell)

The huge air intakes on the XB-70 are clearly visible here, with the splitter plate almost retracted. The size of the intakes are given scale by the people milling around the aircraft during the roll-out ceremony. (*North American Rockwell*)

further back. The aft position provided the most stable operation and basically precluded the shock from being expelled through the front of the duct.

Excess inlet air was jettisoned overboard through six pairs of bypass doors located on the upper surface of the wing between and slightly forward of the vertical stabilizers. The six sets of doors were divided into two sets of trimmer doors and four sets of primary doors. Each pair of doors was interconnected (one door opened downward and the other opened upward). The bypass doors provided from zero to 2,400 square inches of bypass area.

The three panels in the throat of each inlet were perforated so that slow-moving turbulent boundary layer air was bled to ambient pressure on the other side of the panels into four separate plenums, each bleeding boundary air from a different section of the forward duct. This air was discharged at the rear of the step just aft of the nose wheel well. The remaining boundary layer air was diverted into the engine compartments to provide cooling and exited from ducts around the engines. North American believed that ducting inlet bleed air around the engines would also effectively cloak the afterburner from infrared detection. However, little could be done about the miles-long trail of hot gases generated by the six J93s.

Two pairs of unstart sensors were in a support package located between the throat panel hydraulic actuating cylinder and the outboard wall of the forward weapons bay. An inlet unstart was regarded as 'an undesirable condition resulting from the expulsion of the terminal normal shock wave during flight when it is desired to have it located inside the duct'.

The air induction control system package was located in the aft weapons bay, complete with its own environmental control system, but would have been relocated in any production version.

Inside the right hand air
duct during the
construction phase,
looking forward to the
splitter plate.
*(North American
Rockwell)*

The engine 'Six Pack'

All this air had to go somewhere – and it was straight into one of six General
Electric YJ93-GE-3 turbojet engines, unofficially called the 'six pack'. The engine
was a continuous flow gas turbine incorporating a multi-stage axial flow
compressor, a fully annular combustor, a two-stage impulse reaction turbine, and
an afterburner equipped with a variable area convergent-divergent exhaust nozzle.
Compressor speed was governed by a hydro-mechanical fuel control with an

Inside the same duct,
looking rearwards
towards the forward
mounts of three J93
turbojets.
*(North American
Rockwell)*

The afterburner end of the famous 'six pack' of YJ93-GE-3 engines. They number 1 through 6, starting on the left in this view, and so engine No.2 shows an open exhaust nozzle, unlike the others.
(North American Rockwell)

electrical temperature override for exhaust temperature at maximum speeds.

The engine was designed for continuous afterburner operation. The publicised thrust was '...in the 30,000- pound class' in afterburner, but the actual figure was usually not given. In reality, the -3 engine made 28,800 lb in afterburner at sea level. Non- afterburning performance was approximately 19,000 lb.

The YJ93-GE-3 was a big engine for its day – 237 inches long and 52.5 inches wide; its intake was 42 inches in diameter. The thrust-to-weight ratio was 6:1, considered very good for the time but paling into insignificance when compared to modern turbofans. Moving most accessories to the airframe allowed for a much simpler engine installation than was traditional. An engine could be replaced in 25 minutes – a feat demonstrated on several occasions. The engine was designed to use JP-6, basically an improved kerosene derivative with improved heat stability and resistance to the formation of solids in the exhaust.

The J93 was the first engine to use air-cooled turbine blades and also the first to use blades made from titanium alloy. This allowed operating temperatures several hundred degrees higher than was normal practice at the time. The blades proved somewhat more fragile than their steel counterparts, and at least 25 engines suffered foreign object debris damage during the flight test programme.

Despite a protracted development effort, the YJ93-GE-3 was completed on schedule and passed its 68-hour preliminary flight rating test in 1961, in time for the original XB-70 first flight date. By the time the first aircraft was actually rolled out in Palmdale, the J93 had accumulated over 5,000 hours of test time – including 600 hours at more than Mach 2. As part of the engine test programme. General Electric built a Mach 3 test facility, and also used a similar facility at the Air Force Arnold Engineering Development Center in Tullahoma, Tennessee. Engine inlet tests were also conducted at AEDC, with 52 hours of tests involving 154 engine starts, 109 engine stalls, and over 200 inlet unstarts. The inlet in these tests was a 0.577-scale model using an actual small jet engine. Despite the fact that the idea had been cancelled along with the B-70 production programme, the -3 engine had also been flight tested aboard a B-58 (55-662) – designated NB-58A – where

The No.2 engine is removed from AV 1. Engine access was so good, that a crew could change an engine in 25 minutes.
(North American Rockwell)

it was housed in a specially-configured centreline pod. Some doubts exist as to wether this aircraft/engine combination ever flew – certainly a few NB-58A ground runs were made with the J93 engine in place, but the day before the first flight was scheduled to take place, the funding for the NB-58A project was cancelled, and it has been claimed that the NB-58A/J93 combination never took to the air. The special pod was removed and the NB-58A itself was converted to a TB-58A and later flew chase missions for the XB-70A at Edwards AFB.

The YJ93 fuel system consisted of an engine-driven, dual element, constant displacement gear-type pump that incorporated a centrifugal boost element that supplied 32 dual-orifice fuel nozzles in the main combustor. An additional 32 fuel injectors fed the afterburner as needed. The ignition system consisted of a low-tension capacitor discharge unit that housed 4-joule and 20-joule circuits. During

The General Electric YJ93-GE-3 engine was was very advanced for its day and was designed for continuous afterburner operation. The box-like structure under the nose is the engine hydraulic system, plus gearbox and shaft take-off to drive aircraft systems.
(GE Engines)

The jacks supporting the weight of AV 2 were massive – they had to be! AV 2 awaits the installation of the engines. *(North American Rockwell)*

normal ground starts the 4-joule circuit was used; during low-temperature ground starts and for all air starts both the 4- and 20-joule systems were used.

Each engine was equipped with a 3,500-psi hydraulic pump that was separate from the airframe-mounted pumps and was used only for engine control. The engine used hydraulic power to move the front and rear variable stators, and the primary and secondary exhaust nozzles.

Because they were prototype engines, and the XB-70A test programme was not expected to fly into known icing conditions, the engines were not equipped with anti-icing systems. However, the basic J93 design incorporated all the necessary structural facilities (internal piping for air supply, mounting pads, etc.) for an anti-icing system.

The XB-70A was ahead of its time in providing a 'thrust-by-wire' system. The throttle levers in the cockpit sent electrical signals to each engine control system. This in turn provided a mechanical linkage to the engine that integrated the operation of the main fuel control, afterburner fuel control, and primary nozzle area control. In addition to the conventional throttles, emergency thrust control switches were provided on the centre aisle console and also in each escape capsule. Having electric control of the engines was one of the keys to providing limited aircraft control from within the sealed escape capsules, but oddly, the engine thrust could only be reduced from inside the capsule. The concept was that once the aircraft slowed down and lost altitude, the pilots could open the capsules and control the aircraft normally.

'Three Greens...'

Cleveland Pneumatic manufactured the tricycle landing gear had dual steerable nose wheels and four wheels on each main wheel bogie. The 12,000 pound weight gear retracted into environmentally controlled compartments in the lower fuselage. Nose gear retraction was aft; the main gear went through a complicated folding and rotation sequence to fit into relatively small compartments while not interfering with the air intakes or engine plenum chambers. The wheel well doors were kept closed except when the gear was being extended or retracted.

Each main gear consisted of a main shock strut, drag braces, actuators, and a folding bogie assembly with four 40-inch diameter main wheels and 40 x 17.5-inch 36-ply B.F. Goodrich tyres, two brakes, and a 16 x 4.4-inch brake reference wheel. The tyres had higher load ratings than had ever been achieved before within the 40 x 17.5 envelope and operated at higher speeds than ever before on a heavy aircraft.

The tyres themselves had a silver colour as a result of a heat-resistant material being impregnated into the rubber during construction and also painted on the exterior surface. The brakes were somewhat unique, with a stack of 21 stationary and 20 revolving disks located between opposing wheels and shared between them. The stationary discs were splined on a stator ring cage and the rotating discs splined to the torque tube to which the wheels were attached. The wheels ran on bearings fitted directly to the H-11 forged steel bogie instead of on an axle. Since the brake discs were separated from the wheels, much more efficient cooling was achieved. Still, at maximum effort the brake temperatures exceeded 2,000° F and absorbed over 200 million foot-pounds of kinetic energy.

The 'brake control system of the B-70 was a new concept of fully automatic regulation of braking the air vehicle upon a given input command by the pilot. Braking torque on each of the four brakes was individually and automatically controlled to provide maximum retarding force, regardless of runway conditions, without skidding the tyres. The braking system was not of the conventional anti-skid ('On'-'Off') type but a much more refined type of control which utilized a 'fifth wheel' to provide a true ground speed reference

This small fifth wheel and one main wheel contained speed sensors that sent data to the anti-skid computer. The difference in rotational speeds between these two sensors indicated the amount of slippage. Since the fifth wheel had no

The main wheel bogie retraction sequence was somewhat complicated, in that the wheels, struts, brakes and axles had to fit into a very small space.

First the trailing wheel rose upwards until vertical, the entire bogie truck rotated inboard through ninety degrees. Once that was complete, the strut was able to rotate backwards through ninety degrees into the wheel well as shown in this sequence.

Note the dotted reference line painted on the fuselage and struts. This was used as a visual reference in order to check positions.

The so-called 'fifth wheel' used for the anti-skid is visible between the two mains. *(all North American Rockwell)*

loads, it was assumed that it always recorded actual speed. If an excessive speed differential existed, the computer then relieved some brake pressure to that bogie.

The nose gear consisted of a shock strut, drag brace, torque links, actuators, a steering servo actuator, and two 40-inch wheels and 40 x 17.5-inch 36-ply BF Goodrich tyres. The nose wheels could be steered up to 58 degrees either side of centre at taxi speeds, or up to 35 degrees either side of centre during take-off and landing.

Three 28-foot diameter ring-slot nylon drag parachutes were housed in an environmentally-controlled compartment on top of the fuselage, eighteen feet from the rear of the aircraft. A 30-inch diameter spring-loaded pilot parachute pulled an 11-foot diameter extraction 'chute which in turn deployed the three main 'chutes. The upward-opening compartment doors were locked in the open position when the pilot commanded the chutes to deploy, which could be at speeds up to 200 knots after the main gear was firmly on the ground.

The design, manufacture and installation of the landing gear was not straightforward, as North American's Design/Programmatic Impacts log shows for just one period.

28 June – 5 July 1963 – Rework of the main landing gear up lock box required due to negative stress margin (61%) due to a combination of gear retraction snubbing loads and wing bending loads.

30 Aug – 9 Sept 1963 – Replaced one nose landing gear trunnion fitting on AV 1 due to cracks and distortions that occurred after weld rework. Engineering simplified design to reduce machining

18 Oct – 15 Nov 1963 – The L H landing gear was damaged during railroad transit to NAA. Rail car bumping apparently caused wire tie downs to break allowing gear to shift. Tyres were badly chaffed and declared unusable Other components were also damaged. No structural damage to the main strut and bogie beam assembly.

13 March – 8 June 1964 – Operational test on AV 1 showed drag chute door operational speed so excessive that it could cause structural damage.

Actuator change to decelerate action was accomplished on the Drag Chute and operations completed 8 June.

3 April – 10 April 1964. During cycling of AV 1 RH main landing gear down lock H 11 support fitting failed due to cracks induced by weld beef up. The first reworked part was delivered to Engineering Structure Lab for destruction testing. During test one of the supporting components failed. Previously (6 April) B-70 Management decided to make one set of substitute parts of 4340 steel as a backup. On 9 April the fitting completed the 500 cycles of limit load followed by one ultimate load application without failure.

18 June – 2 July 1964. Due to erratic operations of the landing gear on AV 1, the emergency landing gear 4 position valves required rework to reduce surge effort, Engineering was released on 18 June for valve rework. In addition new line, restrictors and check valves were added to the hydraulic installation. Additional rework was required due to thread strippage of the arm attach bolt on the bogie beam. The thread stripping was due to extreme force action during operations. The bolt was redesigned and the method of rotate sequencing was revised. On 1 July the RH bogie fold lock arm failed on AV 1 during operations.

The AV 2 part was installed on AV 1 to continue operations. Cleveland Pneumatic, the gear supplier were on strike at this time. A strengthened part was designed at NAA, made from U3UO steel and approved by Cleveland Pneumatic, to be made locally to support AV 1, 2 and spare.

The massive main landing gear – each truck was made from H-11 tool steel. The tyres were specially made by BF Goodrich of heat-repellant aluminium impregnated 'silver' rubber.

The upper picture shows the brake discs between the wheels.
(North American Rockwell)

Machining titanium

When titanium alloys were first introduced as a structural material, they were considered very difficult to machine compared to more common materials. Research and experience proved that they could be machined at rates economically comparable to other aerospace alloys and that good surface finishes could be obtained. Even so, extreme care was necessary in developing and controlling procedures in selecting tool materials, coolants, and the right combination of speeds, feeds, and tool geometry.

Maximum rigidity was essential in any equipment used in machining titanium to the close tolerances necessary. Cooling of parts during a machine operation was critical because of the great need for maximum heat dissipation and to prevent chips from welding to the cutting tool edge. The best cooling was achieved with a mist generator as atomized coolants provided a much higher cooling rate than that accomplished with flooded coolants, and the force of mist application removed the chips from the cutter and work contact areas, thus minimizing chip welding. Non-chlorinated cutting fluids were used to prevent possible stress-corrosion cracking in titanium.

Much experimentation revealed that sharp helix angles on cutting tools produced a better shearing angle and thus a better swarf-chip clearance and removal. It was also discovered that a single heavy cut produced better results than a series of smaller ones. In the words of one machinist '...*you do not tickle titanium!*'

Today chemical milling is commonplace – but at the time it was a new, patented process, developed by North American, and was recognized as a principal method for removing excess metal to meet close tolerances, particularly on curved surfaces where conventional machining is all but impossible. It became widely used for aluminium and steel, as well as for titanium.

Development and evaluation of etchants and maskants used to chemical-mill titanium and its alloys had been done in conjunction with the X-15 and XB-70 programmes. Metal removal rates of 0.06 inch per hour with tolerances of ± 0.002 inch were regularly achieved by several commercial sources, enabling the process to be cost-competitive with conventional machining methods. The importance of this process in providing a way to remove excess weight from parts made from sheet titanium for the XB-70 cannot be over-emphasized.

Extensive testing was performed on chemically milled titanium to determine if the surface roughness was affected. The effect was determined by roughness measurements and by fatigue-testing. Results indicated that a properly controlled bath reduced the acuity of surface scratches somewhat, but no effect was found in the fatigue behaviour of chemically milled samples when compared to the results of parent metal fatigue tests.

Hydraulics and Electronics

Six airframe-mounted accessory drive system (ADS) gearboxes, each shaft-driven by a corresponding engine, were mounted in separate compartments forward of the engines. All six gearboxes drove 4,000 psi hydraulic pumps, and Nos. 2, 3, and 4 engines also drove AC electrical generators. The aircraft was normally powered by two generators (Nos. 3 and 4), but any one of the three was capable of supplying the entire load if required. The constant-speed (8,000 rpm) generators

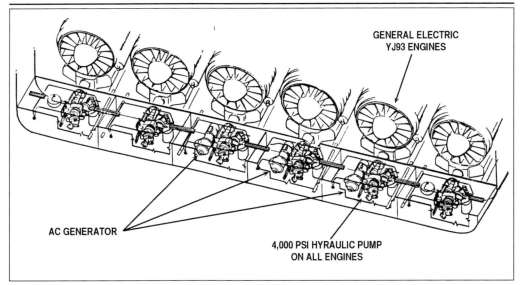

GENERAL ELECTRIC
YJ93 ENGINES

AC GENERATOR

4,000 PSI HYRAULIC PUMP
ON ALL ENGINES

provided 240/416-volt, 3-phase, 400 hertz power through step-down transformers. The hydraulic pumps could be run 'in reverse' and were used to start the engines. Having the accessories mounted on the airframe instead of on the engine allowed easier and more rapid engine maintenance.

Altogether, each XB-70A used 85 linear actuators, 50 mechanical valves, 44 hydraulic motors, and about 400 electrically-actuated solenoid valves.

More than a mile of various size tubing contained 3,300 brazed and 600 mechanical joints. To avoid the large weight penalty of providing a cooling system, all the actuators and valves were designed to withstand high temperatures.

Conventional couplings were not used in the various fluid systems (hydraulic, fuel, oil) to save weight and (unsuccessfully) eliminate the possibility of leakage. Instead, all high-pressure fluid line connections were brazed; low-pressure lines were welded. North American estimated that the technique saved over 10,000 pounds.

Approximately 220 gallons of a special high-temperature hydraulic fluid called 'Fluid 70' (actually named Oronite 70) were used. This fluid could operate continuously at 450° F and intermittently up to 630° F. Although the fluid was much better than the original Oronite 8200 that had been selected, it still left much to be desired and required constant replacement due to breaking down after prolonged exposure to high temperature.

Six engines, six 4,000 psi hydraulic pumps external to each engine and three AC generators. (North American Rockwell)

Electronics

Each aircraft was equipped with two AN/ARC-90 UHF command radios providing 3,500 channels between 225.00 MHz and 399.95 MHz, and had a built-in guard receiver tuned between 238-248 MHz. On AV 1 only one of the UHF sets was active, the other being in standby mode. On AV 2 both sets could be used simultaneously. Antennas were located on both the top and bottom of the forward fuselage. An AN/AIC-18 intercom allowed the two pilots to talk to each other. An AN/APX-46 transponder (IFF) set was installed on both aircraft, more for air traffic control purposes than anything else. Again, antennas were located on the top and bottom of the forward fuselage.

Opposite page: The front page of NAA Skywriter Employee Report dated September 1964 showing the progress of construction of Air Vehicle One. Interestingly in some places the aircraft is called the XB-70, in others it is referred to as the XB-70A. (NAA),

EMPLOYEE REPORT

SEPTEMBER, 1964   NORTH AMERICAN AVIATION, INC.

SPACE-AGE MILESTONES: XB-70 IN MAKING

POISED — North American's XB-70A, manufactured by the Los Angeles Division, is poised proudly on the flight line during final preparations for first flight at Palmdale plant. At right is view of aft engine section of triplesonic craft. Shot was taken during late night tests at Palmdale facility.

AIRCRAFT ASPECTS — Wooden mold, left, is used as tooling aid for fabrication of engine splitters, which are used to channel air intake from main engine duct to respective engine compartments. Center, Earl Harrison, LA B-70 Enginering, reviews main landing gear shock struts. At right is phase of ground vibration test, which was conducted to determine structural stiffness of air vehicle No. 1 and to determine in-flight flutter boundaries.

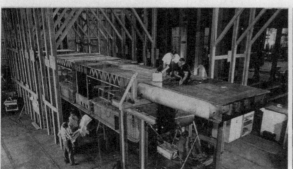

WING WORK — Fabricated aft intermediate test specimen, shown with workmen, was used to test wing bending, simulated loads in duct region, and for fuel tank verification. Here men prepare to move completed section into Structures Lab. Right picture demonstrates unusual configuration of XB-70A wing as men on top perform series of actuator tests. When craft reaches higher Mach numbers, wing tips fold down to achieve flight stability.

Each XB-70A was equipped with an AN/ARN-58 instrument landing system and a standard AN/ARN-65 TACAN radio navigation system. The TACAN installation was a far cry from the sophisticated bombing-navigation system developed by IBM, and was generally considered only marginally acceptable for test flights. Without the IBM bomb-nav system, the XB-70As did not have an inertial navigation system and were forced to rely on dead-reckoning and TACAN. Fortunately, the chase aircraft generally had better navigation systems, and the XB-70s were always under positive radar surveillance.

Military systems

As delivered, neither XB-70A had any military systems installed, other than a non-functional weapons bay. AV 3 would have been equipped with a functional weapons bay and prototype offensive avionics. The planned capabilities were impressive, however.

The weapons bay was sized to house a multitude of bombs, including thermonuclear devices up to 10,000 pounds each, 20,000-pound conventional bombs, various smaller conventional bombs, chemical and biological weapons, or up to two new air-to-ground missiles. The missiles were to have a range of 300-700 nm and an accuracy of less than a mile. Other missiles (probably GAM-87 Skybolts) were to be carried on external hard points under the wings, at least in some variations of the B-70.

The IBM-developed AN/ASQ-28(V) bombing-navigation and missile guidance subsystem was intended to be used by both WS-110A and WS-125A before the nuclear-powered bomber was cancelled. The bomb-nav system would have incorporated a star tracker – an improvement of a unit originally intended for the Navaho intercontinental cruise missile – to allow precise navigation without the use of radio aids. At some points in its development, the ASQ-28 was to

Just how far AV 2 was off the ground is visible in this photograph. Part of the fuselage is still unpainted, and there are still elevons to be fitted. (North American Rockwell)

incorporate both forward- and side-looking Doppler radars – the side looking units were intended to allow relatively 'stealthy' approaches to the targets.

The system was designed to be equally accurate at low level or at 2,500 knots and 100,000 feet. The search radar had a range of 200 nautical miles, and could accurately track targets at 125 nm. A resolution of 200 feet at a range of 50 nautical miles was expected. The avionics used various components: the radar data processor from Goodyear , an X-band radar from General Electric, with General Precision Laboratories providing the Doppler processor. At least limited testing was undertaken using C-54, RC-121, JB-29, JRB-57, and RB-66 aircraft as surrogates.

As originally envisioned, the defensive avionics would consist of five elements: active and passive warning devices, threat evaluation equipment, electronic countermeasures, infrared countermeasures, and chaff dispensing rockets. Again, at least initially the systems being developed for WS-110A would also have been used on the WS-125A nuclear aircraft. Early thought was given to adapting the AN/ALQ-27 jamming system being developed for late-model B-52s to the B-70, but the physical differences in the aircraft made this impossible. A revised system, using many of the techniques developed for the ALQ-27, was to be capable of noise jamming thirty radars simultaneously and track breaking against a further ten simultaneous radars. It would cover almost the entire frequency range from 50 to 16,000 megacycles. At various times, the Air Force and North American explored the application of defensive missiles, including a unique 'flying saucer' design called a 'lenticular defense missile' as well as more conventional designs such as modified GAR-9s. One study (SR-197) endorsed equipping these missiles with a 'neutron kill' warhead that would render the enemy missile warheads inoperative without exploding them.

The B-70 Weapons System Office provided diagrams for all the ground servicing equipment that would have been needed should the B-70 have entered operational service. (AFMC)

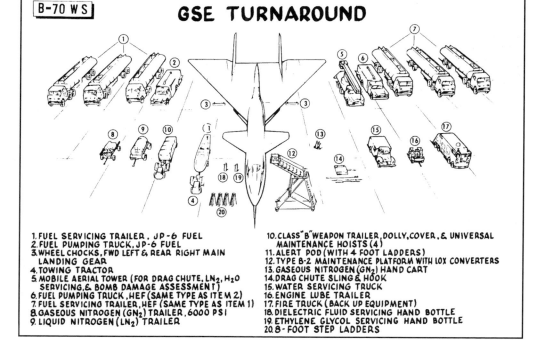

B-70 WS

GSE TURNAROUND

1. FUEL SERVICING TRAILER , JP-6 FUEL
2. FUEL PUMPING TRUCK, JP-6 FUEL
3. WHEEL CHOCKS, FWD LEFT & REAR RIGHT MAIN LANDING GEAR
4. TOWING TRACTOR
5. MOBILE AERIAL TOWER (FOR DRAG CHUTE, LN_2, H_2O SERVICING, & BOMB DAMAGE ASSESSMENT)
6. FUEL PUMPING TRUCK , HEF (SAME TYPE AS ITEM 2)
7. FUEL SERVICING TRAILER, HEF (SAME TYPE AS ITEM 1)
8. GASEOUS NITROGEN (GN_2) TRAILER, 6000 PSI
9. LIQUID NITROGEN (LN_2) TRAILER

10. CLASS "B" WEAPON TRAILER, DOLLY, COVER , & UNIVERSAL MAINTENANCE HOISTS (4)
11. ALERT POD (WITH 4 FOOT LADDERS)
12. TYPE B-2 MAINTENANCE PLATFORM WITH LOX CONVERTERS
13. GASEOUS NITROGEN (GN_2) HAND CART
14. DRAG CHUTE SLING & HOOK
15. WATER SERVICING TRUCK
16. ENGINE LUBE TRAILER
17. FIRE TRUCK (BACK UP EQUIPMENT)
18. DIELECTRIC FLUID SERVICING HAND BOTTLE
19. ETHYLENE GLYCOL SERVICING HAND BOTTLE
20. 8-FOOT STEP LADDERS

Alert Pod

One of the more interesting systems being designed for the operational B-70 was the Alert Pod developed by Beech Aircraft. This was envisioned as a means to provide the B-70 with a self-sufficient ground power system during deployments to relatively austere bases.

One of the operational requirements defined by SAC was that the B-70 should be ready for takeoff in less than three minutes after the crew entered the aircraft. In order to accomplish this, many of the B-70 systems would have to have already been powered-up to maintain them at correct operating temperatures. This would require external power.

Instead of relying on transport aircraft to carry the external power carts for the B-70, a decision was made to design all of the necessary systems into a streamlined pod that could be carried by the B-70 itself, at least during subsonic flight. This pod would provide all necessary hydraulic, electrical, and pneumatic power to the aircraft while it was on ground-alert status, and also during maintenance activities.

The pod was designed to attach to the centreline of the lower fuselage behind the weapons bay, roughly under engines No. 3 and 4. It was equipped with its own retractable wheels that were used after it was detached from the aircraft. While sitting on its wheels, the pod was approximately 6 feet high and 30 feet long. Three built-in hoists (two at front and one rear) allowed the pod to be mated to the B-70. The pod contained two small gas turbine engines driving six hydraulic pumps (one for each J93) and two generators. The hydraulics allowed each of the accessory drives on the B-70 to be powered in order to start the J93s. The pod could also cool and/or heat the B-70 crew compartment and equipment bays as needed. An area in the rear of the pod allowed the ground crew to store tools and minor parts, while a large JP-6 fuel tank at the front was sufficient for nine hours of unrefueled operation of the turbines. The pod could be controlled locally by the ground crew, or from the crew compartment at the copilot's station.

Each operational B-70 was scheduled to have its own alert pod. Beech and fourteen other companies submitted proposals for the pod to North American

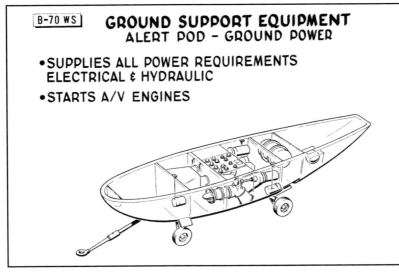

B-70 WS **GROUND SUPPORT EQUIPMENT**
ALERT POD - GROUND POWER

- **SUPPLIES ALL POWER REQUIREMENTS ELECTRICAL & HYDRAULIC**
- **STARTS A/V ENGINES**

Also proposed was a ground support 'Alert Pod' that would have enabled the B-70 to be scrambled from alert in just three minutes. It was designed to supply all electrical and hydraulic requirements needed to start the engines. *(AFMC)*

on 27 October 1958, and North American announced Beech as the winner on 23 April 1959. At the time the pod was considered highly classified and was described only as 'a special power device'. A mockup was inspected and approved on 1 August 1959. A prototype unit was supposed to have been completed by 1 October 1961, with production units available from August 1963, but with the cancellation of the production run, no alert pods were completed.

Air Vehicle 3

Very little has ever been written about AV 3, the third Valkyrie. AV 3 was to carry tail number 62-0208, but it was canceled on 15 February 1964, and never completed. The design for AV 3 was completed on 31 October 1963, and because many of the previous technical problems such as the complicated brazing techniques, the redesign of the honeycomb panels for fabrication, and the elimination of assembly problems had already been solved, it was not long before the construction of AV 3 was under way.

As we have already seen, during the construction of the third aircraft, the Air Force was desperately searching for ways to save the programme. They had devised numerous plans to save something of AV 3. All the alternatives were based on pared-to-the-bone proposals that would hopefully yield information on high-performance vehicles, including data on speed, payload, altitude, and duration of flights at high speed. Some eventually happened – in particular the NASA-funded SST programme testing, but much was not to be.

Over the years many myths have arisen over the third Valkyrie. Some would have it that it still survives in a partially built state, allegedly tucked away in Site 8 of the former NAA plant at Palmdale, along with the unaccounted for remainder of the J93-3 engines built for the programme along with the wooden mock-up.

Certainly it is true that a large part of the third machine was on contract with 100% of the raw honeycomb and sheet metal requirement already met, and around 90% of the extrusions already supplied to NAA. Records also suggest that the Cental Air Data System and the Auxiliary Gyro Platform System had completed acceptance tests and was awaiting installation.

However, it seems that everything was scrapped years ago and nothing of the third machine survives.

And finally – a Finish

One comment often said about the B-70 was that it was a huge target. The concept of 'stealth' was very much in its infancy in 1960, but engineers at Lockheed and North American already understood that reduction of the radar and infrared signature of strategic aircraft would at least delay detection by the enemy. The shape and materials used by Lockheed in the A-12 Oxcart and RS/SR-71 Blackbird were specifically intended to lower its radar signature. Several detailed studies into the signature of the B-70 were made, and provided a basis for reduction attempts.

During the short YB-70 development period, the Air Force directed North American to investigate means to reduce the probability that the B-70 would be detected. Preliminary investigations were made into applying various radar absorbing materials to the airframe, particularly the insides of the air intakes.

However, most of the North American effort appears to have concentrated on reducing the infrared signature of the aircraft. Exhausting cool air around the J93 engines was one means of achieving this.

As part of its research, North American developed a paint 'finish system' that provided a low emittance at wavelengths used by Soviet infrared detecting devices, while radiating most of the excess heat from the surface in wavelengths not normally under surveillance. The finish utilized a low emittance base coat with an organic top-coat that was transparent to energy in the 1 to 6 micron range. The top coating was strangely opaque and highly emissive at wavelengths between 6 and 15 microns. This finish was relatively invisible to infrared detecting equipment, while still allowing the skin to radiate excess heat overboard to maintain its structural integrity.

Two different coatings were developed, one for areas that reached a maximum of 485° F, the other for areas up to 630° F. The first, Type I, consisted of Englehard Industries Hanovia Ceramic Metallic Coating No. 2 that was 0.004 mm thick. Over this was applied a 11 mm thick mixture of 85% Ferro Enameling No. AL-8 Frit and 15% Hommel No. 5933 Frit.

'Frit' is the term applied to a ceramic composition that has been melted and then fused in a special oven, quenched to form a glass, and then granulated. Frits form an important part of the batches used in compounding enamels and ceramic glazes; the purpose of this pre-fusion is to render any soluble and/or toxic components insoluble by causing them to combine with silica and other added oxides.

The Type II base coat was a mixture of 40% Hanovia Silver Resinate and 60% Hanovia L.B. Coating No. 6593 applied 0.004 mm thick. The top coat was a mixture of 74% 3M Kel-F No. 2140, 24% 3M Kel-F No. 601, and 2% A1203 applied one millimetre thick. The Type I coating was actually test flown, having been applied to one panel on the vertical stabilizer of the X-15 rocket aircraft. No observable physical changes occurred during the Mach 4.43 flight. In probability the top coats would have been an opaque silver instead of the white finish used on the two XB-70A prototype aircraft.

The finish system was difficult to apply to an aircraft as large as the B-70s, but the engineers expected that further development would yield improvements in the process. The most difficult problem was that the underlying surface had to be highly polished prior to applying the base coat. In addition, the base coat of both finishes had to be cured at 750° F, while the topcoat of the Type II finish had to be cured at 1,000° F, creating almost a ceramic finish. Accelerated environmental tests indicated that the surface would prove durable on the stainless steel sections of the aircraft, but its long-term adhesion to titanium appeared to be weak and additional work would be needed to cure this problem. Both finishes were relatively immune to exposure to hydraulic fluid, fuels, oils, and other substances expected to be encountered during operational service. Each could be readily cleaned with soap and water.

'It was time...' as some commentators said *'...to see what this puppy could do!'*

IT FLIES!

The two XB-70As were assembled in a new facility on the north side of Air Force Plant No. 42 in Palmdale, California, although almost all of the major sections were manufactured elsewhere.

To provide an efficient means of complete system development and to accurately demonstrate in-flight performance and safety prior to flight, a full scale functional mockup of the B-70 flight control system was designed and built. This flight control system simulator was designed to verify the system design, to allow evaluation of system performance including actual representation of system non-linearities which were difficult to describe for system analysis, to demonstrate compatible subsystem integration, to provide system familiarization for flight maintenance crews, and to some degree, demonstrate reliability and isolate potential reliability problems. The simulator consisted of those systems and components normally used in aircraft control,

The simulation effort in the development of the flight control was continuous beginning at initiation of preliminary analysis and ending at completion of flight test support. Initial simulations consisted of complete analogue representations of pilot, control system and aerodynamics. As the system development progressed

Before flight 62-0001 - otherwise known as AV 1 - had to undergo landing gear tests. *(NAA)*

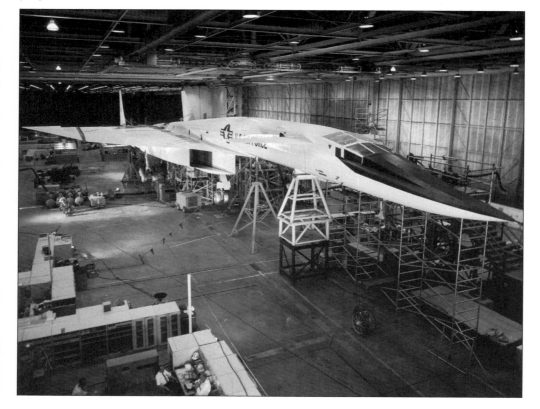

and experimental or actual equipment became available, the analogued simulations of the control loop were replaced by their real counterparts with the complete system available and in operation before flight.

The flight control system simulator permitted complete pilot evaluation of the system throughout the mission of the B-70 while in a realistic environment, while the development phase emphasized the testing associated with system performance and the effects of component characteristics.

The flight control simulator provided a complete air vehicle control installation, within practical limits, for development testing. This generally included all major cockpit controls and displays, all significant control linkages which affected control or feel, all surface actuators and hydraulic and electrical power similar to that provided in the actual aircraft. Air vehicle hardware and components fabricated to production drawings were used wherever possible.

The pilots' forward view in the simulator was the same as that in the air vehicle. Optical displays external to the simulator were provided to indicate particular phases of flight.

The development programme was established as three phases. Phase One was classified as Evaluation and Finalization of overall system requirements and components affecting feel characteristics and handling qualities. Phase Two covered evaluation of preliminary control configuration for design verification

AV 1 sits inside the hangar, ready to be pulled out to meet the public.

AV 1 outside, being prepared for flight - the number of ground support vehicles and equipment required is noticeable. (both NAA)

Detail drawings of the main landing gear (right) and nose gear (below).

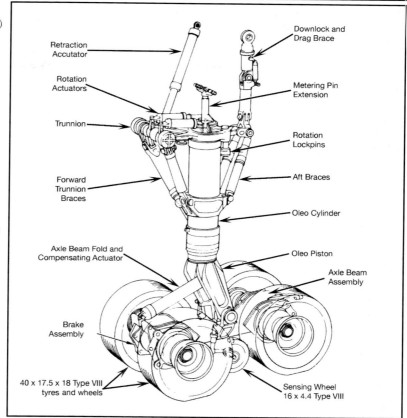

Retraction Accutator

Rotation Actuators

Trunnion

Forward Trunnion Braces

Axle Beam Fold and Compensating Actuator

Brake Assembly

40 x 17.5 x 18 Type VIII tyres and wheels

Downlock and Drag Brace

Metering Pin Extension

Rotation Lockpins

Aft Braces

Oleo Cylinder

Oleo Piston

Axle Beam Assembly

Sensing Wheel 16 x 4.4 Type VIII

In its time they were one of the largest and strongest multi-wheel landing gear systems.

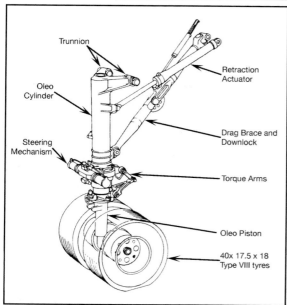

Trunnion

Oleo Cylinder

Steering Mechanism

Retraction Actuator

Drag Brace and Downlock

Torque Arms

Oleo Piston

40x 17.5 x 18 Type VIII tyres

and integration compatibility. Phase Three covered evaluation and verification of final control configuration, demonstration of flight control and safety prior to flight.

Experimental and prototype flight instruments were installed as part of the cockpit of the flight control simulator and were subjected to performance evaluation.

Hydraulic power supplied to the flight simulator came from actual air vehicle system components. System design parameters such as pressure, flow, response, temperature, service life, vibrations, fluid compressibility and surge characteristics were verified. Characteristics of the individual pumps, various combinations of redundancy, and master slave arrangements were all evaluated. Additional work included verifying the braking and steering sub-

Al White and Joe Cotton discuss details with the layout of the cockpit mock-up layout with the engineers. *(NAA)*

system and pilot familiarization and training.

NAA Reports indicate that the cumulative 'flight time' in the simulator complex through to July 1964 was 758 hours, with 382 hours for test pilots and 376 hours for engineers. 'Flight time' was defined as simulator operation time with a pilot at the controls performing manoeuvres for handling qualities or control equipment evaluating, or flying mission profiles.

Roll out of AV 1

Air Vehicle One was rolled out of the hangar on Monday, 11 May 1964. The ceremony was hosted by General Alfredo 'Fred' Ascani, commander of the Systems Engineering Group and deputy commander of the Research and Technology Division at Wright-Patterson AFB, in front of many assembled guests.

The flight programme was to be run by the Air Force to gather data for military programs, but NASA had already signed-on to provide instrumentation for a

number of SST-related experiments. It was hoped that the Air Force programme would be sufficiently successful to justify a follow-on programme that would probably be run by NASA and aimed more directly at SST research.

Two months after the rollout, continuing fiscal problems forced the elimination of the partially-built AV 3 and the reduction of the flight test programme to only 180 hours - hardly enough to justify the expense of the two remaining vehicles.

The four months following roll-out were spent performing the tests that are always done on first-of-a-type vehicles - including low and high speed taxi tests on Palmdale's long runway, plus engine runs and fuel system tests.

The great white bird is rolled out to meet the public for the first time!

The size and span of that huge delta wing is particularly noticeable. (both NAA)

Air Vehicle One dwarfed
its surroundings...

The first taxi test occurred on 9 August, when numerous problems with nose wheel steering, brake chatter, loss of the primary No. 1 hydraulic system, and ammonia fumes ingested into the cockpit caused the tests to be aborted. The nose wheel steering problem was two fold: one was an apparent drift and the other was an apparent lack of authority. The control valve of the steering unit was replaced which fixed the drift and an indicator was installed in the cockpit to provide the pilot with the nose wheel position to aid in engagement of steering. The authority of the nose wheel steering was continually 'squawked' throughout the flight test programme; however, the condition was minimized to some extent by pilot technique.

From up high or at ground level, the Valkyrie looked as if it was travelling supersonically even when at rest. *(Both North American Rockwell)*

Above; AV 1 is rolled out at Palmdale on 11 May 1964. General Ascani is at the podium on the right.

Guests invited to the roll-out ceremony gather around the aircraft and provide some scale as to the height above the ground *(Both North American Rockwell)*

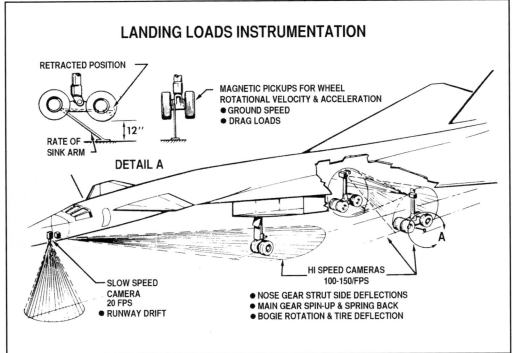

LANDING LOADS INSTRUMENTATION

RETRACTED POSITION

MAGNETIC PICKUPS FOR WHEEL
ROTATIONAL VELOCITY & ACCELERATION
- GROUND SPEED
- DRAG LOADS

12"

RATE OF
SINK ARM

DETAIL A

SLOW SPEED
CAMERA
20 FPS
- RUNWAY DRIFT

HI SPEED CAMERAS
100-150/FPS
- NOSE GEAR STRUT SIDE DEFLECTIONS
- MAIN GEAR SPIN-UP & SPRING BACK
- BOGIE ROTATION & TIRE DEFLECTION

A

Brake chatter was believed to be caused by the brake linings not being 'bedded-in' - that is they were not seating in to the discs. However, a switch was installed so that fore and aft brakes of each bogie could be selected so that bedding in could be accomplished during the next taxi. The Primary No. 1 hydraulics was lost due to a line break at a coupling in ADS Bay No. 1.

Ammonia fumes in the cockpit were caused by contaminated make-up air from the engines which had ingested the overboard exhausted ammonia fumes. This condition could only happen during taxi and ground operations where there was insufficient wind to clear the area forward of the inlets of fumes. To correct the unacceptable condition, a ground lockout relay was installed which closed the make-up air valve during ground operations.

The second taxi test was made on 16 August with the first pass to 35 knots indicated airspeed satisfactorily completed. However, the second pass was aborted due to a hydraulic leak caused by a ruptured line at a manifold fitting in ADS Bay No. 1. During the taxi tests at low speed, the brakes still chattered so badly that it caused the landing gear doors to open and the No. 3 engine nozzle to go full open. The bedding in of the brake linings was scheduled to continue during the next taxi tests.

The third taxi tests were conducted on 24 August with two passes up to 65 knots indicated airspeed satisfactorily completed. However, after the second pass a hydraulic leak was found in ADS Bay No. 6 which was caused by a primary pump valve manifold seal failure. It was subsequently found that the left- hand brake actuator was also leaking, which resulted in installing a new Viton seal in all brake actuators. On 25 August the fourth taxi tests were satisfactorily competed with no

Details of the Landing Loads Instrumentation package installed on the XB-70. The landing gear was filmed in operation, and there were also cameras in the nose to check runway drift on landing.

Left to right: Colonel Joe
Cotton, 'Fitz' Fulton, Van
Shepard and Al White

problems encountered. Two passes were made; the first up to 86 knots indicated airspeed (75 knots ground speed) and the second up to 122 knots indicated airspeed (100 knots ground speed). During the second pass, the drag chute was satisfactorily deployed at 122 knots indicated airspeed and jettisoned at 80 knots indicated airspeed with subsequent deceleration accomplished by moderate to heavy braking.

The fifth and sixth taxi tests were satisfactorily completed on 14 September 1964. The fifth taxi test consisted of one pass at 87 knots indicated airspeed while the sixth consisted of one pass at 97 knots indicated airspeed. After the sixth taxi test, the aircraft was put back up on jacks, all eight main gear tyres were replaced due to wear and the landing gear cycled twenty times in preparation for the first flight. In addition, several binding hydraulic valves were replaced and the No. 4 and No. 6 engines had to be replaced due to foreign object damage (FOD).

Alfredo 'Fred' John Ascani
(29 May 1917 - 28 March
2010) Major General and
test pilot of the United
States Air Force and was
considered father of
Systems Engineering at
Wright Field.

The extensive prior-to-first flight taxi tests were conducted to allow the pilot to evaluate the low and high speed characteristics of the new aircraft. This included radius of turn, steering, braking, intermediate speed directional control, high speed directional control and nose wheel lift-off or longitudinal control power. It also allowed the pilot to evaluate visibility and get the feel of the machine, such as establishing reference points, during these critical phases of just before flight. It also allowed the collection of valuable engineering data. Since these conditions were evaluated on Air Vehicle No. 1, the No. 2 air vehicle taxi tests were completed in one day; 10 July 1965.

On 21 September 1964, Air Vehicle One was declared ready for its first flight. As initially planned, the one and three-quarter - hour hop would be rather spectacular for a maiden flight. Since Plant 42 was in a semi-populated area, caution would be exercised immediately after takeoff - the landing gear would remain down and the airspeed low. But once the Valkyrie was

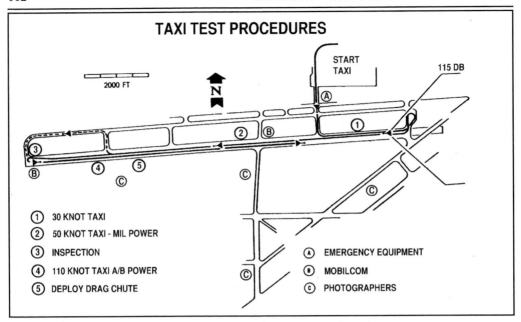

TAXI TEST PROCEDURES

2000 FT

N

START TAXI

115 DB

(A)

(1)

(2) (B)

(3)

(4)   (5)

(B)

(C)   (C)

(C)

(C)

(1) 30 KNOT TAXI
(2) 50 KNOT TAXI - MIL POWER
(3) INSPECTION
(4) 110 KNOT TAXI A/B POWER
(5) DEPLOY DRAG CHUTE

(A) EMERGENCY EQUIPMENT
(B) MOBILCOM
(C) PHOTOGRAPHERS

over Edwards AFB, the plan called for retracting the landing gear and accelerating through the speed of sound at 30,000 feet. If the aircraft went supersonic on the first flight. North American would receive a $250,000 bonus from the Air Force.

At 05.30 Alvin S 'Al' White, North American Chief Test Pilot, and Colonel Joseph E 'Joe' Cotton, Air Force B-70 Chief Test Pilot, began the preflight inspection, although the ground crew had checked the aircraft so carefully that there was little chance that anything had been overlooked.

At 06:10, White and Cotton climbed aboard AV 1 to begin the pre-flight checklist. Engine No. 1 was started and brought up to operating temperature 35 minutes later. In the process of starting the second J93, however, caution lights indicated a failure in the engine's cooling loop. Both engines were shut down. A few minutes later, the problem was traced to a tripped circuit breaker.

The process of starting the engines began again at 07:14. With 132,000 pounds of fuel in the tanks, AV 1 began taxiing towards the Palmdale main runway. Taxiing was a delicate affair - the XB-70A had already demonstrated a major problem with braking at low speeds for there was a violent chatter that caused the XB-70A's braking distance from just 5 mph to be 400 feet. This had

Details of the plans for the taxi-trials at Palmdale.

AV 1 taxies out sometime after the fourth flight. (USAF)

still not been fully solved, thus making manoeuvring a tedious affair. During taxiing, the XB-70A also exhibited another trait - with the pilots so far in front of the nose wheel, they experienced something of a roller-coaster ride as the cockpit porpoised up and down as the nose wheel rode over the joints in the concrete taxiway. This was magnified by the long neck of the Valkyrie and so the nickname 'Cecil' - from 'Cecil the seasick sea serpent' who featured in the Beany and Cecil animated cartoon series created by Bob Clampett - was rapidly adopted. The nickname seemed particularly apt and was used by many of the people involved with the programme.

Finally, at 8:24, the Valkyrie was aligned on the runway. Al White advanced the six throttle levers to the maximum afterburner position, and the XB-70A began its takeoff run. At 193 mph, White rotated the long neck of the XB-70A into the air, establishing a nine degree angle-of-attack for the wing. At 205 mph and at 4,853 feet down the runway, the 387,620 pounds of the Valkyrie lifted into the sky for the first time. As per the flight plan, speed was held at 310 mph

62-0001 - AV 1 - is prepared for its first flight. The height up to the cockpit entry door is noticeable. *(NAA)*

and the gear left down for the flight to Edwards. No unusual handling problems occurred during this time.

Numerous photographs have appeared over the years claiming to be of flight number one - and often they are wrong, for there is a little known, but easily identifiable feature of AV 1 that can discount many of these 'first flight' pictures - the lower fuselage around the engines was left in bare metal finish for the first four flights.

At 08:51, the XB-70A was over Edwards, and, having met up with all the chase planes involved, Cotton attempted to retract the landing gear for the first time. A minute later, waiting for the retraction indicators to go 'green', one of the chase aircraft called out that the retraction had failed. The right side main gear had stopped midway through the retraction sequence.

The chase aircraft pilot reported that the main landing gear legs had stopped moving after only completing the first motion - they had only rotated

AV/1 62-0001 is seen seconds into her maiden flight from Palmdale. Flown by Al White and Joe Cotton for the first time on 21 September 1964, the 107-minute flight was to Edwards AFB. Of interest is that the rear of the 'six pack' is almost all bare metal - this was not fully painted until after the fourth flight. *(NAA/USAF)*

XB-70 "Maiden Flight"

"I KNOW YOU ALWAYS TAKE AN EXTRA MEASURE OF PRECAUTION COLONEL COTTON, BUT..."

No Comment!
(AFFTC History Office Collection)

AV 1 climbs away from Palmdale en route to Edwards. *(NAA/USAF)*

perpendicular to the direction of flight. He also reported seeing blue streaks on the fuselage behind the landing gear doors, and that some kind of fluid appeared to be leaking out. A leak in the hydraulic system was the suspected culprit, but in mid-flight, the only thing to do was to re-extend the landing gear quickly before a loss of pressure made it impossible to do so. Cycled back to the extended position, the gear locked itself back into place, and the Valkyrie continued on her alternate flight plan, proceeding with some low speed handling tests, which showed stability and control to be more than acceptable - and was better than the B-52!

Half an hour later, the number three engine was showing 108% rpm, and so was shut down as a precaution. White and Cotton then proceeded to line up for landing on the 15,000 foot runway at Edwards. Sitting almost 110 feet in front of the main landing gear, combined with the nose-up attitude required to land the big delta wing, it was difficult for the pilots to judge their altitude above the runway, or the actual point of touchdown. It was not until the tenth flight that Al White stopped using the chase planes to call out his altitude. Aiming for touchdown 2,000 feet down the long runway, White smoothly set the XB-70 on the ground.

How North American headed their press releases with a pressure-suited airman and the outline of the Valkyrie.

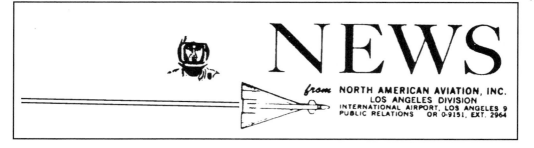

NEWS *from* NORTH AMERICAN AVIATION, INC.
LOS ANGELES DIVISION
INTERNATIONAL AIRPORT, LOS ANGELES 9
PUBLIC RELATIONS   OR 0-9151, EXT. 2964

The end of the maiden flight of 62-0001 at Edwards AFB, showing the fire during the landing roll and it's aftermath. It took eight hours to repair the machine to a point where it could be moved. *(all NAA/USAF)*

Immediately trouble set in. Although White and Cotton couldn't sense it, a pressure surge in the brake system had locked the rear wheels of the left side main gear, causing a fire during the rollout. Notified of this, White let the Valkyrie coast to a stop, using 10,800 feet of runway. Once the fire was extinguished the aircraft remained on the runway for over eight hours while it was de-fueled and the landing gear was repaired. Then the XB-70 could be moved.

North American never received their quarter of a million dollar bonus for going supersonic on the first flight.

TO WORK – TO TEST

With the completion of the only partially successful maiden flight of AV 1 it was time to get down to the serious business of 'wringing out the wrinkles' of the new design and exploring the envelope of the aircraft.

On 5 October 1964, White and Cotton took AV 1 into the air again with the full intent of going supersonic. If they were successful on this flight, North American would receive a $125,000 bonus. If however they failed, North American would be assessed penalties – beginning at $125,000 – for each additional flight until the XB-70A broke the sound barrier.

Following takeoff, with a chase aircraft on each side, the landing gear was retracted, then lowered, then retracted again without a problem. With the landing gear up and stowed, the XB-70A climbed to 28,000 feet and accelerated to Mach 0.85 (600 knots). Then a new problem appeared – the No. 1 utility hydraulic system began losing pressure, and White headed back to Edwards. On the final approach, the landing gear had to be lowered using the emergency electrical system. The touch-down on the lake bed was uneventful, and AV 1 rolled to a stop after 10,000 feet, despite one of the main drag chutes refusing to deploy. Again, there was to be no bonus for North American.

A week later, on 12 October 1964, A V 1 accelerated through the sound barrier for the first time, reaching Mach 1.11 at 35,400 feet for 15 minutes before decelerating beneath the sound barrier and breaking back through several times to check transonic stability. Again, one of the drag chutes opened late during landing, but did not seriously affect the rollout.

The fourth flight, on 24 October, fulfilled the Phase One test objectives of demonstrating the basic airworthiness of the aircraft. White and Cotton were again at the controls for a flight that lasted 1 hour and 25 minutes with AV 1 reaching

AV 1 undergoing pre-flight checks prior to her second flight on 5 October 1964. Note the amount of ground equipment surrounding the aircraft, not made any more tidier by the collection of cars parked on the side of the taxiway. *(AFFTC History Office Collection)*

Mach 1.42 at 46,300 feet. For the first time, the wingtips were lowered to their mid-down 25-degree position. The XB-70A remained supersonic for 40 minutes, establishing a new record for sustained supersonic flight.

After the second flight 62-0001 started to show signs of paint-peeling. (USAF)

The aircraft returned to Palmdale at the end of this flight for a series of structural tests. They would be non-destructive in nature since the programme had not built a dedicated structural test airframe, although a number of 'test specimens', had been built, including most of the rear fuselage that was used for wing bending tests, loads in the engine duct region and fuel tank verification.

While at Palmdale, engineers puzzled over why some of the white paint peeled off during three of the first four flights. It was finally determined that too-thick paint caused by several re-paintings – allegedly done in order to impress various VIPs – was being cracked as the Valkyrie flexed in flight, and was then torn away by the airstream. During the winter stay at Plant 42, AV 1 was stripped and repainted with a single thin coat of white paint. A major exterior change was that the bottom fuselage around the engines was now painted white instead of being left natural titanium finish as it had been for the first four flights.

It has often been quoted that AV 1 suffered paint loss during early flights due to having been painted too many times to impress visiting VIPs who came to see the great white bird... *(North American Rockwell)*

Structural testing completed satisfactorily, Phase Two testing began on 16 February 1965, when Al White and Joe Cotton took the Valkyrie on its fifth flight. For the first time, the wingtips were lowered to the full 65-degree position, and the manual air inlet control system (AICS) throat ramps were cycled. This flight lasted 1 hour and 10 minutes, including 40 minutes at Mach 1.6 and 45,000 feet.

However, this could have been due to poor adhesion properties of the 'finish system' used to reduce the infrared signature of the aircraft – a finish that was highly secret at the time. *(North American Rockwell)*

Continuing an unhappy trend, the drag chutes again failed to deploy completely, and AV 1 required 11,100 feet to rollout.

The sixth flight, on 25 February 1965, marked the first time someone other than White and Cotton was at the controls. Lieutenant Colonel Fitzhugh 'Fitz' Fulton – later to be NASA's chief test pilot – flew as copilot with Al White. But again, hydraulic leaks cut the flight short. Engineers at North American worked to modify the hydraulic systems to end the constant leakage problems that had disrupted every flight. These changes and 'fixes' were never totally effective on AV 1, but greatly benefited AV 2 during its construction.

The normal climb schedule for the XB-70A aircraft consisted of a series of accelerations, combined with variations in canard flap and elevon deflections, windshield ramp slope adjustments, engine air inlet/throat and wingtip geometry changes; the landing gear was cycled soon after takeoff. The VG wingtips were lowered to mid-down, or 25 degrees, anywhere from 400 to 630 knots. Steady acceleration followed to Mach 1.5, where the VG wingtips were lowered to full-down, or 65 degrees. A Mach number of 1.5 was generally maintained to an altitude of 50,000 feet. Then, if desired, varied rates of accelerations to Mach 3 at 70,000 feet followed. The best recorded time to 2,000 mph and 70,000 feet was 25 minutes after rotation.

On 4 March, the seventh flight had White and Fulton sustaining supersonic flight for 60 minutes, reaching a top speed of Mach 1.85 and 50,200 feet. North American's Van Shepard made his first flight as co-pilot during the eighth flight on 24 March 1965 reaching Mach 2.14 and 56,100 feet – 40 minutes were spent above Mach 2; another 34 minutes above Mach 1.

The 12th flight was on 7 May 1965, with Al White and Fitz Fulton at the controls. Travelling at Mach 2.60 (1,690 mph), a 'thump' was heard in the cockpit, followed by a multitude of engine-related alarms going off in the cockpit – engines number 3, 4, 5, and 6 were shut down as a precaution. As the chase aircraft caught up, they reported that the horizontal splitter – the very apex of the huge delta wing right up close to the fuselage, had torn away. The resulting debris had been sucked into the intakes and done severe damage to the engines. For the final approach, the No. 5 engine was restarted to provide some thrust from the right side, and AV 1 landed on the long lake bed without major incident. All six engines, nearly one-sixth of the 38 built, were considered damaged beyond repair. After this flight, the splitter itself was replaced with a single solid piece of titanium alloy in place of the honeycomb unit that had failed.

A photograph that must have been taken on one of the first four flights of AV 1, for it shows the unpainted engine area that was later painted white. The picture also shows the standard 'escorts' the XB-70 had on every flight.(USAF)

The results of the honeycomb failure on the 12th flight.

Below – Looking up at what was left of the damaged horizontal splitter.

Right: No.5 engine with damaged intake vanes and guides.

Below right: Damage to engines No.1 and No.2 can be seen, along with the gash in the fairing between the two power plants caused by the horizontal splitter.*(USAF)*

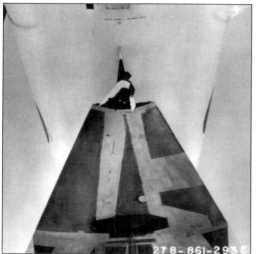

A view down the inlet duct for engines 4,5 and 6 showing the vane and guide damage. This duct, as big as a small room, also sustained damage to the 'floor' through flying debris.*(USAF)*

At this point, concerns about the integrity of the honeycomb began to surface, and the next four flights concerned themselves with 'heat soaking' the skin for sustained periods of time. For the first time, the ability of the XB-70A to reach Mach 3 was being seriously considered.

On 1 July 1965, during the 14th flight, AV 1 recorded Mach 2.85 at 68,000 feet for 10 minutes. On this flight, several sheets of honeycomb skin were lost from the fuselage and upper wing surface; fortunately no debris was ingested by the engines. Mach 3 was getting closer, but doubts persisted.

AV 2 joins the programme.

Most of the major problems that plagued AV 1 were cured on AV 2, which was rolled out on 29 May 1965. In addition to having a functional No. 5 fuel tank, AV 2 had 5-degrees of dihedral on the main wing, versus the zero degrees on AV 1. This small, but important visual difference provided the observer with a valuable identification feature when the aircraft's serial was not visible.

This change was a result of wind tunnel testing that showed AV 1 would have poor roll stability with the wingtips fully lowered. The tradeoff was that, at low speeds with the wingtips up, AV 2 suffered from a 'dihedral effect' where sideslip caused one wing to drop. The pilot, sensing the low wing but not spotting the sideslip, would use the elevons to bring the wing back up – causing more sideslip, forcing the wing to drop lower. The only solution was for the pilots to closely watch the sideslip indicator. It was expected that any production aircraft would cure this anomalous behaviour with changes to the stability augmentation system.

Internally, AV 2 featured a revised hydraulic system to reduce the leaking that continued to trouble AV 1. Techniques to build the honeycomb skin had also improved as experience was gained in its manufacture, resulting in a stronger material that was unlikely to separate.

An automatic control for the AICS was installed in place of the manual system on the first aircraft. The most visible external difference was that the radome for the non-existent bomb-nav system was painted black on AV 2; it was white on AV 1. This again was a useful identification aid when the serial was not visible.

On 17 July 1965 AV 2 joined the flight test program. With much better luck than had accompanied AV l's first flight, the wingtips were lowered 65 degrees, and a top speed of Mach 1.41 at an altitude of 42,000 feet was reached before landing at Edwards AFB. The second flight of AV 2 was significant in that it was the first time that Al White was not the pilot-in-command of an XB-70A – he and Joe Cotton swapped seats on 10 August 1965 while AV 2 recorded Mach 1.45 at 41,000 feet.

Initially, AV 2 was not completely trouble-free. Brake chatter continued to be a problem during low-speed taxiing; it was suspected that this stemmed from the lack of return springs for the brake pads. Far more troubling though was the problems in the automatic AICS system, which would inexplicably recycle during supersonic flight, causing an 'unstart'.

The normal climb schedule for the XB-70A consisted of a series of accelerations, combined with variations in wingtip, windshield, and air inlet geometry. The landing gear was retracted early. Wingtips were lowered to mid-down anywhere from 400 knots to 630 knots to provide extra stability in the transonic region. Steady acceleration to Mach 1.5 at 32,000 feet followed, then

62-0207 - AV 2 - is prepared for flight. The black painted area of the nose 'radome' is noticeable in this view. The truck in the foreground provided high-lift capability for cockpit entry.

AV 2 is rolled out into the Californian sunshine on 29 May 1965.
(Both North American Rockwell)

the wingtips were lowered to their full down position. Mach 1.5 was maintained to about 50,000 feet, and then varying rates of acceleration were applied until Mach 3 (2,000 mph) at 70,000 feet was reached. The best-recorded time to Mach 3 was 25 minutes from rotation.

From Mach 2 on, the rectangular air inlet ramps began to close. As the speed increased, their geometry changed to provide the optimum pressure recovery through a series of sequential shocks; beginning with an oblique shock from the splitter plate, ending with a terminal shock as the air reached the throat areas. Introducing the initial shock wave was 'starting' the inlet ramps. If the shock wave refused to enter, or popped back out of the inlets, it was called an 'unstart' condition.

Al White described an unstart at Mach 3 as '*...sudden and violent, accompanied by a large reduction in engine thrust. The aircraft rolled, pitched, and yawed, accompanied by considerable buffeting*'. Normally one inlet

unstarted with a bang and as the pilot was recovering the other inlet would unstart. Similar problems also affected the Lockheed Blackbirds – it was one of the hazards of very high speed flight. While not particularly dangerous, unstarting was one problem facing supersonic transport designers. Passengers aboard an SST would not appreciate such an occurrence in flight and it took the joint design teams of Aérospatiale, the British Aircraft Corporation and Rolls Royce to come up with a viable solution.

62-0001 along with the TB-58A escort over the Arizona desert. (USAF)

There was another, potentially more serious problem. Sometimes, speed and throat ramp settings would create a condition where the shock wave was right at the boundary of the inlet, jumping in and out. This 'buzz' had to be corrected quickly – if it continued for more than a few minutes the stresses could cause structural damage.

Despite the problems, by its eighth flight AV 2 had reached Mach 2.34 at 57,500 feet. However, Al White's post-flight report recommended waiting until the AICS was fixed before attempting a Mach 3 flight.

Meanwhile AV 1 continued to go faster. Finally, on 14 October 1965, the aircraft recorded Mach 3.02 at 70,000 feet. As the aircraft and crew accelerated through Mach 3 Al White reported *'There's that big magic number'*. For just over two minutes everything appeared fine. Suddenly, White and Cotton heard something behind them. Although no caution lights had come on, White decided to decelerate and let the chase aircraft catch up to see if anything was wrong. Chase soon reported that about two feet of the left wing leading edge was missing from the Valkyrie. As luck would have it, the damaged section of the wing was far enough outboard so that the debris was not drawn into the engine inlets. So, after 56 weeks and 17 flights, AV 1 had finally reached its goal – but it would never fly at Mach 3 again. Alarmed with the ongoing skin separation problems, and hoping that manufacturing improvements in AV 2 would finally solve the problem, the Air Force imposed a strict Mach 2.5 speed limitation on AV 1. However, AV 1 was the largest and heaviest aircraft to have ever flown Mach 3, even if was only for two minutes!

An unusual and stunning photograph taken from the back seat of the T-38 Talon chase aircraft with reflections everywhere. It is thought that this is AV 2. *(USAF)*

During its 15th flight, on 11 December 1965, AV 2 reached Mach 2.94 briefly, but ran at Mach 2.8 for 20 minutes without any indications of skin separation. Ten days later, after 7 minutes above Mach 2.9, the oil pump for the No. 4 engine failed. Shutting down the engine, White and Cotton headed back to Edwards, when an over temperature caution came on for the No.6 engine, which was also shut down as well. After landing, it was discovered that, despite the early shut-down, loss of lubrication had destroyed engine No.4 – now the flight programme only had 29 airworthy engines left. The No.6 engine was removed and sent back to General Electric for repair.

In less than six months after its first flight, AV 2 reached Mach 3 on its 17th flight – coincidentally the same number of flights that AV 1 needed to reach Mach 3. A top speed of Mach 3.05 (2,010 mph) was recorded for 3 minutes. The post-flight inspection revealed no sign of skin damage. Great concern was still being expressed about the likelihood of more honeycomb separation, and AV 2 twice more went beyond Mach 3 for just a few minutes before sustaining 2,000 mph at 73,000 feet for fifteen minutes during her 22nd flight on 17 February 1966.

Air Vehicle Two at Edwards AFB. The sleekness of the design, and the distance the cockpit is ahead of the nose gear is noticeable. *(USAF)*

Flight Test recording

Today, recording of flight data during any flight would all be done on microchips. Back in the time of the XB-70 the Flight Test Instrumentation System for the XB-70 air vehicle was very advanced for its time, but would be looked upon as being archaic today. It was developed to provide the capability of obtaining data required to establish safety or flight limits, to evaluate sub-system functional operations, and to define gross problem areas within the realm of the various flight test tasks. The airborne instrumentation system also contained provisions for obtaining Supersonic Transport (SST) data and supplemental cockpit instrumentation for special flight monitoring requirements. The primary data acquisition media was magnetic tape recorded in both digital and analogue formats. In addition, selected parameters were telemetered to the Ground Station and displayed in real time on chart recorders concurrent with the flight.

The high capacity airborne instrumentation system developed for the flight test programme, provided the capability of subsystem test sharing during each flight of the XB-70's. This provided an equivalent test hour total five times actual flight test hours plus the invaluable capability of 'looking' at all sub-systems for gross problems during the first phase of flight testing. This 'gross look' at all sub-systems provided early detection of problem areas which resulted in a timely progression of the flight test programme.

Six basic types of parameters were recorded by the airborne instrumentation system. They were miscellaneous, acceleration, position, temperature, strain, and pressure. To acquire the parameter data, three sensor or transducer installations were employed. The conventional or normal approach was where the transducer was added at, or near, the point of measurement. The second type was where an air vehicle sub-system configuration had an electrically isolated sensor incorporated as part of the basic configuration and was furnished as an integral part of that sub-system. This avoided the requirement for making a direct electrical connection and afforded maximum isolation and safety. The third type of installation was the direct pick-off method and applied only to the measurement of electrical quantities, such as, voltage, current, frequency or to parameters already existing in electrical form.

In the course of building up the overall data acquisition system it was necessary to meet requirements for data sensors which were capable of operation in high temperature and vibration environments. Much was purchased from outside vendors, but sensors for the measurement of linear positions, rotary positions, air flow directions, and high vibration hydraulic pressures were not available. These items, therefore, had to be designed and developed within the Instrumentation Group. High temperature bonded strain gauge and variable reluctance techniques were applied in the construction of these devices.

The instrumentation package was the heart of the airborne data acquisition system. This was a specially designed package which could be lowered out of or raised into the air vehicle forward weapons bay. The equipment section was divided into four areas, three of which were compartmented for installation of modular chassis employing rack and panel connectors. The fourth area contained the tape recording equipment, the programme panels, circuit breakers, operational controls and displays for performing pre-flight and checkout operations. Cooling air, in metered amounts, was forced through each chassis from a self-contained environmental control system which employed liquid nitrogen for cooling and pressurization. Temperature was regulated between limits of 40 and 160° F. Pressure was maintained so that it was never less than that corresponding to 8000 feet altitude. Environmental control provisions were dual, providing back-up operation in the event of an in-flight failure of the system. The instrumentation package was entirely independent of any air vehicle system with the exception of electrical power.

The digital system and analogue system were the primary media of data

The instrumentation package as installed in the weapons bays of AV 1. The weapons bays on both the XB-70s were inoperable as such, for they could not be opened in flight, and carried no weapons suspension racks. The package could be lowered for maintenance. *(AFFTC History Office Collection)*

acquisition, and were some of the earliest in use for this type of work. Although technical in nature, this pioneering system deserves description.

The digital system provided for the recording of around 800 channels of quasi-static data with a maximum frequency response of 20 cycles per second for selected channels. A wide variety of parameters were recorded and with the exception of thermocouples, all data channels were individually signal conditioned. The following sub-paragraphs describe the major functions of the digital system.

Multiplexing: a scheme of time multiplexing was employed to sample, digitize, and record each data channel in accordance with a prescribed repetitive pattern. Fifty channels of master commutation received signals sequentially from two pre-digitized data channels and 48 sub-commutators.

Filtering: to limit the signal frequency spectrum to that which could be recovered from the recorded data at the digitizing rates provided, preceded the signal operation.

Commutation: was accomplished, at low level, by solid state switches which switched both sides of the signal lines. The switching rate for each master channel was 400 times per second which set the total system and sampling rate at 20,000 times per second. Switch and system sequencing commands were derived by dividing down from a master crystal controlled clocking oscillator. A system time code which was recorded as data, was also generated from this source. Switching was followed by amplification to bring the signal to the +/-3 volt level required by the analogue to digital converter. Five sequentially gated amplifiers performed this function.

From the Final Report comes this diagramatic representation of the Airborne Instrumentation System. (North American Rockwell)

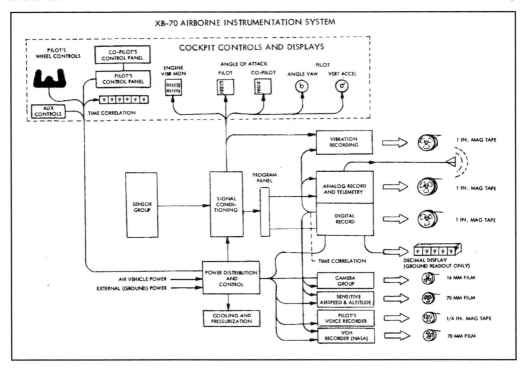

With landing gear and flaps down, AV 2 turns onto final approach to the main runway at Edwards AFB. *(USAF)*

Digitizing: digitizing was completed in 15 micro-seconds at a repetition rate of 20,000 times per second. The digital resolution provided was 1 part in 1024, corresponding to conversion into 10 binary bits. The converter was self-clocking, but received its command to digitize from the system programmer.

Recording; recording of the digitized output was in parallel binary bit format on 16 track 1 inch magnetic tape. Though data words were normally 10 bits in length, the recording system was capable of accepting up to 20 words of 13 bit length as derived from shaft encoders or other externally generated digital inputs. These longer words were recorded on the tape by gating them into the recorder at preset times in the data sampling sequence. Additional bits were also recorded on tracks, not used for data, to provide readout clocking and to indicate lateral parity, commutation frames and cycles, and system operational modes. The packing density on the magnetic tape was 667 words per linear inch with the tape recording speed of 30 inches per second. Two digital tape machines were employed for data acquisitioning. The switch over from the first to the second recorder occurred automatically when tape on the first machine was exhausted. A total of between 48 and 96 minutes of recording time was available depending on the thickness of the tape used; however, during the flight test programme a thin tape was used so that the recording time was approximately 96 minutes.

The analogue system, which provided for the acquisition of high frequency data, employed frequency multiplexing to record up to 144 data channels in banks of up to 12 channels per data track on to a 14 track 1 inch magnetic tape. Track 13 was used for tape speed servo control only, and track 14 was used for correlation data only.

Recording: one analogue tape recorder was used with a recording tape speed of 15 inches per second for acquisitioning the higher frequency parameters of the airborne system. At this tape speed and with thin tape, 90 minutes of recording time was provided.

Telemetry: the real time display of 36 selected parameters, via telemetry, for the full duration of the flight, proved useful in monitoring flutter and certain other

important parameters. Such monitoring made it possible to follow predicted versus actual flight conditions to guard against exceeding given limitations. It also permitted extensions of the flight envelope during the course of the test. The composite data signals appearing on analogue tape tracks 1, 2, and 3 were telemetered to the ground on three UHF radio links operating on 228.2, 250.7, and 259.7 Mc. These data were displayed on chart recorders, and provided a permanent record of the flight. Correlation with the in-flight records was provided by the analogue time code format, and data record start and stop signals.

VGH Recorder: the NASA VGH recorder provided a time history of airspeed, altitude, and normal acceleration. Normal acceleration was measured at both the centre of gravity and the pilot's station. The data were recorded on a 200 foot roll of 70mm photographic paper which advanced at the rate of two and a half feet per hour in a removable recording drum,

Cockpit Camera: a 16mm pulse-operated camera, installed between the pilot's and Co-Pilot's capsules, was focused on the cockpit instrument panel. The field of view

AV 1 rests between tests, with all the static ports plugged and tow-tug attached. The obvious way of telling AV 1 and AV 2 apart was that AV 1 did not have the lower radome area painted black.

The converted school bus seen in both these photographs was North American Aviation's 'Mobile Command Center' used to support the XB-70 programme.
(both USAF)

included all of the pilot's engine and flight instruments. The camera was pulsed at two frames per second, and recorded only during the instrumentation recording period.

Pilot's voice recorder: a compact, quickly removable tape recorder was installed in the cabin equipment compartment to record flight comments. The recorder was also wired into AIC-18 Audio Bus to record all inter-com conversation, and transmitted or received radio communications. A total of four and a half hours of recording time was available at a recorder speed of fifteen-sixteenths of an inch per second.

Landing gear camera: a 16mm camera was located in each main landing gear well to record the behaviour of the gear at the touchdown point. These cameras operated at 100 frames per second for a 40 second duration.

Sensitive Airspeed and Altitude Recorder: a NASA recorder of the VGH type was used to record sensitive airspeed and altitude. These data were recorded on 70 mm film operating at the rate of two and a half feet per hour.

Landing on tip-toe

On 7 March 1966 the 37th flight of AV 1 showed the type of adversity that could be overcome by a pair of experienced test pilots. Van Shepard was the pilot and Joe Cotton was copilot. Halfway through the planned flight, both hydraulic systems began to fail. Shepard quickly brought the Valkyrie home as Cotton extended the landing gear. No green indicators came on, and that was soon followed by a call from the chase aircraft that there was trouble with both sets of main gear. On the left side, the gear had not fully lowered before rotating to meet the direction of travel, leaving the rear wheels higher, rather than lower, than the front set of wheels.

The right side gear was in worse shape as it hadn't lowered at all before rotating. Even more alarming, it hadn't rotated completely in line with the

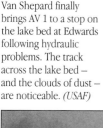

Van Shepard finally brings AV 1 to a stop on the lake bed at Edwards following hydraulic problems. The track across the lake bed – and the clouds of dust – are noticeable. *(USAF)*

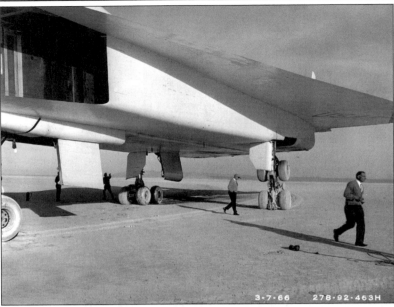

Landing on tip-toe!
7 March 1966 and AV 1 is
brought in for a very
gentle landing following
hydraulic problems. The
path taken by the aircraft
as it swung can be clearly
seen.(USAF)

direction of travel, although it was close. Neither the backup or emergency system corrected the problem. After what must have seemed like hours in the cockpit, engineers on the ground called up to the pilots with their plan. Shepard would land the Valkyrie on the dry lake bed, so there would be plenty of room. The engineers believed that, on touchdown, the left gear would level itself out, the weight of the XB-70A forcing the gear into its normal position. As for the right gear – being behind the centreline of the main strut, it was unlikely to level out,

AV 2 at Edwards AFB. This picture shows the height and complexity of the crew boarding ladder. What is not so clear is just how small the crew entry door was! *(USAF)*

but hopefully the landing would at least cause the gear to finish swinging into the direction of travel, and the wingtip would still clear the ground, although the right side would be much lower than the left.

Van Shepard set AV 1 down on the lake bed, and each main gear did what the engineers expected. The aircraft was down and rolling, but it wanted to turn sharply to the right – threatening to ground loop, which, although probably not fatal to the pilots, would probably destroy the aircraft. So Shepard kept applying power to the No. 6 engine to help keep the XB-70A something like straight.

After rolling almost three miles across the lake bed, the XB-70A came to a stop, having swung over half a mile to the right and turned 110 degrees. Only the size of the lake bed made this landing possible.

The damage, such as it was, was quickly repaired and AV 1 returned to flight on 22 March piloted by Cotton and Shepard on a 2 hour and 11 minute flight that only reached Mach 0.97 at 32,000 feet.

The only time an XB-70A would travel anywhere other than Edwards or Palmdale was on 24 March 1966 when Fulton and White took AV 2 to the air

Three images from a contact strip showing the take-off in the pre-dawn light with full afterburner of Flight 54 – the 22nd flight of AV 2. *(USAF)*

FLT-54 303-92-12

show at Carswell AFB, Texas. The Valkyrie spent only 13 minutes at Mach 2.71 before slowing down, ending up at 6,000 feet over Carswell just 59 minutes after takeoff. For the next half hour, AV 2 thundered around the skies of Texas before landing. The return flight two days later was the only flight during the entire programme where performance data was not recorded, as Cotton and White flew back at subsonic speeds, taking a little over three hours to return to Edwards AFB.

62-0001 comes in to land at Edwards AFB, watched by the mandatory rescue helicopter hovering in the distance. (USAF)

It was not unusual for the XB-70A to experience engine unstarts during the test programme. For instance, on 12 April 1966 AV 2 was on a high-speed flight that had been scheduled to fly at Mach 3 for 30 minutes, but Al White and Joe Cotton decided to cut the high-speed run short after an inlet unstart. The internal shock wave moved forward from its optimum position while the flight crew was experimenting with the manual vernier controls for 'fine tuning' the engine inlets to achieve maximum performance. The unstart was aggravated by

The two flight-test vehicles in one of the hangars at Edwards AFB. The cut-outs in the end wall were to let the rudders through.(USAF)

a turn manoeuvre – turning always affected inlet airflow, but was usually compensated for by the automatic inlet control system.

During the 20-minutes spent at Mach 3.08 and 72,800 feet, the maximum free-stream temperature reached 624° F at stagnation points on the wing and inlet leading edges. The highest previous free-stream temperature had been 610° F during a 16-minute Mach 3 flight on 8 April. The higher temperature on this flight was attributed to atmospheric conditions and not the duration of the flight.

The 'Paperclip' Flight

Not to outdone, AV 2 also experienced a landing gear problem – this time on 30 April 1966 the 37th flight. Shortly after takeoff, Cotton retracted the landing gear. However, a short-circuit in the landing gear retraction system permitted wind forces to blow the nose gear back into the partially-retracted gear well door, slashing the tires. An attempt to lower the gear using the normal hydraulic system failed. Trying the backup electrical system, Cotton heard a 'pop' as that system went dead.

White first brought the XB-70A around for a touch-and-go, hoping that a hard impact on the main gear would knock the nose gear loose and let it fall to the extended position. Even after a second try, however, the nose gear remained jammed. At this point, bailing out and losing the aircraft was quickly becoming the only option.

But there was fuel to burn, so White and Cotton circled around Edwards while engineers on the ground attempted to sort things out and come up with a solution. After more than two hours the problem with the backup system was traced, so they hoped, to a circuit breaker. Now all Cotton had to do was find a way to short circuit the unit. Of course, the Valkyrie had no onboard toolkit – that would have made things too simple. But Cotton had brought along his

Neither up nor down. The nose gear of AV 2 during its 37th flight. It took a paperclip to resolve the problem. *(USAF)*

AV 2 comes to a halt on the main runway at Edwards AFB after the 'paperclip' flight.

Fire trucks spray foam over the main wheel units after three of the four brake assemblies stayed locked on.

The aftermath; four sets of ruined tyres and wheels, with plenty of foam to be cleared from the runway. (USAF)

Two views taken out in the desert at Edwards. AV 1 is moved by a ground tug. This head-on view of the Valkyrie was and still to this day is always dramatic.

briefcase with his various notes and plans, and opening it, he found a binder-type paperclip. Straightening out the paperclip, then grasping the middle of it with a leather glove. Cotton carefully reached in and short circuited the breaker. It did the trick.

However, the malfunction also caused hydraulic pressure to remain on three of the four main wheel brakes, which were thus locked when the aircraft landed at 173 knots. Fire fighters at Edwards prevented any serious damage to the aircraft, which flew again a little over two weeks later.

On 19 May during flight number 39, AV 2 flew at Mach 3.06 at 72,500 feet for 33 minutes. In just 91 minutes, the Valkyrie traveled over 2,400 miles – an average

Both machines on the ground at Edwards. Sadly, they never took to the air together – imagine what a formation shot that would have made! *(both USAF)*

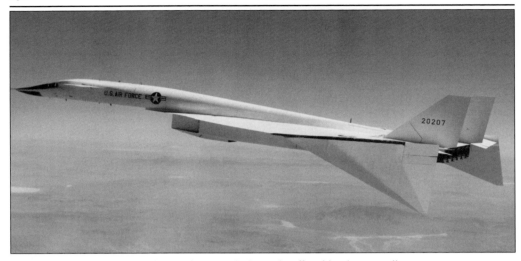

speed of more than 1,500 miles per hour, including takeoff and landing. Finally, A truly stunning picture of
all remaining concerns about skin separation were laid to rest. The Valkyrie could   62-0207 in flight with the
now certainly lay claim to being a true Mach 3 cruiser.   wingtips in the full down
                                                                                        position. *(USAF)*
    Three days later AV 2 thrilled the spectators at the Armed Forces Day show at
Edwards, including a couple of supersonic passes over the crowd. Test data on
stability and control issues were recorded during the 2-hour and 22-minute flight
that reached Mach 1.51 and 36,500 feet.

    With all systems tested, the XB-70A prepared to move into Part 2 of Phase
Two test program, where NASA would become much more involved, and
extensive sonic boom and handling tests would begin. New pilots would join the
programme, including NASA chief test pilot Joseph A. Walker, who had just come
from the X-15 programme. Not only did Walker have an 'astronaut' rating (given
to Air Force pilots who flew higher than 50 miles altitude), he had flown the X-15
beyond Mach 6 (4,100 mph) in level flight. Mach 3 would seem slow. Also joining
the programme was Air Force Major Carl Cross. At the same time, both Al White
and Joe Cotton began to gradually ease out of the programme, with Cotton going
on to test other aircraft for the Air Force, and White to work on other projects at
North American.

    AV 2 was refitted with additional instrumentation and data recording
equipment – more than a thousand sensors, recording devices and telemetry
equipment were installed. These instruments would give a better look at a number
of phenomena that couldn't be thoroughly tested in a wind tunnel including body
flex, flutter, and pressure distributions. At the same time, NASA began setting up
a large number of ground sensors to precisely measure the effect of sonic booms.

    But tragedy awaited.

THE DEMISE OF AV 2

Like all accidents, it only happened as a coming together of a chain of events that, if the chain had been broken at any stage could have so easily never occurred. General Electric started the ball rolling for this particular photographic mission sometime in mid-May of 1966, when GE chief test pilot John M Fritz approached a senior representative of North American at the Edwards AFB Flight Test Center.

Fritz was asked by General Electric to see whether it would be possible to arrange for in-flight photos of the XB-70A in formation with other supersonic aircraft using General Electric engines. The North American representative said it might be worked out, depending on the availability of the XB-70.

John Fritz then contacted Colonel Joe Cotton. He agreed to the inclusion of the photo session at the end of a test flight as long as it did not interfere and if large demands were not made on the Air Force Flight Test Center (AFFTC). Colonel Cotton had permitted North American to take in-flight photos of the Sabreliner and the XB-70A on a non-interference basis. He felt consideration should be given to General Electrics request. He also felt that General Electric responded positively to the flight test programme.

On 2 June 1966, Colonel Cotton requested and received approval for the flight from his supervisor, Colonel Cate, the deputy for Systems Test, AFFTC. Colonel Cotton:

'The main thing here, when I realized we were going to have a formation, was I didn't think it was appropriate to see a five- or six-ship formation someplace without folks here at home knowing it. I felt it was important to discuss it with the boss and tell him it was a request for General Electric and to point our that we had done it before, and see what he thought about it and get his guidance on it'.

Joe Cotton (left) and Al White after an earlier Valkyrie flight. Note the XB-70A 'patch' on each light suit.

No further approval was sought or secured, except for the briefing of Colonel Cate by Colonel Cotton on the details. Once a decision had been reached, John Fritz started the arrangements for a number of aircraft to participate in the flight. He wanted one of the XB-70s, and an AFFTC T-38 was scheduled to participate in the flight as a chase aircraft. F-104N (N813NA) supplied by NASA for the photo mission by Joe Walker, who was the chief research pilot for NASA at Edwards. The request for this aircraft by John Fritz was backed by Colonel Cotton even though it was not needed for chase flight. The flight was scheduled by Joe Walker as a chase operation, which was under his authority at NASA (although his superiors did not know of the photo mission). Fitz also requested a US Navy F-4 Phantom from Point Mugu Naval Air Station, California. This was secured by John Fritz with Commander Jerome Skyrud, head of Air-to-Air Weapons Branch, Naval Missile Center with E J Black in the back. It was approved by the operations coordination officer as a routine training flight in support of what was assumed to be an approved Air Force mission. There was also an F-5 - Air Force-owned, but bailed to General Electric under unrelated engine component improvement programmes. In the technical sense there was a requirement that all flights of bailed aircraft must be approved. This was complied with, but the F-5 did not perform the engine airstart evaluations (the 'official' reason for its inclusion) as stated by John Fritz in the documentation for this flight.

John Fritz also attempted to arrange for an Air Force B-58, but was unsuccessful. He also unsuccessfully tried to arrange for Air Force photo coverage, so a civilian Gates Learjet flown by H Clay Lacey was contracted by General Electric to photograph the formation.

The XB-70A had a reason to be in the air along with the T-38 aside from the photo session. The F-104N was also considered to be of importance since Joe Walker had flown chase on the XB-70A a number of times and was training to be a XB-70A pilot. His first familiarization flight was slated for 10 June.

The photo session was officially added to the research flight on 2 June 1966. It was tagged to the end of an airspeed calibration run and a familiarization flight for Major Carl Cross. On 7 June a third objective was added to the list: a sonic boom run for the SST programme. In the official paperwork for preflight reports, only these three missions were mentioned.

62-0207 is prepared for another flight from Edwards AFB. *(USAF)*

A preflight briefing was held on 7 June. North American handled the technical end of the flight while John Fritz handled the photographic session. A 'loose vee' formation that was going to be led by the XB-70A was proposed rather than a close formation. The F-104 was assigned the inboard position and flown by Joe Walker from NASA. This was off the right wing of the XB-70A. Commander Jerome Skyrud in the F-4 was given the inboard position on the left side. John Fritz was assigned the right outboard position in another F-5, and Captain Pete Hoag, in the Air Force T-38, was in the left outboard position, with Colonel Cotton in the rear seat. The Learjet was out of the formation.

By all accounts, there were no specific separation distances discussed and no formation commander assigned, although it seems everyone assumed that Colonel Cotton was in charge.

Three pilots from the proposed flight were not present at the briefing: Al White, who assumed command as XB-70A pilot on June 7 when the original pilot had to drop out for another flight; Commander Skyrud, who kept in contact with John Fritz via telephone; and H. Clay Lacy, who was the Learjet pilot briefed by John Fritz before takeoff on June 8. On the Learjet, there was a General Electric test pilot who was familiar with Edwards AFB procedures and had attended the preflight briefing.

John McCollum, the director of research vehicles for the aeronautical systems division and who served as the XB-70A system programme director was also involved. At the time, he was visiting Edwards AFB to discuss the next phase of the XB-70A test programme with the Test Center, NASA, and contractor personnel. On 7 June, he helped in the scheduling of the sonic boom run and was invited to attend the preflight briefing. He was the highest-ranking Air Force official at the

Momma hen and her chicks.
Closest to the camera is John Fitz, in an F-5. Then there is Commander Jerome Skyrud in and US Navy F-4. XB-70 62-0207, then Joe Walker in the NASA F-104. Outboard right is Capt Peter Hoag and Colonel Cotton in an Air Force T-38. *(USAF)*

62-0307 flies in formation with the other aircraft. As far as is known, once the formation was created, all remained in the same relative positions until after the collision.

briefing and he knew about the photographic aspect to the mission. Since he did not object, it seemed that this was taken as his unexpressed consent. If he did object, the mission would not have been able to go on, as it was within his jurisdiction to take the XB-70A out of the flight.

XB-70A AV 2 took off at approximately 07:15 to run the airspeed calibration tests. As usual, there was a chase aircraft following it - this time a T-38. When the XB-70A started to climb for a sonic boom run, the T-38 had to land to refuel; another T-38 in the area checked the XB-70A to make sure that the cooling doors were closed. The sonic boom run was completed by 08:30 and all indications suggest that the rendezvous portion of the mission was completed at about 08:45. There were clouds in the area that made a change in altitude necessary - from the prescribed 20,000 feet to 25,000 feet. Location and direction were also changed from north-south to east-west, the latter resulting in a much shorter fight path.

It is clear from the backgrounds, that they were searching to find a suitable backdrop to show off the formation to its best advantage. *(both USAF)*

This image has appeared innumerable times, but going back to the original source shows it to its best advantage with less cropping. (USAF)

Recorded radio 'chatter' was to hint at what was happening. XB-70A pilot Al White: *'Roger, I'm going to have to climb slightly or I'm going to lose everybody in the clouds'.* White also had restricted vision from the XB-70A - especially to the rear and at one stage was heard to ask *'How many airplanes have I got with me?'*

Joe Walker replied: *'You got two now and there should be a T-38 and an F-5 plus the photo Learjet'*

Fritz: *'I'm joining now. A T-38 is on the way. Would it be possible to make a left-hand turn here for a little bit and let this Lear jet catch up?"*

White: *'Oh, okay. I'll have to go around this cloud thing here.'*

It seems that the clouds were a continuous problem and White spoke of them several times as he moved above 25.000 feet, still surrounded by cumulus but straining to let the photo plane catch up. Once he said: *'My problem is I can't go any higher... I'm afraid I'll lose them if I go... I'm just milling around in these things. That's why I wanted to go out east.'*

Walker: *'I think you're right Al. Over east is a lot better and you can stay lower.'*

The situation improved. The XB-70A dropped down and slowed to 300 knots. Then Fritz spoke up from his position just outboard of Walker: *'...You got all your chickens.'*

White: *"Great. What do we want them to do? Just fly like this and get some pictures ...okay?"*

No problems were reported with the formation and it continued on its way. At around 09:00, an Air Force photo aircraft on a return from another mission had 100 feet of unexpended film. That flight asked for and received permission to film the formation in progress. At 09:15, the Learjet was questioned about additional time, since the already-planned-for 30 minutes had elapsed. The Learjet requested an additional 10-15 minutes. The Data Record transcript tells the story: 'Two Zero Seven' is the call-sign for the Valkyrie:

09:20:02:   DATA CONTROL: *Ah, yes, this is Data Control. Is tank eight feeding now?*
                 AV 2 (Cross): *Affirmative tank eight is feeding properly now.*
                 DATA CONTROL: *Rog.*

09:21:24   INTERPHONE(Cross): *They must have had that Learjet full of film or they'd be out of business by now.*

                 AV 2 (White): *Yes—He was sitting there but he's up here now. This hole is getting smaller and smaller too.*

The formation keeps station while the camera aircraft circles it *(USAF)*

09:22:47   #813 (Walker): *We must be helping the cumulus activity along with all this hot air.*

09:24:48   RAPCON: *Two zero seven. Traffic. Two zero miles east of your position, orbiting Three Sisters two four zero, two seven zero.*
                 AV 2 (White): *Roger, Thank you.*

A close-up of Joe
Walker's F-104. The
Valkyrie's wingtip is just
visible.
(USAF)

09:25:05   AV 2 (White): *We got a contrail out there—but, I don't ah, it looks like he's higher than that.*
INTERPHONE (Cross): *Probably—*

09:25:23   #601 (Cotton): *Learjets Lear—Another four minutes the Learjet said.*
AV 2 *(White): Thanks, Joe.*

09:25:42   DATA CONTROL: *Two zero seven, the Learjet says about three more minutes.*
AV-2: *OK, Zeke.*

09:26:06   RAPCON: *Two zero seven, he's off your left wing now ah, below the clouds.*
AV 2 (White): *Roger, thank you.*
RAPCON: *The B-58's speed run is now one five miles east of your position westbound three zero zero or above.*
AV 2 (White): *I have him, thank you.*

09:26:26   ??: At this time there was one carrier burst followed by a longer carrier, of one second maximum duration, sounding like a live microphone in an open cockpit.

09:26:28   ??: There were two or more carriers on the frequency with resultant signal clash, followed by
#601 (Hoag): Mid-air, mid-air, stand by for—
#601 (Cotton): You got the verticals, this is Cotton, you got the verticals—came off left and right. We're staying with ya, no sweat, now you're holding good, Al.

The NASA F-104 collided with the XB-70. The first contact was with the left

horizontal stabilizer and the canted right wingtip of the XB-70. The F-104 then
pitched up, rolled to the left, and hit the right leading edge of the XB-70's wing.
The F-104 continued its roll inverted into the XB-70's top right vertical stabilizer
and took the top off the left vertical stabilizer. The F-104 was cut just aft of the
cockpit, its nose hit the XB-70's left wing, and the fuselage of the F-104 went
streaking aft in flames.

09:26:40   #601 (Hoag): *Joe Walker ran into him and I think he's had it.*
                 (Cotton): *The B-70 went upside down, it's rolling now, the left
                 wing—*
                 #601 (Hoag): *Bailout, bailout, bailout—*
                 #601 (Cotton): *Bailout, bailout, bailout.*

09:27:09   #601 (Cotton): *OK, the B-70 is spinning to the right—*
                 #601 (Hoag): *Something came out, it looks like—*
                 #601 (Cotton): *Looks like a capsule came out. It's spinning to
                 the right, the nose is slightly down.*

09:27:23   #601 (Hoag): *No chute—*
                 #601 (Cotton): *. . . see no chute yet. The main gear is down, the
                 nose gear is up.*

09:27:28   #601 (Hoag): *Chute, chute, good chute.*

09:27:28   #601 (Cotton): *There's a chute, there's a capsule (pause). There's
                 one chute.*
                 #601 (Hoag): *B-70 wing up here to our right.*

09:28:02   #601 (Cotton): *The B-70 wing is to our right. We're at fifteen
                 thousand. The B-70 is going down. I see one chute, one capsule.*   Moments after the
                 #601 (Hoag): *The left one.*   collision, Joe Walker's
                 #601 (Cotton): *The airplanes in a flat spin. The airplane is*   F-104 drops away
                 stable in a flat spin slightly nose down. Most of the left wing is   streaming flames. The
                 gone. Got several pieces around us. There's a burning piece to   XB-70A continues to fly,
                 the northwest. The airplane is flat. We're staying clear of the   but as can be seen, both
                 capsule.   verticals have been
                ripped away... *(USAF)*

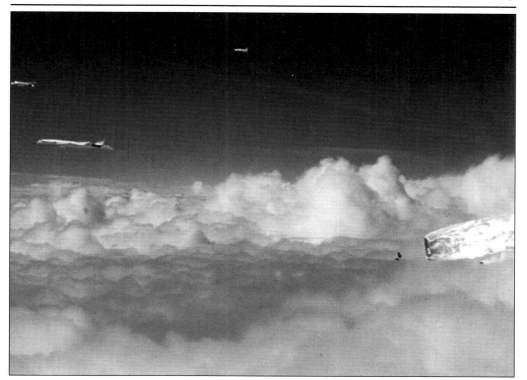

... a few seconds later the Starfighter continues to burn and break up as the formation starts to open up to give the XB-70A some space. (USAF)

As Al White said afterwards: *"I heard a good loud thump - an explosion - and I heard somebody yell 'Mid-air' But with all that length and mass behind me, I didn't know it was us. My immediate impression was that two other planes had collided. Even when I heard Cotton call about a vertical being gone, I still wasn't sure it was us. If I had heard the plural. I'd have understood."*

The XB-70A was the only plane in the sky with two vertical fins.

Cotton, knowing the plane was done for but hoping for a stable ejection condition, called his encouragement to White and Major Cross. Then the XB-70A abruptly surrendered to its wounds.

Al White again: *The airplane yawed abruptly and very violently to the right. It was so violent I thought the nose would break off. Then it was upside down and nose down, and then right side up and nose up. It did this twice and the second time around a big piece of the left wing broke off.*

These were unstabilized rolls and the G forces were fierce. It was probably the Gs that finally tore the wing off after it had been weakened when Walker fell on it. The force on me was violent, throwing me ahead and to the left. I couldn't move against the Gs. But then it settled into a flat spin. This gave it a more or less fixed axis somewhere back along the fuselage and it was more stable but out of control, of course. Centrifugal force was still shoving me forward, but at least I could move a little.

When it nosed up out of the second tumble, I began trying to encapsulate'

To encapsulate and eject from an XB-70A required two conscious, deliberate actions on the part of the pilot to touch off a finely integrated sequence of events,

Slowly, inexorably the XB-70A starts to slide out of the sky.

Above: With the formation now spread wide open, the XB-70A enters the last few seconds of stable flight...

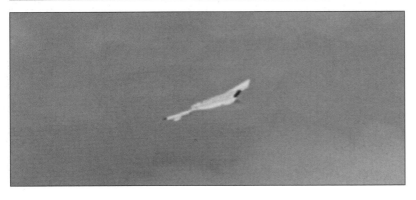

Right: Before dropping nose down...

Bottom: and then falls over onto it's back...
(USAF)

More pictures taken
from the Lear.

The XB-70A spirals
down, fuel streaming
from the damaged fuel
tanks.

The cloud cover below
forms a reference point
to orientate the view,
especially when no part
of the Lear is in the
frame. The lower picture
is often reproduced
'upside down' as if to
show the aircraft was
rotating a lot worse than
it was.

Nevertheless the
streaming fuel shows
that the aircraft was no
longer flying.
(USAF)

most of them powered by explosive charges.

The first action was to pull up either or both hinged, yellow hand-grips built into the front edges of the armrests. The second action was squeeze either left or right or both triggers set into the yellow handles. This simultaneously slammed the pilot's seat back about one and a half feet deep into the upright box of the capsule and jerked his shoulder harness so rigidly tight that he can scarcely move. It also shoved the aircraft's control column forward to provide room for the capsule's clamshell doors to snap shut from top and bottom. The doors respond to an involuntary human act when, being whipped back into the capsule, the pilot's heels whack into a pair of 'kickers' as his legs are being doubled up into a near-fetal position.

When all this has been done, the pilot is sealed up tight in an individual metal box which carries its own life-support system.

The pulling of the triggers set off the final sequence: first the overhead hatch blew off, rapidly followed by the firing of al rocket which shot the capsule, pilot and all, 300 feet above the aircraft.

Major Carl S Cross.

White's first action slammed him back into the capsule recess and, according to plan, jerked his shoulder harness tighter than any corset. His heels struck the door-triggering device and set off that charge. But he was immediately conscious of excruciating pain. Fighting the forces of the XB-70's spin, his right elbow had been doubled outward as he pulled the yellow handle, and now it was trapped outside the capsule at the hinge point of the clamshell doors. As a result the doors could not close shut, six inches of his own doubled elbow was outside the capsule and, with the shoulder harness straining backward, his right hand jammed against the yellow handle and the elbow locked outside, he could not get free.

'*The capsule not only had me trapped, but it hurt like hell. I was sure the arm was broken—at the minimum.*' White recalled later.

Using his left hand, White pried painfully at his right fingers, trying to work them loose from the yellow handle. They would not come free. He could have

Joseph Albert 'Joe' Walker, (1921-1966)

pulled the left trigger and fired his capsule out of the plane. But the clearance between the ejecting capsule and edge of the hatch frame was only four inches. Had he pulled the trigger, part of his elbow would have been sliced off as though by a guillotine. Spinning, in agony, and being hauled in two directions, he knew what the prospect was.

'*It didn't help any that, with that crazy tumbling and the spin, I was completely disoriented. And I could see Carl Cross. His head was bobbing around as though he was working real hard at something himself. I don't know why, but I knew he hadn't begun to encapsulate because he was still forward in the thing: his seat didn't move back. That was why I could still see him out of the corner of my eye. I wanted to talk to him and tried to yell, but I guess with the pain and confusion I was only grunting.*'

The doomed Valkyrie was falling fast and White, having been pulled away from the instruments, had no way of knowing how soon the XB-70A would hit. He wrestled frantically with his arm.

'I stopped once. It sounds insane, but I debated whether to eject and cut my arm off or stay and go in with the airplane. And there was Carl to think about, even though there was no possible way I could physically help him."

Then White's left hand worked one right finger free, then another, then all of them and he pulled the now unlocked hand away from the yellow handle. In agony, he finally dragged the wounded arm and elbow inside with him. White said that it seemed as if minutes passed while he wrestled with the arm, but actually just about 86 seconds elapsed between the time the XB-70 began toppling out of control and his chute blossomed.

"Once that arm was in I didn't waste any time, I didn't know where we were

The XB-70's escape capsule seen in the correct configuration during testing. The clamshell doors at the front are closed. The stabilizing 'arms' are deployed to the rear, each with their own drogue chutes and the cushioning 'attenuator bag' has been deployed. *(USAF)*

or how close to going in. I pulled the trigger, the rocket fired and I went out with the capsule doors still open. The shot gave my head a hell of a jerk on top of the snap in the neck I'd got when the seat went back."

The capsule doors were still open when he ejected. Since he was now well below 15,000 feet, his chute opened almost immediately. A new peril was immediate - the spinning XB-70A swung past what seemed like only inches from his capsule.

'That long nose went by and I thought God, the next time that big bastard comes around it's going to get me. At that point the airplane and I must have been falling at the same speed. It scared me."

The capsule doors were still wide open and White wanted them closed. Although the charge which should have closed them was gone they could be closed manually by pulling a handle on the upper door.

White wanted them closed for two reasons. He felt exposed with only the nylon straps of his harness between him and the void. The second reason was more imperative: his trapped arm had interrupted one more vital event in the escape sequence. At that altitude an XB-70A capsule, weighing with pilot approximately 800 pounds, falls fast even with its parachute open - 32 feet per second compared to the approximate 22 fps of a man with an ordinary parachute. To absorb the shock of landing, a pneumatic cushion - called the 'attenuator bag' - should have inflated automatically as the main chute deployed. But it had not

Smoke billows up into the sky after 62-0207 hit the ground. The aircraft had impacted near 'Three Sisters' a few miles from Barstow, California.
(USAF)

done so because the bag could not inflate with the lower door open and swung down against it. Al wanted the door closed so he could inflate the bag with a manual backup system.

'I didn't want to hit without that bladder blown up. The engineers had calculated that to land without the bag might cost a man a broken back. But it didn't work. Even after I got the doors closed I couldn't find it. I was still disoriented and concerned about a lot of things: Carl, whether he was out: the junk falling around me: and a terrible coldness. Shock, I guess - that on top of the sweat from working to free my arm.

Then I heard the XB-70A hit. It made a terrible explosion and an enormous plume of smoke came up.

Cotton watched the descending parachute and thought for a time that White would fall into the XB-70's pyre. But then he saw that an easterly wind would carry the capsule clear.

At five minutes and 22 seconds after the accident and four minutes and 11 seconds behind his dead aircraft. White's capsule was about to hit.

"I saw a big Joshua tree coming up and thought God, I'm going in fast,"

Without its shock bladder, the capsule slammed down on a rocky slope close by the XB-70s severed left wing and about a mile from the main wreckage. The engineers later calculated that the capsule's impact created a 45 G-force. Somehow White managed to avoid the predicted broken back - it was probably a help that the seat fastenings gave away and gave his body some cushioning effect. Nevertheless, he hit so hard that his right boot heel stamped a deep indent on the capsule floor

Al White's escape capsule where it came to rest on the desert floor.
(USAF)

and one knee left its mark in the lower door. Al White was badly hurt.

At six minutes 25 seconds after the collision. Cotton and Hoag - who had made a number of low passes over the wreck site in their T-38 - reported no activity around the capsule which had tipped over on its side and faced downhill.

Inside Al White was struggling to break free. One big can of capsule equipment had broken loose was jammed against his helmeted head - he was also pinned down on his injured right arm, so once again he had only his left hand to work with.

'I was really moaning. I could hear myself. And I was freezing cold and

Left: Part of a wing tip of 62-0207 hit the ground. The main wreckage once the fires had gone out.
(USAF)

The remains of Joe Walker's F-104. *(USAF)*

stiffening up fast, but I wanted out of there. I wanted my feet on the ground. I tried to pry open the top door and did crack it, but it snapped down again. The second time, I got my helmet off and into the crack and worked it back toward the hinge like a wedge. When I had the door open about eighteen inches, I stuck my head and shoulders out. I saw the T-38 go by and waved."

Cotton saw the wave. At 13 minutes and one second after the collision - seven minutes and 56 seconds after the capsule hit - Cotton reported: *"There is activity at the capsule... The capsule is on its side... The position has been changed and we saw waving.'*

White was able to force his body all the way out but then, sweating from the work he had done and bone cold with shock, he crawled back in to get his flight jacket. It wasn't enough, and so he staggered up the slope and wrapped himself in the parachute. That may have been a mistake, for when the first of the rescue helicopters arrived from Edwards about 35 minutes after he landed, he was in trouble again.

'It was too rocky and steep for the chopper to land, but the downwash of its blades inflated my chute and I was almost airborne again'.

The helicopter dropped off a rescue team about 50 yards from where White lay. As they got to White with a stretcher panic set in. He may have recently fallen 25,000 feet, but now White begged the stretcher-bearers, *'Don't drop me, don't drop me!'*

The wreck site was a few miles north of Barstow, California. Major Cross's body was found in the XB-70A with his seat still forward in the ejection capsule. He may never have been able to begin the escape sequence, perhaps because of the same violent forces which had nearly killed Al White.

Ten miles from the wreckage of the XB-70, neither the charred ruins of Joe Walker's Starfighter nor his decapitated body could reveal anything about why he had died.

President Lyndon B Johnson issued a statement at 17:00, read by Bill D Moyers, Special Assistant to the President, at his news conference from the White House. *'Joe Walker and Major Cross gave their lives in advancing science and technology. Their deaths remind us how dependent we are on men of exceptional ability in the development of new vehicles in flight. They died while training for demanding assignments in a new field of major national interest- research on supersonic transport flight. They added immeasurably to the progress this nation is making in that effort.*

I extend my deepest sympathies to their families'.

Lets all play the blame game

With any major test programme there is always a higher than normal risk of incidents and accidents - that's why its called flight test.

By the week's end, as the Air Force convened a 62-member board of inquiry, few thought that Walker could have carelessly rammed the bomber; there was speculation that turbulence or the B-70's backwash might have caused the collision. But the circumstances surrounding the accident raised other questions. Though it was standard procedure for manufacturers of Air Force equipment to take pictures of their craft in flight, both for publicity and research purposes, even Pentagon officials conceded that last week's spectacular line-up was hardly standard.

In Washington, Chairman George Mahon of the House Appropriations Committee, declared: *"The loss of these men, and an aircraft in which more than $500 million has been invested, while accommodating the public relations department of a private company, is indefensible."*

In fact, the B-70 cost closer to $750 million, but what was not measurable in dollars were the lives of two pilots and the future hours of supersonic research that were lost in the Mojave desert.

The furore that followed the crash was hard to believe. Fingers were pointed in every direction and it became obvious that scapegoat creation had begun. General Electric bore the brunt of a great deal of unfair and undeserved criticism. The photo session had been requested under the same rules, formal or informal, that had been followed dozens of times before, and the Air Force approved the routine request. After the accident, industry and Air Force heads were on the chopping block. Congress and the Administration wanted to see someone - anyone - disciplined, and there were plenty of 'expendable' people to choose from. Careers were about to be destroyed and lives were about to be ruined.

The accident took place on 8 June 1966 - the final report of the Accident Board, signed by its president, a USAF colonel, was issued just forty-nine days later on 27 July 1966. It all seemed remarkably quick - so quick in fact that some have doubted that it was as thorough as it should have been.

At first look the report appears to be thorough, but a closer study and a certain amount of thought indicates that it may well have been hurried. Indeed, the report was published before all the wreckage had been recovered and examined!

The accident involved the loss of two lives and the loss of a $500-million airframe, that was highly advanced in both materials and construction and was equipped by many new and unproven systems. It also involved the destruction of half of a research 'fleet' that had a programme cost of nearly $1.5 billion. One can

George Herman Mahon (22 September 1900 - 19 November 1985). He called the loss of AV/2 *'...indefensible'.*

understand why so many suspected that no matter how obvious the circumstances of the mid-air collision, the investigation appeared to be short to the point of a cover-up. Was pressure put on the writers to put the past behind them as soon as possible?

It appears there was an effort within the Air Force to complete the investigation and then try to forget it. Following publication of the report, Secretary of the Air Force Harold Brown wrote a summary on the report to Secretary of Defense Robert McNamara on 12 August 1966, making it very clear that he was not going to accept responsibility for the crash. He mentioned 'instructions' and 'procedures' that were not followed and made reference to a lack of coordination with the assistant Secretary of Defense for public affairs. The Air Force leadership was not going to acknowledge the photographic mission as standard procedure, even though the memo never spelled out which regulations were violated. It contained nothing about why such photo missions had been taking place openly for years without comment from Air Force leadership.

Brown stated that under established procedures, requests for Air Force assistance in the production of commercial films required approval at a high level. He indicated that this procedures list included not only theatrical motion pictures, but also industrial motion pictures of advertising value. The director of information for the Air Force was supposed to be the sole authority.

The director of information was supposed to coordinate with the assistant Secretary of Defense (Public Affairs), who had the primary responsibility for relations with industry. In view of Secretary of Defense McNamara's desire to micro-manage all of the press and PR releases for all the services including NASA, this practice would not seem unusual.

Other directives prohibited flights of USAF aircraft not in the direct interest of government business. Air Force participation in contractor-sponsored special events was restricted and was not to be used to support commercial advertising, publicity, or promotional activities. Office of the Secretary of Defense approval was required on all aerial reviews not otherwise authorized.

Brown made it clear that the XB-70A flight in question never had such approval for the General Electric part of the flight. Brown concluded that the Air Force officer who assisted General Electric with this exercise used poor judgment, and that this officer's superior was also to blame because he didn't exercise good judgment in his duties. Two other Air Force officers were cited: *'an Air Force information officer and an official at the next higher level of the XB-70A program, both of whom were aware of the formation flight but failed to do anything about it.'*

Brown drew his prologue to a close, stating that further measures taken to ensure that the lessons of this accident were learned.

In his report Brown reviewed all the contracts held with North American Aviation and General Electric. There were, of course, no provisions made for photography for nongovernmental purposes - they were not authorized or required. The photographic aspect to this mission was therefore *'...outside the terms of these contracts and could not properly have been undertaken unless approved in accordance with the procedures on pictorial and industrial relations activities noted at the outset'*. This statement says that this was an illegal flight sanctioned by the Air Force, which said that its officers acted incorrectly.

Brown's summary of the XB-70A disaster showed just how hurriedly this report was put together, presumably so that it could be swept under the rug. Nothing could have pleased Robert McNamara more. Not only was there resistance to finding out the real reasons for the accident, but Brown also seemed insistent that General Electric was to be blamed. The apparent attitude was that none of this would have happened if General Electric hadn't asked for the photo flight.

Colonel Cotton would be assigned the blame for not refusing the request and overriding North American Aviation's reluctance to cooperate. Colonel Cate would take the blame for his limited view of his approval authority - which, incidentally never seems to have been challenged before in other photo-opportunity issues. And, of course, McCollum would be blamed for not stopping the flight altogether. No one ever questioned why this practice had occurred so many times before without objections.

According to Brown, all those people and companies were working in complete '*...ignorance of the prescribed procedures, rather than with intent to violate them*'. He questioned the judgment of the people who made this whole episode possible: the Air Force, the civilian contractors and, of course, the General Electric Company. Conveniently not mentioned was the office of the Assistant Secretary of Defense (Public Affairs), apparently because they had not been informed of the flight.

Brown strongly implied that this accident would never have happened at something as legitimate as an Armed Forces Day event. Such a flight would have required the approval of the Air Force director of information, and the assistant Secretary of Defense (Public Affairs). He cited the earlier instance where merely for the XB-70A to appear an air show at Carswell AFB, Texas, the request had reached the highest level of the Air Force chief of staff and the Secretary of the Air Force, and then the appearance was limited to a static display. Why it would take the approval of the Air Force chief of staff to approve a static display, but a formation flight could be approved by a secretary of an aircraft in the line of duty, way past the initial flight test stage. Accidents happen. It's an unfortunate fact of life. Could the loss of the second XB-70A have been prevented? We may never know. Bureaucracy played a large part in the inquest that followed the accident. Heads rolled, blame was handed out, and changes were made; but they were largely futile political solutions that came too late and settled nothing.

Many questioned the competency of Joe Walker. It was said by a well-known test pilot that Walker had no business being in that formation. Was he was out of practice? Walker was a pilot with almost 5,000 hours of flight time, and over 750 hours in the F-104. No one really knows exactly what happened up there. Some assume Walker wasn't prepared to fly formation, others think he took his eyes off the Valkyrie to watch a B-58 that was coming down the corridor, or maybe he just got caught in the vortex of the XB-70A after allowing his aircraft to creep disastrously close to it.

After all the bloodletting, the political punishment exercise was unable to bring two dead pilots back to life or to replace a $500-million aircraft.

SO HOW **DID** IT FLY?

The XB-70 was an incredibly complex piece of equipment. Preparation for each flight took the many 'departments' many man-hours to complete. The aircraft had twenty-one servicing points, all of which needed attention. Apart from the JP-6 fuel - of which no alternative was allowed - the aircraft needed liquid nitrogen, demineralised water in the form of ice shaped specifically to fit the containers, special lubricants... the list was huge.

The aircraft's requirements and size may have been large, but the cockpit itself was tiny. It was dominated by the two escape capsules, and then almost all of the rest the available volume was crammed full of dials, switches and levers. Both machines had a somewhat strange mixture of rotational and linear dials that today confuse the eye and the mind.

To take off - from the cockpit

Both the pilot and the co-pilot had specific duties according to the Flight Manual. However, much of the detailed pre-flight inspection was left to the maintenance personnel: *'Due to the size and complexity of this airplane, it is assumed that maintenance personnel have completed the preflight inspections. The exterior inspection performed by the flight crew is only an inspection of the readily accessible and flight safety items and is based on the flight crew accepting the airplane for flight with emphasis on the items affecting safety of flight. Check the airplane as outlined in Section 2.1. Information on non-accessible items is listed in the 'Pre-Flight Inspection Record'. Ground crew will be at the airplane to discuss the status of the airplane and its system'.*

The twelve external areas of inspection contained thirty seven specific items that excluded checking that all ground equipment was connected and working. Once on board there was a further twenty three point list to be completed before the cockpit could be 'set up' for flight.

Once in their seats the flight crew faced pages and pages of pre-flight 'instructions'. As each of the two aircraft varied slightly, there were sections specifically relating to whichever machine was being readied for flight. Engine start occurred at the bottom of the seventh page.

The normal starting sequence is engines No. 4, 6, 5, 3, 1, 2. When the first throttle is moved

Section 2.1 Pre-flight Exterior Inspection.
1 - Forward fuselage area.
2 - Right canard area.
3 - Right inlet area.
4 - Nose wheel area.
5 - Weapons bay area.
6 - Right main landing gear area.
7 - Right wingtip area.
8 - Rear fuselage area.
9 - Left wingtip area.
10 - Left main landing gear area.
11 - Left inlet area.
12 - Left canard area.

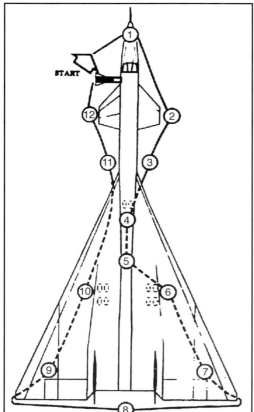

from OFF to IDLE the cooling loop fuel pump caution light goes out. However, as each engine is started one cooling loop fuel pump caution light comes on and stays on until engine rpm is between 35 and 40%.

After the first engine is started, and during the start of each successive engine, observe that engine and ADS oil pressure lights come on when each throttle is advanced to IDLE and goes out after start. This provides a check on the pressure switches and electrical circuits.

There were then another twenty pages of actions brought about by call and responses between the two crew on board before the aircraft was ready to taxi.

It was then instructions to the ground crew: *'Landing gear safety pins, wheel chocks and clear airplane to taxi. The three landing gear safety pins will be displayed to the pilot where he can see and count them.*

Nose wheel steering selector switch - TAXI. Nose wheel steering selector switch - ENGAGE, check nose wheel steering - ON indicator light ON, then move switch to FAILSAFE.

Hydraulic pressures, fluid levels and pump status indicators CHECK. Ground intercom - have ground crew disconnect. AGPS magnetic and great circle headings - CHECK. AGPS mode switch - MAG. Apply brakes and release pedals. Check that Brake Hold light goes out.

Before taxiing be sure that there is proper clearance for the airplane. (see Fig 2.4 for minimum turning radius). Note over the nose vision with the nose ramp retracted to runway level is about 90 feet in front of the airplane.

The idle thrust of six engines is adequate for taxiing. Directional control should be maintained by nose wheel steering rather than differential thrust or braking.

During taxiing five more points on the long list had to be covered. The brakes

Air Vehicle One under tow at Edwards AFB. In the background can be see Air Vehicle Two. *(USAF)*

Figure 2.4 from the Flight Manual - the minimum turning radius of the XB-70A, based on the nose wheels turned 58 degrees from centre, with the nose wheel steering switch in the TAXI position.

1 - The pitot boom tip = 142 feet.
2 - Wingtip = 97 feet.
3 - Nose gear = 54 feet.
4 - Left main gear = 40 Feet.
5 - Right main gear = 27 feet.

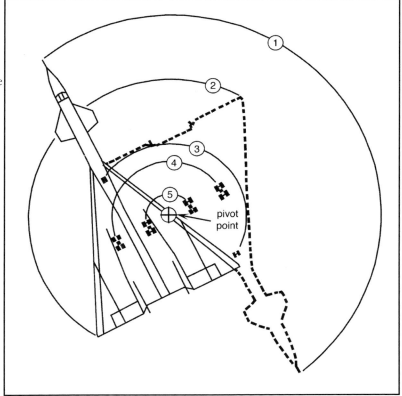

were checked, along with the hydraulic pressure, as was the nose wheel steering. Both crew's turn needle, ADI and HSI were checked, with the attitude director and horizontal situation indicators were working in the correct manner. The wheel brake control switch was set to AUTOMATIC. Both braking systems were checked by using the wheel brake test switch held to SYS 1 then SYS 2 and applying the brakes with the switch in each position.

On arrival at the take-off area the aircraft was brought to a complete stop for another series of checks/actions.

1. *AC voltages - Check. Check each phase (A, B and C) of AC voltage for each ac bus (LH PRI, RH PRI, and essential). Voltage should be 115 volts +/-3 volts. When the check is over leave the bus selector switch to ESSENTIAL.*

2. *Co-pilot - Air Induction Control System - Check. Bypass area should be 0000 square inches and Throat Mach schedule indicator should be at 1.67.*

3. *Secondary exhaust nozzle standby pressure knob - check set at field elevation.*
   Caution - if the nozzle standby knob is improperly set, the automatic transfer of the ambient pressure signal to the nozzle standby circuit in the event of central air data computer failure may cause loss of thrust.

4. *Co-pilot - Liquid Nitrogen quantity indicator - check quantity.*

5. *Co-pilot - IFF Master Switch - NORMAL.*

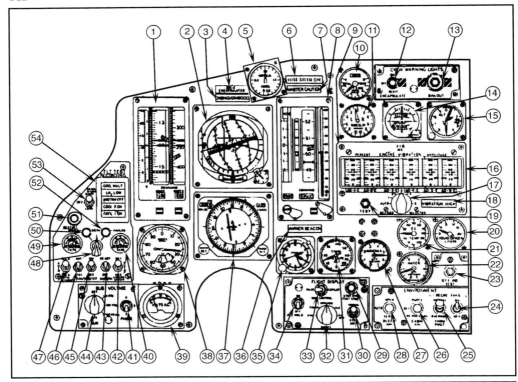

Pilot's Instrument Panel

1   Airspeed/Mach Number Indicator.
2 - Attitude Director Indicator
3 - Cabin over 42,000ft Caution Light.
4 - Crew Encapsulation Indicator Light.
5 - Vertical Accelerometer (shroud mounted).
6 - Nose wheel Steering ON indicator light.
7 - Master Caution Light.
8 - Altitude - Vertical Velocity Indicator.
9 - Let-Down Chart Holder Location (plug in).
10 - Total Temperature Gauge.
11 - Sideslip Indicator.
12 - Encapsulate Caution Light Switch.
13 - Bale-Out Warning Light Switch.
14 - Standby Altitude Indicator.
15 - Standby Altimeter.
16 - Engine-ADS Gearbox Vibration Indicators.
17 - Engine-ADS Vibration Record Selector Switch.
18 - Engine-ADS Vibration Caution Light.
19 - Engine-ADS Vibration Indicator Test Switch.
20 - Liquid Oxygen Quantity Gauge
21 - Electronic Equipment Compartment Air
     Temperature Gauge.
22 - Water Quantity Gauge.
23 - Quantity Gauges Test Button.
24 - Air Recirculating Fan Switch.
25 - Air Recirculating Fan Terminal Protection Switch
26 - Cabin Air Switch.
27 - Ammonia Quantity Gauge

28 - Bleed Air Switch.
29 - Standby Gyro Fast Erect Button
30 - Attitude Director Indicator Selector Switch.
31 - Cabin Pressure Altimeter
32 - Flight Director Mode Selector Switch.
33 - Command Control Switch.
34 - Flight Director System Altitude Hold Switch.
35 - Clock
36 - Marker beacon Indicator Light.
37 - Horizontal Situation Indicator.
38 - Standby Airspeed Indicator.
39 - AC Voltmeter.
40 - Analogue Tape Remaining Indicator.
41 - AC Voltmeter Phase Selecting Switch.
42 - Instrumentation Package Cooling System
     Selector Switch.
43 - Camera Switch.
44 - AC Voltmeter Bus Selector Switch.
45 - Instrumentation Master Switch.
46 - Telemetering Switch.
47 - Digital Recorder Selector Switch.
48 - Recording System Selector Switch.
49 - Digital Tape Remaining Indicator.
50 - Digital Recorder Indicator Light.
51 - Recording Restart Button
52 - Analogue Recorder Indicator Light.
53 - Interval Record Switch.
54 - Instrumentation Caution and Indicator Lights.

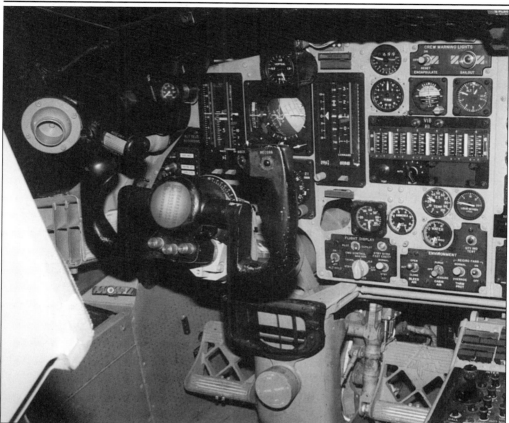

The diagram from the Flight Manual and corresponding picture of the pilot's instrument panel. *(Author)*

6. *Tires and brakes - have ground crew check. Ground crew will check brake temperatures and visually check tires for cuts, abrasions and proper inflation.*

7. *Flight Controls - check for freedom of movement.*

8. *Canard Flaps - Have ground crew check position.*

9. *Take-off Trim Button - Press and hold until light comes on, then release.*

10. *Hydraulics pressures, fluid levels and pump status indicators - Check.*

11. *Take off data - review.*

12. *Engine Overspeed Arming Lever - OUT.*

   Note - When take-off conditions (ambient air temperature above 50° F require engine overspeed (104% RPM) operation to provide extra thrust, the overspeed arming lever should be pulled back into its armed (ARM) position before the throttles are advanced from IDLE. The overspeed armed caution light comes on push either master caution light to extinguish both master caution lights and to reset master caution light circuit.

13. *Anti-collision light switch ON.*

   Caution - Operation of the anti-collision lights on the ground should be limited as much as possible, as the bulbs may be damaged by overheating.

   Note - Operation of the anti-collision lights on the ground shall be held

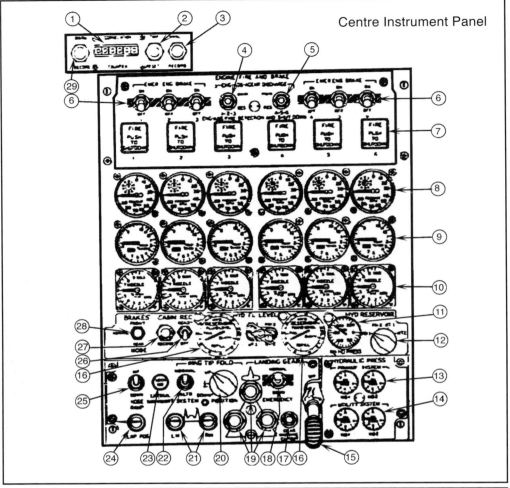

Centre Instrument Panel

1 -	Correlation Counter	14 - Pair of Utility Hydraulic System Pressure
2 -	Correlation time and Counter Reset Button	Gauges.
3 -	Analogue Recorder Indicator Light	15 - Landing Gear Handle
4 -	Fire Extinguisher Agent Discharge Switch	16 - Hydraulic Reservoir Fluid Level Gauge.
	(No 1, 2 and 3 engines)	17 - Landing Gear Audible Warning System
5 -	Fire Extinguisher Agent Discharge Switch	Cutout Button.
	(No 4, 5 and 6 engines)	18 - Landing Gear Emergency Lowering Switch.
6 -	Engine Emergency brake Switches.	19 - Landing Gear Position Lights.
7 -	Fire Warning Lights/Engine Shutdown	20 - Wing Tip Position Selector Switch.
	Buttons (line of six)	21 - Wing Tip Position Indicators.
8 -	Tachometers (line of six)	22 - Wing Tip Fold Mode Switch.
9 -	Exhaust Temperature Gauges (line of six)	23 - Lateral Bobweight Indicator (fitted to 62-001
10 -	Primary Exhaust Nozzle Position Indicators	only)
	(line of six).	24 - Flap Position Indicator.
11 -	Hydraulic Reservoir Gaseous Nitrogen Head	25 - Nose Ramp Switch.
	Pressure Gauge.	26 - Cabin Recorder Switch.
12 -	Hydraulic Reservoir Head Pressure Selector	27 - Cabin Recorder Indicator Light.
	Switch.	28 - Wheel Brake Mode Switch.
13 -	Pair of Primary Hydraulic System Pressure	29 - Digital Recorder Indicator Light.
	Gauges.	

The diagram from the Flight Manual and corresponding picture of centre instrument panel. Note there are some differences between the flight manual - which is dated 25 June 1965 - and the interior photograph, which was taken after the last flight of 62-0001. *(Author)*

to a minium because ground emergency vehicles have similar lights. The operation of the anti-collision lights could confuse and hamper ground rescue operations.

14. Ammonia and water quantity gages - check that sufficient amounts of ammonia and water are available for completion of the mission. Caution - If ammonia is below 275 pounds, or water is below 4000 pounds, abort the flight until ammonia or water tank is refilled.

15. Co-pilot - On aircraft 62-001 - Bypass area and Throat Mach - check both bypass areas closed and both throat indicators at 1.67

16. On aircraft 62-0207. Co-pilot - AICS mode switches check both STBY.

17. Co-pilot - Fuel quantity - Tanks 8L and 8R - check quantity at 13,500 pounds or less on 62-001. Tank 5 - check quantity at 26,000 pounds or less on 62-0207. If fuel quantity in specified tank is above the recommended level, move corresponding fuel pump switch to OFF until fuel level is reduced.

18. Co-pilot - Fuel tank pump switches AUTO. Move No. 6 fuel pump switch to AUTO and check increase in tank No.3 quantity, then move all

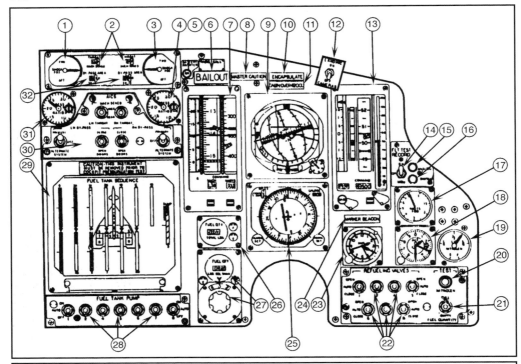

Co-pilot's Instrument Panel

1 -   Left Inlet Shock Wave Position Indicator
2 -   Left and Right Inlet Throat Mach Schedule
　　　Indicators.
3 -   Right Inlet Shock Wave Position Indicator
4 -   Right Inlet Pressure Ratio Gauge (62-001 only)
5 -   Battery Inverter Indicator Light.
6 -   Bale Out Warning Light
7 -   Airspeed mach Number Indicator.
8 -   Master Caution Light.
9 -   Attitude Director Indicator.
10 - Encapsulate Caution Light.
11 - Cabin over 42,000 feet Warning Light.
12 - Landing Camera Switch (shroud mounted).
13 - Altitude - Vertical Velocity Indicator.
14 - Instrumentation Record Switch.
15 - Analogue Record Indicator Light.
16 - Digital Record Indicator Light.

17 - Standby Airspeed Indicator.
18 - Standby Altimeter.
19 - Liquid Nitrogen Quantity Indicator.
20 - Liquid Nitrogen Quantity Indicator Test Button.
21 - Fuel Quantity Indicator Test Switch.
22 - Refuelling Valve Switches.
23 - Clock.
24 - Marker Beacon Indicator Light.
25 - Horizontal Situation Indicator.
26 - Total Fuel Quantity Indicator
27 - Selected Fuel Tank Quantity Indicator and
　　　Selector Knob.
28 - Fuel Transfer Pump Switches (line of seven)
29 - Fuel Tank Sequence Indicator.
30 - AICS Panel (typical).
31 - Left Inlet Pressure ratio Gauge.
32 - Left and Right Inlet Bypass Area Indicators.

　　　remaining fuel switches to AUTO.

19.　*Co-pilot - Tank No.3 check at high level. Make sure fuel is transferring*
　　　properly to No.3 sump tank. The sump tank tape will indicate full if
　　　proper transfer is taking place.

20.　*Ground Intercom - Have ground crew disconnect.*

21.　*Both pilot and co-pilot to remove Capsule flight status safety pins.*

22.　*Co-pilot. Pitot heater Switch ON.*

Once permission was granted from Air Traffic Control, the Valkyrie could enter
the active runway, line up and then hold while:

The diagram from the Flight Manual and corresponding picture of co-pilot's instrument panel. *(Author)*

1. *Nose wheel steering selector switch - TAKE-OFF LDG.*
   Note - nose wheel steering remains engaged when switch is moved from TAXI to TAKE-OFF LDG.
2. *Nose wheel steering engage switch - FAIL SAFE*
3. *Throttles - advance to 81%.*
   Caution - To prevent possible engine vibration, the following 'detented' throttle technique is recommended. When making throttle bursts from IDLE to MIL (or greater) accelerate to 80% or 90% RPM and hold this speed long enough to observe stable rpm. If vibration is within limits accelerate engine to throttle position as required. During all flight conditions where flight idle is greater than 80% rpm, throttle movements are unrestricted.
4. *Co-pilot - Refrigeration switch ON. Electronic Air Equipment Temperature Gauge - Check decreasing. Water-Ammonia caution light out.*
5. *Throttles (if required) - MIL. If Military Thrust check has not been made before line-up, advance all throttles to MIL and allow engines to stabilize for 30 seconds. Make sure all conditions are correct and within limits and check exhaust nozzle position indicators are at about 40%.*
6. *Throttles 85% rpm*
7. *Throttles 70 degrees. Advance throttles 3 and 4 rapidly to MIN A/B and, after afterburner light-off, continue to advance throttles to 70 degrees. Repeat procedure from engines 2 and 3, and then for engines 1 and 6.*

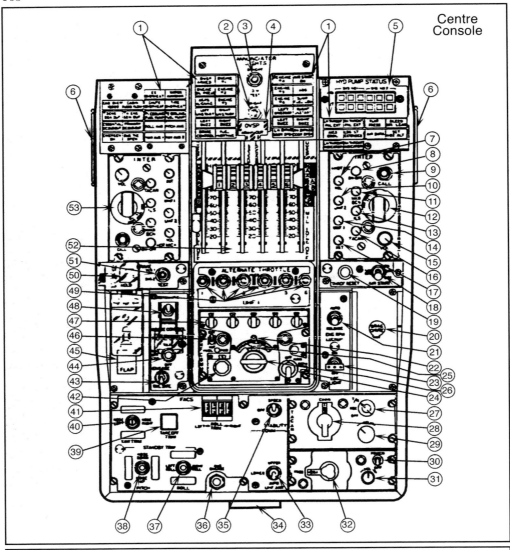

Centre Console

1 - Annunciator Lights.
2 - Annunciator Light Intensity Switch.
3 - Annunciator Light Test Switch.
4 - Engine Overspeed Arming Lever.
5 - Hydraulic Pump Status Lights.
6 - UHF Frequency Card Holder.
7 - 'Hot' Microphone Volume Knob.
8 - 'Hot' Microphone On/Off Switch
9 - Intercom Call Button.
10 - UHF No.2 Mixer Switch.
11 - Marker Beacon Mixer Switch.
12 - Function Selector Switch.
13 - ILS Marker Switch.
14 - UHF No. 1 Mixer Switch.
15 - Master Volume Knob.
16 - TACAN Mixer Switch.
17 - Intercom Mixer Switch.
18 - Air Start Switch.
19 - Throttle Reset Button.
20 - Drag Chute Handle.
21 - Engine RPM Lockup Switch.
22 - UHF Manual - Preset - Guard Sliding Selector.
23 - Landing Light Switch
24 - UHF Function Switch.
25 - UHF Channel Indicator
26 - UHF Channel Selector Knob.
27 - TACAN Function Switch.
28 - TACAN Channel Selector Switch

The diagram from the
Flight Manual and
corresponding picture of
the Centre Console.
(Author)

29 -	TACAN Volume Knob.	45 -	Flap Handle.
30 -	ILS Power Switch.	46 -	UHF Modulation Selector Switch.
31 -	ILS Volume Knob.	47 -	VHF Manual Frequency Selector Knobs (line of five)
32 -	ILS Frequency Selector Knob	48 -	Wheel Brake Control Switch.
33 -	UHF Antenna Selector Switch.	49 -	Alternate Throttle Switches (line of six)
34 -	Console Release Handle.	50 -	Wheel brake Hold Switch.
35 -	Flight Augmentation Control System Speed Stability Switch.	51 -	Wheel Brake Test Switch.
36 -	Flight Augmentation Control System En Button.	52 -	Throttles (line of six)
37 -	Standby Trim Roll Switch.	53 -	Intercom panel (same as items 7 to 18).
38 -	Standby Trim Pitch Switch.		
39 -	Take-off Trim Button/Light.		
40 -	Yaw Trim Switch.		
41 -	Primary Roll Trim Knob.		
42 -	UHF Volume Knob.		
43 -	Nose Wheel Steering Engage Switch.		
44 -	Nose Wheel Steering Selector Switch		

NOTE
The centre console is constructed in two parts to aid
entry and exit into both the pilot's and co-pilots
capsules. The U-shaped outer portion can be raised
by releasing the console release handle in the lower
centre.

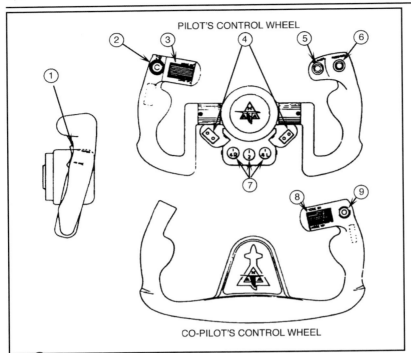

PILOT'S CONTROL WHEEL

CO-PILOT'S CONTROL WHEEL

1 - Intercom Microphone Swith (on outboard grip of each control wheel).	Use applicable stop selector pin to obtain desired wheel rotation. For a
2 - Flight Augmentation Control System Disengage Button.	3/4 turn stop, use opposite 1/4 selector pin. (To select stop, push pin
3 - Primary Pitch Trim Knob.	in and turn 90 degrees. To release,
4 - Wheel Rotation Stops (Instrumentation Installation)	turn pin right 90 degrees. Pin is sprung-loaded out).
5 - Event marker Button.	8 - Primary Pitch Trim Knob.
6 - Instrumentation Record Button.	9 - Flight Augmentation Control System
7 - Wheel Rotation Stop Selector Pins.	Disengage Button (Roll and Pitch only)

Caution - to preclude stalling the other engines if one engine stalls, engage only one afterburner at a time per inlet.

Because the operation in the minimum afterburner range may cause unstable combustion, which could result in compressor stalls and/or engine flame out, avoid afterburner operation with the throttle between 61- and 70 degree settings.

8.   *Engines Instruments - check.*

9.   *Wheel brakes - release. Use nose wheel steering for directional control at speeds up to nose wheel lift off (approximately 10 knots ISA below take-off speed). It is not recommended that directional control be maintained by use of wheel brakes because braking action greatly increases take-off roll.*

10.   *Throttles MAX A/B or OVSP. Advance all throttles simultaneously to MAX A/B or, if above 50°F and overspeed is required, through the MAX A/B setting to OVSP. Monitor engine instruments.*

Caution - Selected overspeed operation should not be used for take-off below 50°F. Exceeding overspeed limitations may damage engine turbine section.

Note - to go into overspeed after throttles have been moved to MAX A/B, the throttles must be retarded slightly to release the overspeed solenoids. The overspeed arming lever is placed in ARMED and then the throttles moved to the overspeed position.

The pointers of the exhaust nozzle position indicators should be within the green arc for maximum afterburner or in yellow arc for overspeed operation.

11.   Acceleration speed - check. The acceleration should be checked and a decision to either continue take-off or to abort. At about 20 knots ISA below take-off speed for the gross weight, begin to rotate the airplane at such a rate that it will assume the pitch angle required for lift-off at the recommended take-off speed. Maintain take off attitude after breaking ground until sufficient airspeed and altitude are attained to prevent settling back on the runway.

Warning - The airplane should not be rotated to take-off attitude before the nose wheel lift off speed has been attained. A high angle of attack prior to take-off speed will reduce acceleration and increase take-off distance.

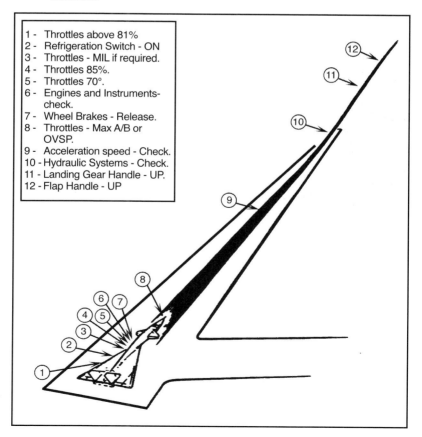

1 - Throttles above 81%
2 - Refrigeration Switch - ON
3 - Throttles - MIL if required.
4 - Throttles 85%.
5 - Throttles 70°.
6 - Engines and Instruments-check.
7 - Wheel Brakes - Release.
8 - Throttles - Max A/B or OVSP.
9 - Acceleration speed - Check.
10 - Hydraulic Systems - Check.
11 - Landing Gear Handle - UP.
12 - Flap Handle - UP

From the Flight Manual comes this typical initial take-off and climb away procedure.

Standardising flight reporting

In April 1972 North American Rockwell produced the 'B-70 Aircraft Study Final Report'. Within it were a number of pilot's flight reports - some in summary, others specific. This was a complete section that described the aircraft, its handling and operation is detail. It was compiled by Al White, who made use of the Cooper-Harper rating scale in applying subjective valuation to the aircraft. This was and is a set of criteria used by test pilots and flight test engineers to evaluate the handling qualities of aircraft during flight test. The scale ranges from 1 to 10, with 1 indicating the best handling characteristics and 10 the worst. The criteria are evaluative and thus the scale is considered subjective.

The Cooper-Harper scale came about after World War Two, when the various U.S. military branches sent different models of their operational aircraft to the Ames Aeronautical Laboratory located at Moffett Federal Airfield in Mountain View, California for evaluation of the planes' flight performance and handling qualities. The laboratory was operated by NACA, the predecessor of NASA. Most of the flights were conducted by George Cooper, Bob Innis, and Fred Drinkwater and took place at the remote test site at the Crows Landing Naval Auxiliary Landing Field in the central valley area east of Moffett Field.

What may be the most important contribution of the flying qualities evaluation programs and experiments conducted on the variable stability aircraft at Ames was George Cooper's standardized system for rating an aircraft's flying qualities.

The Cooper-Harper Ratings Scale used by test pilots to evaluate aircraft under test.

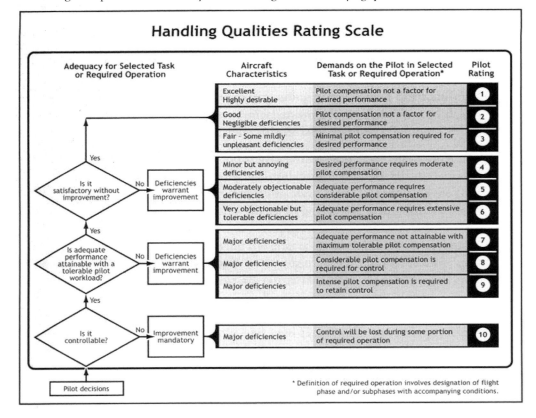

Cooper developed his rating system over several years as a result of the need to quantify the pilot's judgment of an aircraft's handling in a fashion that could be used in the stability and control design process. This came about because of his perception of the value that such a system would have, and because of the encouragement of his colleagues in the United States and England who were familiar with his initial attempts.

Cooper's approach forced a specific definition of the pilot's task and of its performance standards. Furthermore, it accounted for the demands the aircraft placed on the pilot in accomplishing a given task to some specified degree of precision. The Cooper Pilot Opinion Rating Scale was initially published in 1957. After several years of experience gained in its application to many flight and flight simulator experiments, and through its use by the military services and aircraft industry, the scale was modified in collaboration with Robert (Bob) Harper of the Cornell Aeronautical Laboratory and became the Cooper-Harper Handling Qualities Rating Scale in 1969, a scale which remains the standard for measuring flying qualities.

The flight test summary both pulled no punches and at the same time sang the designs praise, when they stated '*The XB-70 has proven itself to be a very remarkable*

Air Vehicle One climbs away from the main runway at Edwards AFB. (USAF)

airplane. It has accomplished every milestone that was set down for it. No aerodynamic changes were required in order to achieve the objectives; but in spite of Its tremendous performance, the XB-70 is an unfinished airplane. It was operated in a completely new speed and altitude range, but with off-the-shelf navigation equipment and flight instrumentation that were obsolete for this type of flight operation. This pilot believes that with normal development, including some aerodynamic refinement, some system changes, and better instruments and navigational equipment, this would be a truly outstanding airplane.

In reading this pilot's summary report, consideration should be given to the fact that the combination of this airplane's size, weight, and speed ranges compares to no other airplane in existence; and that the program was primarily a research program with ground rules that allowed only those changes which were necessary to safely accomplish the test objectives. In the normal sequence of development to an operational airplane, many of the opinions and recommendations expressed herein would have been made after the initial airworthiness flights. They are presented now, for the record, and for consideration if improvements can be made for follow-on programs.

In general terms, the XB-70A was an interesting airplane to fly. It had some peculiarities due to size, weight, and configuration that were different from most other airplanes. The movable wing tips introduced some new characteristics in the airplane that had not been experienced before, such as the wide variation in directional stability, roll power, and dihedral effect.

The airplane had a tremendous performance capability and was a thrill to fly from that standpoint, but this capability combined with the fact that the airplane was climbed and cruised very near the boundary of the allowable flight envelope quicker and easier than any other airplane this pilot has flown. The duct pressure limits and the low allowable 'g' aggravated the recovery. All this adds to the pressure on the pilot by requiring greater concentration on his part. This was acceptable in a research program of this

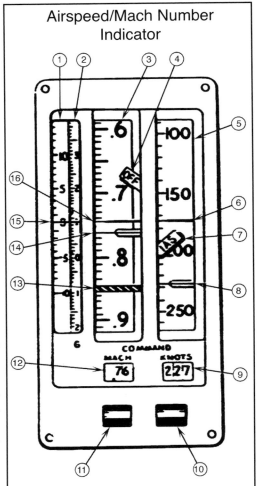

Airspeed/Mach Number Indicator

1 - Angle of Attack Scale.
2 - Acceleration ('G') Scale.
3 - Mach Scale.
4 - Power Off Warning Flag (Mach).
5 - Airspeed Scale.
6 - Fixed Index Line (Airspeed).
7 - Airspeed Warning Flag (Power Off).
8 - Command Airspeed Marker.
9 - Command Airspeed Readout Window.
10 - Command Airspeed Slewing Switch.
11 - Command Mach Slewing Switch.
12 - Command Mach Readout Window.
13 - Maximum Allowable Mach Marker.
14 - Command Mach Marker.
15 - Fixed Index Line (Angle of Attack and Acceleration).
16 - Fixed Index Line (Mach).

Altitude - Vertical Velocity Indicator

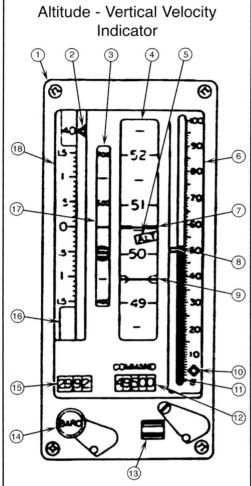

1 - Vertical Velocity Moving Scale (Climb).
2 - Vertical Velocity Index.
3 - Vernier Altitude Scale.
4 - Altitude Scale (sensitive Altitude).
5 - Altitude Warning Flag (Power Off).
6 - Gross Altitude Scale.
7 - Fixed Index Line (Sensitive Altitude).
8 - Command Altitude Marker (Gross Altitude).
9 - Command Altitude Marker (Sensitive Altitude).
10 - Target Altitude Marker.
11 - Gross Altitude Index (Movable).
12 - Command Altitude Readout Window.
13 - Command Altitude Slewing Switch.
14 - Barometric Pressure Set Knob.
15 - Barometric Pressure Readout Window.
16 - Vernier Velocity Moving Scale (Dive).
17 - Vernier Altitude Fixed Index Line.
18 - Vernier Velocity Fixed Scale.

nature, but would certainly not be acceptable in an operational vehicle.

The potential for a great airplane is here, but some refinements are required. More specifically, the pilot's opinions and recommendations are as follows:

Ground Handling Qualities:
Taxiing the airplane was not a difficult operation. Turns from one narrow taxiway to another narrow taxiway was made with acceptable accuracy. However, parking the airplane in a precise location was difficult because of the restricted visibility, configuration of the airplane, and lack of repeatability of the nose wheel steering system, i.e., the nose wheel steering rate varied with the load on the nose gear so that full rudder pedal application did not consistently give the same turning rate. Ground observers were required for parking, but their inputs were sometimes valueless due to the steering system's inability to follow their directions. Cooper Rating of 3.5.

Originally the braking system was unsatisfactory at very low speeds, but with development, the system became marginally satisfactory. The airplane could be stopped without brake chatter as long as the pilot anticipated far enough in advance to be able to apply very light braking to make the stop. If an abrupt stop was required at low speeds, heavy brake chatter occurred. Cooper Rating 4.5.

Checklist - in the cruise
Once the crew had cleared the runway there was no time to relax, for there was a flurry of activity.

1. *Hydraulic Systems - Check pressures, fluid levels and pump status indicators.*

2. *Landing Gear Handle - UP, below 300 knots ISA. Check gear position lights. Note. When landing gear is retracted, the rudder travel is reduced automatically. The +/- 12 degrees available when the gear is down is reduced to +/- 3 degrees when the gear is up.*
   Caution - Landing gear and doors should be completely up and locked before gear down limit speed is reached, otherwise excessive air loads may damage the doors and gear operating mechanism and

Pilot's Side Console

1 - Ground Escape Hatch Jettison Handle.
2 - Roll Augmentation Power Switch.
3 - Yaw Augmentation Power Switches.
4 - Standby Pitch Trim Arming Switch.
5 - Visor Heater Reostat.
6 - Oxygen Toggle Valve.
7 - Lateral Bobweight Switch.
8 - UHF Manual Frequency Selecting Knobs
    (line of five).
9 - UHF Manual - Preset - Guard Sliding
    Selector.
10 - UHF Channel Selector.
11 - UHF Function Switch.
12 - Auxiliary Gyro Platform Lattitude
     Indicator.
13 - Auxiliary Gyro Platform Lattitude Setting
     Knob.
14 - Auxiliary Gyro Platform Magnetic Heading
     synchronisation Indicator.
15 - Auxiliary Gyro Platform Mode Switch.
16 - Secondary Exhaust Nozzle Standby
     Pressure Switch.
17 - Utility Light.
18 - Spare Lamps.
19 - Auxiliary Gyro Platform Slew Knob.
20 - Auxiliary Gyro Platform Alignment Switch.
21 - Auxiliary Gyro Platform Magnetic Variation
     Setting Knob.
22 - auxiliary Gyro Platform Magnetic Variation
     Indicator.
23 - UHF Channel Selector Knob.
24 - UHF Volume Knob.
25 - UHF Transmitter Power Output Knob.
26 - UHF Modulation Selector Switch.
27 - Pitch Augmentation Power Switch.

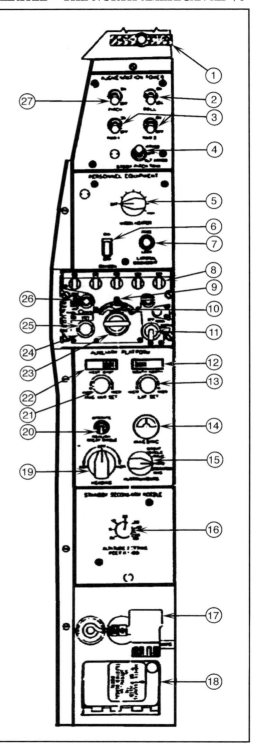

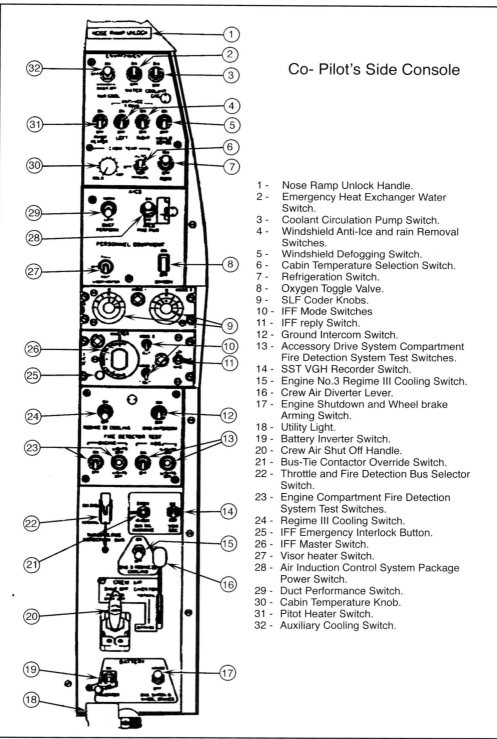

Co- Pilot's Side Console

1 - Nose Ramp Unlock Handle.
2 - Emergency Heat Exchanger Water Switch.
3 - Coolant Circulation Pump Switch.
4 - Windshield Anti-Ice and rain Removal Switches.
5 - Windshield Defogging Switch.
6 - Cabin Temperature Selection Switch.
7 - Refrigeration Switch.
8 - Oxygen Toggle Valve.
9 - SLF Coder Knobs.
10 - IFF Mode Switches
11 - IFF reply Switch.
12 - Ground Intercom Switch.
13 - Accessory Drive System Compartment Fire Detection System Test Switches.
14 - SST VGH Recorder Switch.
15 - Engine No.3 Regime III Cooling Switch.
16 - Crew Air Diverter Lever.
17 - Engine Shutdown and Wheel brake Arming Switch.
18 - Utility Light.
19 - Battery Inverter Switch.
20 - Crew Air Shut Off Handle.
21 - Bus-Tie Contactor Override Switch.
22 - Throttle and Fire Detection Bus Selector Switch.
23 - Engine Compartment Fire Detection System Test Switches.
24 - Regime III Cooling Switch.
25 - IFF Emergency Interlock Button.
26 - IFF Master Switch.
27 - Visor heater Switch.
28 - Air Induction Control System Package Power Switch.
29 - Duct Performance Switch.
30 - Cabin Temperature Knob.
31 - Pitot Heater Switch.
32 - Auxiliary Cooling Switch.

prevent subsequent operation. If the landing gear handle has been moved to UP while the weight of the airplane was still on the gear, the handle must be placed in the DOWN position and then returned to UP (with the weight off the gear) before the gear can retract.

3. *Flap Handle - UP below 270 knots ISA. Move Flap Handle to FLAP UP before reaching the flap down limit airspeed. There will be a nose-down trim change as the flaps are raised. Check flap position indicator and flap pressure caution lights are out.*

4. *Electrical and hydraulics - check voltages, hydraulic pressures, fluid levels and pump status indicators.*

5. *Cabin altitude and oxygen - check at 8,000 feet when airplane is above 8,000 feet.*

6. *Co-pilot - auxiliary cooling switch OFF if electronic equipment air temperature is in green arc.*

7. *Ammonia, water oxygen and nitrogen quantities - check.*

8. *Co-pilot - Fuel system - check, fuel sequencing - check, fuel tank pump switches check empty tanks OFF.*

9. *Wing tips 1/2 at Mach 0.95 or 400 knots ISA whichever is lower. Wing tip fold mode switch check NORMAL. NOTE - do not use ALTR to lower the wing tips. Note a slight nose-up trim change occurs when the tips are lowered.*

For every change of speed there was a series of check list items in the Flight Manual that involved both the pilot and co-pilot, much of which related to the engine inlets. Colonel White continues his report on his experiences in handling the XB-70A:

In-Flight Handling Qualities:

Low Speed: The pitch control in low speed flight regime was very good. Some lack in airplane response could be detected during abrupt pitch manoeuvres; however, the response was satisfactory in all of the normal manoeuvres used in flying the airplane. The long period of the short-period oscillation was different from most other airplanes, but did not cause difficulty in controlling the airplane. The damping in pitch was good in the subsonic flight regime. Cooper Rating of 2.5.

The main difficulty in flying the XB-70 was caused by a combination of characteristics in the lateral-directional sense. These characteristics were: First, that the period of the short-period oscillation was very long as compared to most

Air Vehicle Two with F-104 escort seen from behind. *(USAF)*

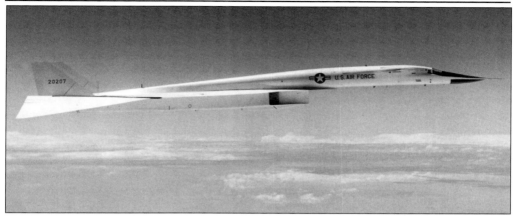

Air Vehicle Two with
the wingtips in the
half-down position.
(USAF)

other airplanes, secondly, the side force per degree of sideslip was low in this airplane. This combination made it difficult for the pilot to sense inadvertent sideslips. In addition to those characteristics, the airplane had a marked positive dihedral effect (particularly #2 A/V) and it had excessive adverse yaw due to ailerons.

Considering these four characteristics together, if an inadvertent side-slip occurred without the pilot's knowledge (who was busy with other system operations), the airplane rolled due to the dihedral effect. Instinctive reaction of the pilot was to counteract the roll with aileron; however, the aileron input increased the sideslip because of the high adverse yaw due to aileron. This increased sideslip caused more roll away from the aileron input and aggravated the situation. The solution was that the pilot had to fly the sideslip or yaw indicator religiously throughout the flight regime. This general characteristic of the XB-70 was most predominant with the wing tips up. Cooper Rating of 4.5.

Placing the wingtips in the one-half position reduced the tendency for the

6 January 1966 and Air
Vehicle One flies in
formation with NB-
52B '008'.

The NB-52B was B-
52B number 52-0008
converted to an X-15
launch platform. It
subsequently flew as
the 'Balls 8' in support
of NASA research until
17 December 2004,
making it the oldest
flying B-52B.
(NASA/USAF)

Air Vehicle One - wing tips fully down. *(USAF)*

situation explained in the previous paragraph, because lowering the wing-tips reduced the roll power by approximately 50%, therefore reducing yaw due to aileron. In addition, the tips down configuration reduced the positive dihedral effect. Cooper Rating of 4.0.

Visibility with the windshield in the up position was unsatisfactory. The pilot cannot see the horizon ahead and must make the flight almost entirely with reference to the pitch attitude indicating system. The poor quality of the heading information, precise heading, climb schedule made altitude flying extremely difficult. In addition, images of light-colored ground such as snow and sandy desert areas reflected badly in the windshield during turns, at times causing vertigo. Cooper Rating of 5.0.

Unstarts:
The inadvertent inlet unstarts encountered in the flight test program, varied in intensity from mild to severe. They were breath-taking to say the least. In the case of a severe unstart, it jarred the airplane rather violently and was followed by heavy buffeting, intense aerodynamic noise, and minor trim changes. At Mach 3, the primary trim change was in roll, but usually did not persist since the other inlet would normally unstart within a few seconds. If the inlet system did not effect an immediate restart, the inlet would go into buzz. The buzz cycle was immediately recognizable to the pilot since it was almost purely a lateral oscillation at about the natural frequency of the fuselage. If it was not corrected, it built up in intensity to a very disturbing, if not destructive, magnitude. In spite of the severity of the transients caused by inlet unstarts, airplane control was considered good.

Return to earth
Descent from altitude followed even more check-lists, before setting the aircraft up for the final phase of the descent and approach to the airfield.
1.   *Brake Control Switch - AUTOMATIC.*
2   *Nose wheel steering Selector Switch - TAKE-OFF LDG*

3. *Engine RPM lockup switch - check RELEASE.*
4. *Co-pilot - Fuel Tank sequence and quantity indicators check and check empty tank pump switches OFF.*
5. *Landing data - compute approach and landing distances before entering the traffic pattern.*

Flare Speed vs Weight

Gross Wt Lbs	CAS Knots	Gross Wt Lbs	CAS Knots
460,000	219	340,000	192
440,000	215	320,000	186
420,000	210	310,000	184
400,000	206	300,000	181
380,000	201	290,000	178
360,000	197	280,000	175

Landing Pattern Speeds

Downwind -	Flare Speed plus 50 knots
Base Leg -	Flare speed plus 30 knots
Final Approach -	Flare speed plus 10 knots

6. *Flight augmentation control system switch - OFF*
7. *Landing Gear handle - DOWN and check gear position lights. Extend gear below gear-down limit speed.*
8. *Flap Handle - FLAP DOWN and check flap position indicator. Lower flaps below flap-down limit speed.*
9. *Electrical and hydraulics - check voltages and hydraulic pressures, fluid levels and pump status indicators.*
10. *Ammonia Quantity Gauge - check.*
11. *Co-pilot - auxiliary cooling switch - check ON*
12. *Co-pilot - Refrigeration switch (if windshield anti-ice and rain removal switches are ON) - OFF.*

The great white bird about to touch down at Edwards AFB after another flight. The nose-high attitude is particularly noticeable. *(USAF)*

The Flight Test Summary provides an insight into what the aircraft was like to fly during the approach and landing phase:

The XB-70 was not a difficult airplane to land. Some care had to be used due to the distance between the pilot and the main gear and due to the crew station height above the main gear at touchdown. Because of these dimensions, it was easy to undershoot the runway. After some practice, all pilots were able to make satisfactory landings without external assistance from chase aircraft.

The wing of the XB-70 experienced a strong ground effect in the proximity of the runway which helped considerably in making relatively smooth landings. The secret to a good landing, like in most airplanes, was a good stabilized approach using a rather low rate of descent (2 to 3 degrees glide scope).

Crosswind landings in the XB-70 were not as difficult as was predicted. The relatively shallow bank angle per degree of sideslip made the wing-down technique rather easy to use with the XB-70.

Landing in turbulent air required additional pilot concentration, primarily due to previously mentioned relationship between inadvertent sideslip, dihedral effect, and yaw due to ailerons. The pilot was required to watch the yaw indicator very closely in making an approach so as not to get into this inadvertent sideslip condition close to the ground. Landing Cooper Rating was 3.5.

The Flight Manual provided all the information and procedures that were needed to make a successful landing.

1.   *Throttles - IDLE at touchdown. Retard all throttles simultaneously. Note! Air Induction System Coolant Caution Light will come on when the weight is on the main gear. However, this does not indicate a malfunction.*
2.   *Lower Nose Wheels.*
3   *Nose Wheel Steering Engage Switch - ENGAGE then FAIL SAFE.*
4.   *Co-pilot - Drag Chute Handle - DEPLOY below 220 knots ISA.*
5.   *Wheel Brakes - as required. Avoid excessive braking unless necessary, as high operating temperatures and excessive tire wear will result.*
6.   *Drag Chute Handle - STOWED JETTISON below 60/70 knots ISA.*
7.   *Co-pilot - Refrigeration Switch - OFF after landing roll.*
8.   *Nose Steering Selector Switch - TAXI.*
9.   *Nose Wheel Steering Engage switch - ENGAGE.*

A close-up of the nose
'ramp' in the raised
position. (USAF)

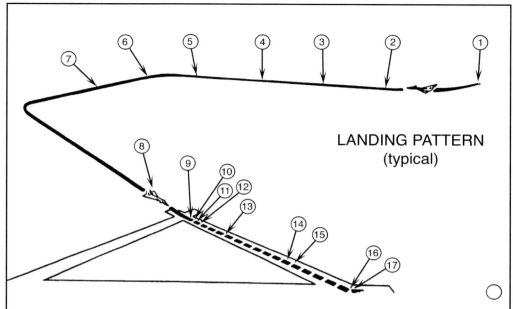

LANDING PATTERN (typical)

1 - Enter Pattern.
2 - Landing Gear Handle - DOWN.
3 - Flap Handle - FLAP DOWN.
4 - Electricals and hydraulics - CHECK.
5 - Ammonia Quantity Gauge - CHECK.
6 - auxiliary Cooling Switch - Check ON.
7 - Refrigeration Switch - OFF (if windshield anti-ice and rain removal switches are ON).
8 - Flare.
9 - Throttles - IDLE at touchdown.
10 - Lower Nose Wheels.
11 - Nose Wheel Steering Engage Switch - Engage then Fail Safe.
12 - Drag Chutes - DEPLOY.
13 - Wheel Brakes - as required.
14 - Drag Chutes - Jettison.
15 - Refrigeration Switch - OFF.
16 - Nose Wheel Steering Selector Switch - TAXI.
17 - Nose Wheel Steering Engage Switch - ENGAGE.

Caution

Control rate of descent with thrust to less than 1,000 feet per minute on final approach.

Do not exceed a 10-degree angle of attack at touchdown as the engine exhaust nozzles will strike the runway.

Normal Landing Technique.

Following entry into the traffic pattern, lower the landing gear and the flaps below landing gear and flap down-limit speeds. Fly the traffic pattern at the previously computed airspeeds, adjusting throttles to control rate of descent. After rolling out of the turn onto final approach, adjust throttles to maintain final approach speed for the specific landing gross weight to control rate of descent to touchdown at the desired speed. Retard the throttles to IDLE after touchdown. Normal landing touchdowns will be at about 10 degrees nose high.

Caution - higher touch down angles should be avoided, as the engine exhaust nozzles will strike the runway when the airplane is at an 11-degree attitude. Besides the angle- of -attack indicator, the windshield nose ramp can be used as a reference to indicate over -rotation. The windshield nose ramp angle is 11 degrees: therefore, when the ramp becomes horizontal during touchdown, the airplane is at 11 degrees angle-of-attack. Over-rotation will be indicated when the nose starts to blank out the horizon.

In compiling the Flight Summary, Colonel White critically describes the cockpit, the controls and the layout:

Capsule; The pressure seals in the capsule doors were torn loose many times when the pilots entered the capsules. Entering the capsule, particularly when wearing the pressure suit, was very difficult due to the lack of space. The seals should be guarded so that they are not damaged in this way.

The original installation of the capsule handgrip seat pins included a lanyard and a take up reel which were installed behind the pilots shoulder. A large percentage of the time the take-up reel did not operate; and when it did operate, the pin was extremely hard to reach to reinstall after flight. A temporary fix was made by cutting the lanyard, thereby eliminating the take-up reel. This worked satisfactorily, except for the minor inconvenience of not having a place to stow the pin.

The emergency parachute and riser cutter handles and the hinge split handle were difficult to see when encapsuled. When the pilot raised his head to see the handles with his helmet on, he had to raise his helmet with his hand in order to see past the bow of the helmet. This was particularly true when the pilot was wearing a pressure suit and was aggravated under the dynamic conditions encountered after ejection.

The pressurization and capsule oxygen gauges were particularly hard to see once in the capsule. The safety belt was almost impossible to adjust after it has been fastened. The seal deflate button was very difficult to actuate due to its location when the pilot was wearing a pressure suit.

The hot mike interphone capability during encapsulation was operable only after the capsule doors were closed. It appears wise, after the experience of the recent ejection, that the hot mike be actuated in another way in addition to the door closure. It should be connected to the handgrips so that when encapsulation is made, the hot mike interphone is available even if the doors are not closed.

With brake-chutes streaming, AV/1 rolls out of its landing at Edwards AFB. *(USAF)*

The manual impact attenuator inflation device was extremely difficult to get to while encapsulated. It was recommended that some thought be given to relocating this device between the pilot's knees for easier access.

The Secondary Nozzle Rheostat: This rheostat is in a poor location considering the number of times it was used during flight. It would be desirable to move it forward In the area near the oxygen and visor heater switches.

Hydraulic Pump Status Indicators; The hydraulic pump status indicators became almost useless in view of the number of times the pump status indicators showed yellow with the pumps operating properly.

Nose wheel Steering System: The nose wheel steering engage button ideally should be mounted on the control wheel. Originally this was not done because of lack of space on the wheel. The pilots believed that the augmentation disengage switch should have the priority location on the wheel. The experience gained in the flight test program indicates that it would be satisfactory to move the augmentation disengage switch to the same area as the augmentation engage button on the console and put the nose wheel steering engage switch on the control wheel.

TACAN; The TACAN instrumentation on the XB-70 was only marginally satisfactory. Early in the program the pilots were requested to list the minimum equipment with which they could accomplish the mission, and one TACAN was

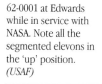

62-0001 at Edwards while in service with NASA. Note all the segmented elevons in the 'up' position. *(USAF)*

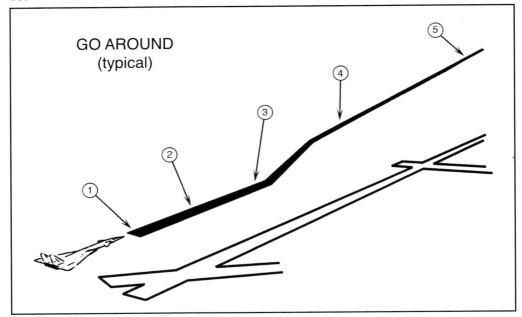

GO AROUND
(typical)

1 -Throttles - military thrust (Max A/B) if required.

2 - Landing Gear Handle UP (only after adequate flying speed has been attained.

3 - Flap Handle - as required.

4 - Climb to traffic altitude or missed approach altitude.

5 - Throttles - retard to obtain desired thrust reduction. Monitor engine instruments.

suggested for navigation. Experience has now shown that without radar tracking and the occasional assistance of the FAA centers, some of the missions would have been extremely difficult to complete satisfactorily due to the quality of this equipment and installation.

Attitude and Heading Information; The attitude and heading information was marginally satisfactory. This added to the pilot's difficulty in navigating the airplane. In view of the above two conditions, it was highly desirable to have a more reliable navigation system. An inertial platform was highly recommended.

AICS Controls: The AICS controls were satisfactory for the development stages, although the controls in A/V #1 were minimum satisfactory. It was highly recommended that this system be reviewed for future use.

Flaps; The flap system was marginally satisfactory. Because of a design problem, the flaps were to be raised for the taxi and lowered just prior to takeoff in order to ensure that they would retract in flight. Occasionally they would not extend for landing, and occasionally they would not retract after landing. The result was that the pilots lost confidence in the flap system. It was recommended that a design change be made to eliminate the necessity of the intricate procedure that was required to operate the flap system.

Map Case: The map case was almost inaccessible to the pilots. In most cases the pilot had to get out of his seat to get the equipment from the map case. Although the map case was of little use to the pilots, it was the only place in the cockpit that extra material could be stored. Check lists and pilot's data cards had to be strapped to the pilot's legs to be of any use. Some consideration should be given to a more convenient stowage space for let-down charts, handbook, and additional maps, particularly if this airplane is to be used for cross-country work in the future.

Wingtip Selector Switch: If the flaps are lowered for landing prior to raising the wingtips to the up position, it would be possible to lose control of the airplane. It was recommended that a safety device be installed to prevent lowering the flaps when the tips were not in the up position.

The airplane had moderate buffet at low speeds with the gear and flaps down. There was a minor change in the buffet level as the gear and flaps were raised. Some buffet persisted and a high aerodynamic noise level existed until the airplane accelerated to .87 Mach number or above, at which time the buffet completely disappeared and the noise was reduced to at least half of the low-speed level.

High Speed: Pitch control during the transonic acceleration and low supersonic speed ranges was very good. Above Mach 2 it became evident that there was some deterioration in the effectiveness of the pitch control. At speeds above 2.5 Mach, the force level required to manoeuvre the airplane was excessive due to

Ground escape from the B-70 for aircrew was by two routes, through the top hatches or out through the main door - in both cases use was made of the 'Sky Genie', a controllable descent device, later used in the NASA Space Shuttle.

Crews were warned that if the entrance door was used, they had to be sure that the pip pins on the escape ropes were firmly anchored in the sockets above the door opening to provide proper location of the descent devices.

If the ground escape hatch was used the crew had to make sure that the escape ropes were fully extended out of the hatch and over the leading edge of the canard to provide a proper location of the descent device.

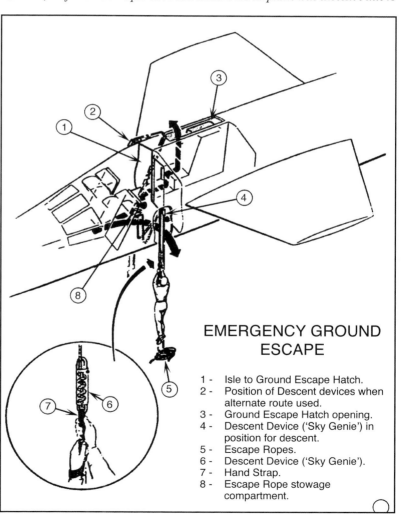

EMERGENCY GROUND ESCAPE

1 - Isle to Ground Escape Hatch.
2 - Position of Descent devices when alternate route used.
3 - Ground Escape Hatch opening.
4 - Descent Device ('Sky Genie') in position for descent.
5 - Escape Ropes.
6 - Descent Device ('Sky Genie').
7 - Hand Strap.
8 - Escape Rope stowage compartment.

From the Safety
Section of the XB-70A
Flight Manual comes
this drawing of how
the escape capsules
could be towed
behind a boat in the
event of a water-
landing.

this deterioration and due to the action of the 'g' bellows. Cooper Rating of 3.5.

The directional control was adequate to take care of three engines out on one side, but was much less effective in producing yaw than were the ailerons. Considering the capability of the rudders alone, they were considered adequate. Cooper Rating of 3.0. However, the powerful capability of the ailerons in producing yaw was considered the most objectionable characteristic in the airplane. Cooper Rating of 4.5.

The roll response of the airplane in the supersonic flight regime was good. The roll response did not seem to deteriorate at the same rate as pitch response, and therefore there was less compatibility in the response of the airplane between Mach 2 and 2.7 than in other areas. As the airplane approached Mach 3, the roll response deteriorated and the yaw due to aileron input was reduced; therefore the handling qualities of the airplane in roll were better at Mach 3 than at any other supersonic speed. Cooper Rating for the roll control system was 3.5.

Although there were minor differences in the flight characteristics between 1.4 and Mach 3 with all augmentation off, the general characteristics were the same. The short-period oscillations in pitch and yaw were four to six seconds in length and the damping in pitch and yaw was relatively poor. The airplane could be flown at all speeds with the augmentation off, except that extreme care had to used in the use of ailerons because of the strong tendency to excite lateral-directional oscillations with the ailerons. This was due to a high roll rate in the unaugmented case and because of the excessive level of yaw due to ailerons. When the pilots left the ailerons alone, the yawing oscillations would damp. Unaugmented supersonic flight: Cooper Rating of 5.0.

Visibility: The visibility with the windshield down was satisfactory. Although some forward visibility was lost after the rotation at takeoff and during the initial part of the climb out, the remainder of the subsonic flight was satisfactory. The visibility for landing was considered good. At no time was the pilot aware of any loss of the runway visibility during approach, flare, and touchdown: Cooper Rating of 3.0.

The longitudinal trim system was very good - Cooper Rating of 2.0. The lateral trim system was also very good, except that the primary lateral trim control was difficult to operate with a high degree of accuracy when the pilot was wearing heavy gloves. Cooper Rating of 3.0.

The directional trim system was very good after the gear had been retracted. It was too sensitive with the gear down, which caused the pilot to over-control when attempting to trim out directionally.

Occasionally some difficulty was encountered when engaging the nose wheel steering system due to the inability of finding the neutral directional trim position. For instance, the pilot would trim out directionally prior to putting the gear down; however, the trim system would not be exactly centered at this time. When the gear was lowered, this minor out-of-trim condition was amplified by a ratio of four to one. Due to turbulence and low speed flight characteristics, this out-of-trim condition would go undetected until after landing when the rudders were released and the nose wheel steering engaged which resulted in an abrupt transient in the steering system. It was recommended that consideration be given to reducing the directional trim rate and incorporating a rudder position indicator. Cooper Rating of 3.0.

The compatibility of the roll and pitch force gradients was satisfactory; however, due to the large differences in the moments of inertia, the airplane responded much quicker in roll than in pitch or yaw. This was not considered to be a discrepancy against the airplane, but a characteristic of a very long and narrow configuration. It required some getting used to by the pilots in order not to over-control in roll, particularly with the tips up. A change should not be made in the response characteristics, but something should be done to reduce the adverse yaw due to ailerons. This would eliminate the primary objectionable characteristics in the airplane. If the pilots were not concerned about generating yaw with aileron inputs, the fighter-like roll response would not be objectionable. Control force compatibility: Cooper Rating of 3.0.

The trim change while operating the landing gear was negligible. The trim change while operating the wing tips was small and occurred at such a slow

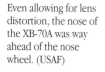

Even allowing for lens distortion, the nose of the XB-70A was way ahead of the nose wheel. (USAF)

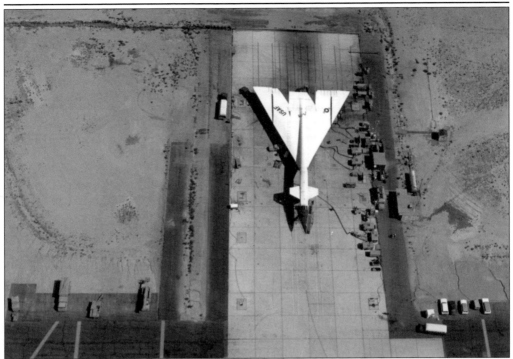

An unusual view of the XB-70 in its parking bay at Edwards AFB, surrounded by ancillary equipment. (USAF)

rate that it was hardly noticeable to the pilot since he took care of it in the normal trimming of the airplane. The trim change due to operation of the flaps was large, but easily manageable with the trim system. Although the trim system did take care of the trim change, when the flaps were lowered the control column moved very near the forward end of its travel leaving very little usable down elevon for manoeuvring, go-around, or flying in turbulent air. This could be extremely hazardous in the instance where the center of gravity was farther aft than normal.

It was recommended that a design change be made whereby more down elevon control would be available with flaps down.

To Mach 3 - and beyond!

Air Vehicle 1 only ever managed to struggle to just over Mach 3 once - and that was only for a precious two minutes.

The first true, sustained Mach 3 flight was flight 39 of AV/2 on 19 May 1966, when Al White as Aircraft Commander and Cotton as Second Pilot reached 3.06 Mach for thirty three minutes.

As usual, for certain stages of the flight the Valkyrie was escorted - Chase One was Capt Hoag and DeLong in T-38 '598'. Chase Two was Captain Livingstone aboard F-104 '817'. Flying support was Lt. Col Fulton and Prahl in B-58 '662'. Rescue was C-130 '132' flown by Sqn Ldr David Cretney (on exchange from the Royal Air Force) and Major Doryland. The flight was to last one hour fifty-nine minutes.

As the flight report stated, the purpose of the flight was Mach 3 for 30 minutes!

Preflight and Taxi

The preflight and engine start phases were completed by 08:14. It was necessary to make a soft start on the #1 engine. Although this was not written up as a discrepancy, soft starts have been necessary for the last three engine starts.

An oil leak was detected from the engine 4 pod vent. No. 4 engine was accelerated to 90 per cent rpm for a short time and on reducing power to idle, the leak had stopped. No further action was taken.

Data was taken for the power advances required during the taxi phase. No brake chatter was encountered at any time on this flight.

Takeoff, Climb and Cruise

Brakes were released for takeoff at 0900 and MAX afterburner was immediately selected. OVERSPEED was not used for this takeoff. The runway temperature was

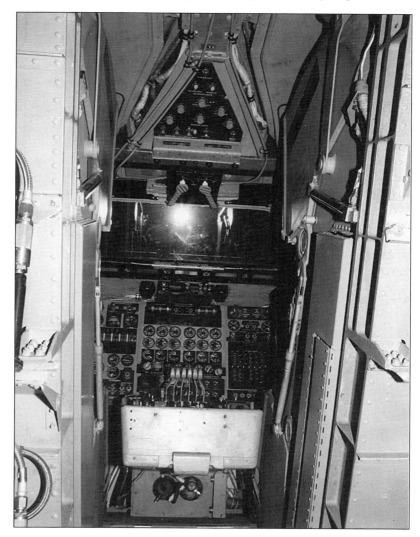

'Go inside the door and turn left...' This is the view that greets you from the tiny isle behind the crew compartment - the cockpit of Air Vehicle One as it was in 1991. The space between the two escape capsules is very tight. *(Author)*

reported to be 69° at brake release. The acceleration check was made using the sensitive airspeed indicator on the pilot's side. According to the handbook, the airplane should have accelerated from 70 to 148 knots in 20 seconds. It actually accelerated from 70 knots to 150 knots in 20 seconds. Rotation started at 195 knots, and the airplane flew off the ground at 210 knots on the pilot's tape airspeed indicator.

The gear and flaps were raised. The #2 utility augmentation channel disengaged during the gear cycle and was immediately re-engaged after the gear was up and locked. The tips were lowered to one-half at 300 knots during the climb. At 0.9 Mach the AICS was reset and switched to the AUTO node. The first turn was made at 32,000 ft. fifty miles east of the Edwards TACAN. The airplane did not accelerate during the turn; consequently, it did not go supersonic until the turn was completed. The windshield was raised for the acceleration and the airplane was accelerated at 32,000 ft. to 575 knots where the climb was continued. During the initial part of the climb, the speed was allowed to build up to 595 knots and then slowly bled off to 575 by 40,000 ft.

The inlets started between 2.13 and 2.16 Mach just prior to reaching 50,000 ft. in the climb. After accelerating to 2.6 Mach, light buffeting was observed in the airplane of the type encountered on previous flights when the bleed air holes were partially plugged. However, this buffeting all but disappeared by 2.7 Mach and was not noted again during the flight.

Both the pilot and copilot had trouble in the climb phase of this flight with the face plate fogging over. The pilot normally runs the heater rheostat at the mid position, but had it on full hot and was still getting some fogging. The copilot reduced the airflow through the eyeball outlets to a minimum, and then turned the cabin heat up one notch in an attempt to help this situation. Later in the flight when the temperature was up, neither pilot had trouble with the face plate fogging. Whatever the cause, it appears that the face plate heating units are not adequate to take care of the moisture expelled in the helmet.

The turn north of Lovelock, Nevada, was made at approximately 2.6 Mach,

The pilot's position, with PILOT XB70 and 20001 stenciled on the side of the capsule. It was remarkably difficult to see around inside due to the lack of lighting - I only really saw the interior when I viewed my photographs later!
(Author)

and up until that time the TACAN indications were very good. The DME function of the TACAN broke lock just before the turn, so the ground station advised the pilot of the turning point. After rolling out of the turn, the TACAN locked on Lake View TACAN station and appeared to be functioning satisfactorily, but the heading information drifted and fooled the pilot into thinking that he was left of course when actually the radar track showed him to be right of course. The TACAN worked very well for the remainder of the flight. Any errors in navigation were caused by the drifting and the sluggishness of the heading information.

The inlet system was switched to HIGH PERFORMANCE at 2.7 Mach. The turn northeast of Boise, Idaho, was made at 2.8 Mach using a 15- to 17-degree bank angle. The airplane did not accelerate in this turn.

During the run between a point north of DuBois to Rock Springs, the airplane was slowly accelerating, but the throat Mne were on the lower limit. At 2.9 Mach the deviation control was set to 000 for the right inlet. At 2.92 the setting was changed to 995. At 2.97 the left inlet deviation control was set to 000. Mach 3 indicated was achieved at 0959 at a point in a turn just southeast of Rock Springs, Wyoming.

The Second Pilot's side of the cockpit, showing the mixture of rotary and linear or 'strip' instrumentation. The centre of the control horns has an outline of the Valkyrie showing the location of the fuel tanks. *(Author)*

Total fuel remaining at that time was 81,000 pounds. The throat Mach numbers indicated 3.06 on the left and 3.02 on the right. Consequently, the right deviation was changed to 990. During the next two minutes, the Mach number built up to 3.025 and then bled off to 3.01 as the airplane climbed above 71,000 ft. Throat Mach numbers were 3.05 on the left and 3.04 on the right. The deviation settings were then changed to 995 on the left and 985 on the right and remained that way for the rest of the Mach 3 portion of the flight. The Mach number varied between 3.02 and 3.06 with several constant periods at 3.03. Altitude variations

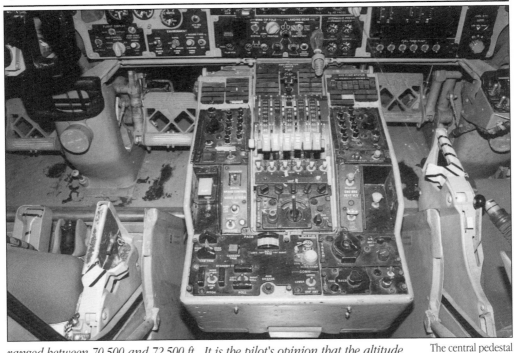

The central pedestal area of the cockpit, the outer area of which hinges up to allow better access to the seats. *(Author)*

ranged between 70,500 and 72,500 ft. It is the pilot's opinion that the altitude variations were caused by very minor errors in pitch attitude, rather than any abrupt pressure changes in the atmosphere, The altitude changes were not sudden; however, the rate-of-climb instrument showed some rather large excursions occasionally during the flight.

A right turn was started at Prescott, Arizona, and the airplane was held in a 15-degree bank. The flight path at the beginning of the turn was approximately ten miles west of the planned flight path, and the airplane overshot the planned flight path by approximately fifty miles on arriving in the Edwards area. No problem was encountered in maintaining speed in the turn, although altitude control required intense pilot concentration.

The throttle settings during the Mach 3 run varied between a 92-degree throttle angle and MAX afterburner. During the early part of the run, the average throttle setting was approximately ninety-eight degrees. During the final ten minutes, the average throttle netting was 95 degrees or less.

The pilot was aware of the minor trim changes caused by fuel burning out of tank 8 and tank 1. In other words, the pilot could sense the point where tank 8 stopped feeding and tank 1 began feeding due to the shift in the CG. This has a minor effect on the precise altitude control, since only minor pitch trim changes will cause rather large changes in the rate of climb.

A marker was placed on the data at C/N 5688 with a call-out for correlation with the ground stations at Edwards during the last five minutes of the run. After at least 32 minutes at Mach 3, the inlets were switched to normal and the deviation controls set at 005. Before the pilot could reduce the throttle to Military Power, the left inlet unstarted. It restarted immediately and the copilot reset the duct.

At approximately this time the right inlet unstarted and went into several cycles of buzz. The copilot selected LOW PERFORMANCE; but even though the airplane was buffeting moderately due to the inlet settings, the buzz lights went out and the side-to-side oscillation associated with buzz ceased. The VIBRATION HIGH light came on with no indication of high vibration on any of the twelve pickups.

Military Power was selected and the deceleration commenced. As the airplane decelerated through 2.6 Mach, the left-hand #1 buzz light came on with no airplane transient. This occurred several times during the descent to Mach 2.

At approximately 2.2 Mach number, in a right turn near Bishop, the windshield was lowered. Total fuel at this time was 26,500 pounds. At a speed just below Mach 2, the #6 engine EOT suddenly increased to 1000 degrees. The throttle was reduced to IDLE, eliminating the over-temperature condition. At .7 Mach number it was noted that the utility pump status lights were on for utility pumps 1, 3, 4 and 5. At approximately 1.2 Mach, the #1 engine nozzle position indicator became inoperative and began to spin counterclockwise. Just after going subsonic with engines #1, #3, #4, and #6 at IDLE, the #3 engine compressor vibration pickup was indicating 60 per cent. The throttle was increased to 80 per cent rpm, which reduced the vibration to 40 per cent. The #2 engine was then reduced to IDLE for the descent.

APPROACH AND LANDING

The normal descent was made to a straight-in final approach. While turning on final approach after having lowered the gear satisfactorily, the flaps were lowered. The flaps came down and then slowly started back up again with the flap switch in the DOWN position. Flaps were raised on the approach and a

Another view of the central area of the instrument panel, plus more details of the first pilot's side that includes details of the centre of his control horns. *(Author)*

Behind the crew cabin
of AV 1 is the
environmental control
system compartment.
(Author)

no-flap landing was made. Touchdown occurred at approximately 170 knots on the pilot's VSI. Two chutes inflated and braking was satisfactory. After turning off the runway, during the Military Power runs, it was noted that the #4 nozzle had failed open. The #4 engine EOT indicated only 500 degrees at Military Power throttle setting, and the nozzle position was 70 per cent.

SUMMARY
This flight should have removed all doubt about the XB-70's capability of accomplishing its objectives. Although some difficulty was encountered in accelerating at the northern end of the course, once Mach 3 was achieved it was no problem maintaining the speed, even in the turns.

It was apparent from this flight that the automatic inlet system has not been fully developed. Evidently more data at Mach 3 is required to optimize this system so that the co-pilot isn't required to manually adjust the automatic schedule so many times in order to satisfactorily complete a mission. Since this is one of the most important, if not the most important, new system in the airplane, it would be very beneficial to schedule sufficient flying at Mach 3 to overcome this deficiency; in fact, this is strongly recommended.

DISCREPANCIES
1. Yaw augmentation -#2 disengaged several times during flight.
2. Pilot and copilot face plate heat inadequate.
3. #6 engine went overtemp at Mil Power during descent.
4. #1 engine nozzle indicator spinning during last portion of flight.
5. Flaps went down and then slowly bled up on final approach.
6. #4 engine nozzle stuck open on Mil Power run after landing.
7. VIBRATION HIGH light on after unstart. Individual reroute were O.K.

BLACKBIRDS AND SUKHOIS

Over the years there has been much speculation that the XB-70 programme was secretly assassinated by Lockheed and Kelly Johnson with their A-12/YF-12 and RS-71 programme by putting pressure on the Oval Office.

Like many conspiracy theories, mysteries tend to conceal half-lies, half-truths. Throw into that mix a large dose of political intrigue, numerous 'black' projects and the Alice in Wonderland world of the Central Intelligence Agency, and even today, you have very murky waters indeed that prove hard to see through.

Here is as good a place as any to dispels one 'urban myth'. The SR-71 designator is actually a continuation of the pre-1962 bomber series, which ended with the B-70 Valkyrie. As we have already seen, the B-70 was proposed for the reconnaissance/strike role, with an RS-70 designation. The 'RS' prefix was allowed as an explicit 'special case' in the original 1962 issue of the designation regulations. When it was clear that Lockheed's A-12 aircraft (then used by the CIA) had much greater performance potential, it was decided to 'push' a USAF version of that one instead of the RS-70. This USAF version was to become the RS-71.

Conventional wisdom now says that President Lyndon B. Johnson messed up the designation in his public announcement and called it the SR-71 - and nobody wanted to correct the President. Because the strike mission had been cancelled anyway, 'SR' was quickly reinterpreted as 'Strategic Reconnaissance'. However, a first-hand witness of those events revealed in *Aviation Week & Space Technology,* that LBJ did not misread anything. In fact, USAF Chief of Staff LeMay simply didn't like the 'RS' designator - he already objected to it when the RS-70 was discussed for the inference was that the prime mission was 'Reconnaissance' not the 'Strategic' aspect - LeMay preferred the 'SR-70'. When the RS-71 was to be announced, he wanted to make sure it would be called SR-71 instead. He managed to have LBJ's speech script altered to show 'SR-71' in all places. Using archived copies of LBJ's speech, it can actually be verified that it reads SR-71 both in the script and on the tape recording. However, the official transcript of the speech, created from the stenographic records and handed to the press afterwards, shows 'RS-71' in three places. It seems that not the President but a stenographer did accidentally switch the letters, and thus create a famous aviation 'urban legend'.

In many ways it is hard to come up with a concrete 'link' between the A-12/YF-12/SR-71 family and the B-70. The Lockheed machines were not designed to perform the same functions as the North American design, despite strident attempts by some members of the Air Force and politicians to cast them both in the same mould.

There were major differences in their construction and operation, as well as their performance. The B-70 was designed as a strategic bomber. It was never intended to be stealthy. It was not designed for reconnaissance work - although the Air Force tried to sell the reconnaissance role to Congress at one point in an attempt to save the programme as the RS-70. The B-70 was never intended to be anything but a high-altitude, intercontinental strategic bomber with Mach 3 capability.

However, that said, there were a lot of similarities. Both programmes had difficulty building out of materials that could withstand the high temperatures associated with high-speed flight. At 80,000-feet altitude, the ambient air temperature was around minus 60°F, but at 2,000 miles per hour the skin temperature would approach 600°F. Each programme found a different solution to this problem.

Development of the XB-70 brought about the first extensive use of stainless steel honeycomb, but only after new autoclaves were designed to support the large sizes required. A new brazing technique had to be developed to make sure that the 'weld' would not be compromised by vibration or heat. Some of the constraints included wearing special gloves so that natural oils from the workers' fingers would not interfere with the integrity of the weld.

Kelly Johnson was well aware of the problems North American were having. He was quoted as saying, with a fine element of sarcasm *'...It was evident very shortly that the Skunk Works was not smart enough to make use of steel honeycomb with its very involved and precise tooling and difficulties in quality control'.*

Clarence Leonard 'Kelly' Johnson (27 February 1910 – 21 December 1990)

Nevertheless, Lockheed was having similar problems with the A-12 - codenamed 'Oxcart' - and its exotic titanium skin. Although it was as strong as stainless steel, titanium was a largely untried material, particularly in the quantities used in the A-12.

Both Lockheed and North American made use of heat sink technology to handle some of the airframe heat loads and in both cases the primary onboard heat sink was fuel. In the A-12, the airframe was largely uninsulated, and though it used heat-resistant titanium, some of the heat was absorbed by the fuel. Fuel also was actually used as a hydraulic fluid for the engine controls. The cockpit was pressurized, but not well insulated, so the pilot had to wear a pressure suit at all times for temperature protection as well as protection against sudden depressurisation.

The XB-70 was a much larger aircraft and carried an enormous fuel load, which made for a very suitable heat sink. In addition, the XB-70 was insulated, aided further by the honeycomb skin. The crew compartment could be kept at a relatively comfortable temperature, and the larger volume of pressurized space within the aircraft meant that any depressurization would be more gradual. The crew of the B-70 could, in theory at least, operate in a 'shirtsleeve' environment.

Weight and payload performance differed greatly between the Oxcarts and the Valkyrie. The B-70 was designed to carry a heavy, destructive payload from the onset that the Oxcarts could never match. The extra payload ability of the B-70 was also utilized for fuel. The B-70 had a longer unrefueled range than the Oxcarts, and the B-70 could take off with a full fuel load. The Oxcarts had to refuel shortly after takeoff to enable them to reach operational speed and altitude. Weight was always a problem for the Oxcarts, and they wrestled with it on a continuing basis.

Certainly there are many indications that Lockheed and NAA were aware of each other's projects and helped where they could. Johnson's log provides numerous instances. '*12 March 1962: It appears that our problem with Viron shows that the material planned for the B-70 is no good either. Sent information and a can of our sealant to Wright Field for use by Ascani to help the B-70*'. *5 December 1962: '... We are helping the B-70 all we can, because they are in real trouble on tank sealing and wiring and other things. I wrote General Ascani a letter promising our assistance, which we have given verbally many times in the past*'. *14 August 1964: 'Fred Rail of ASD and Ed Dawson of North American came here to discuss hydraulic problems on the B-70. I am amazed to find they built no hydraulic mock-up whatsoever and they are into troubles that we solved in 1961. I showed Dawson a letter I had written to General Ascani in 1961, pointing out these problems.*'

The Oxcart's fuel requirement called for low-vapour-pressure fuel with a low volume at operating temperatures; the fuel would also be a heat sink to cool various parts of the aircraft. The J58 engine required lubricants that did not break down at very high operating temperatures of Mach 3.2 speeds. Finding a suitable hydraulic pump was just as difficult. Kelly Johnson finally modified a pump that was being developed for the North American B-70.

There were also operational differences between the two aircraft. There was no quick turnaround system developed for the A-12. It took a minimum of three hours of preflight to get the A-12 into the air. It also required a special start cart with twin Buick auto racing engines to get the J-58 engines up to the 3,000 rpm needed to start.

The B-70 would be able to start up via one engine and an alert pod, which was similar to a stair cart but physically attached to the engine bay. For a combat operational B-70 on alert status, it was supposed to take no more than two minutes from startup to runway. From a cold start it would take only 20 minutes. The quick start feature was never tested in the two XB-70s because they were not intended to be combat operational aircraft, but the procedures were in place for the production model.

Aircraft operations aside, programme operations were different as well. The A-12 was highly classified and the B-70 was not. Publicity for the two programmes was a double-edged sword and they each handled it in their own way. Publicity was not a problem for the B-70 programme. The futuristic bomber was in the media's spotlight, and both the Air Force and North American basked in it, particularly early on in the programme. The B-70 received considerable attention in the

An A-12 'Oxcart' takes to the skies. *(Simon Peters Collection)*

national news, aviation magazines, and other publications. While some aspects of it were classified, it was certainly not a 'black' programme, so money was saved by not keeping it secret. On the other hand, lack of secrecy meant that the B-70 programme was fair game for budget-cutting politicians. Conversely, the Oxcarts had to live in deep secrecy. They lost out on the benefit of the media, but avoided budget cuts, as most politicians did not know they existed.

To see the way forward - we have to look back

In the early 1950s, with Cold War tensions on the rise, the US military required better strategic reconnaissance to help determine Soviet capabilities and intentions. The existing surveillance aircraft were primarily converted bombers, vulnerable to anti-aircraft artillery, missiles, and fighters. It was thought an aircraft that could fly at 70,000 feet would be beyond the reach of Soviet fighters, missiles, and even radar. This would allow 'overflights' - knowingly violating a country's airspace to take aerial photographs.

Under the code name 'Aquatone', the Air Force gave contracts to Bell Aircraft, Martin Aircraft, and Fairchild Engine and Airplane to develop proposals for the new reconnaissance aircraft. Officials at Lockheed Aircraft Corporation heard about the project and asked aeronautical engineer Clarence 'Kelly' Johnson to come up with a design. Johnson was a brilliant designer, responsible for the P-38 Lightning, and the P-80. He was also known for completing projects ahead of schedule, working in a separate division - Advanced Development Projects - jokingly called the Skunk Works after the striking black and white carpet in their entrance foyer.

Johnson's design, called the CL-282, married long glider-like wings to the fuselage of another of his designs, the F-104 Starfighter. To save weight, his initial design didn't even have conventional landing gear, taking off from a dolly and landing on skids. The design was rejected by the Air Force, but caught the attention of several civilians on the review panel, notably Edwin Land, the father of instant photography. Land proposed to CIA director Allen Dulles that his agency should fund and operate this aircraft. After a meeting with President Eisenhower, Lockheed received a $22.5 million contract for the first 20 aircraft.

A NACA registered bare-metal U-2 is prepared for flight.. *(Simon Peters Collection)*

A black painted, civilian registered U-2. *(Simon Peters Collection)*

It was renamed the U-2, with the 'U' referring to the deliberately vague designation 'utility'.

The first flight occurred at the Groom Lake test site (Area 51) on 1 August 1955, during what was only intended to be a high-speed taxi run. The sailplane-like wings were so efficient that the aircraft jumped into the air at 70 knots. Project director Richard M. Bissell assured President Dwight Eisenhower that the aircraft's high altitude of 70,000 feet would render it invisible to Soviet radars. However, the earliest flights, in July 1956, were tracked. On 5 July, an A-100 radar detected Carmine Vito as he flew over Smolensk, en route to Moscow. The operators even calculated his altitude as 65,000 feet , which was later rejected by experts who did not believe that an aircraft could fly that high.

Hartford, Connecticut-born Richard Mervin Bissell Jnr had worked closely with the Office of Strategic Services (OSS), which had helped to organize guerrilla fighting, sabotage and espionage during World War Two. In July, 1947 Bissell was recruited by Averell Harriman to run a committee to lobby for an economic recovery plan for Europe. The following year he was appointed as an administrator of the Marshall Plan in Germany and eventually became head of the Economic Cooperation Administration.

Richard Mervin Bissell, Jr. (18 September 1910 – 7 February 1994)

Bissell worked for the Ford Foundation for a while but Frank Wisner persuaded him to join the Central Intelligence Agency (CIA). In 1954 he was placed in charge of developing and operating the Lockheed U-2. Within two years Bissell was able to claim that 90% of all hard intelligence about the Soviet Union coming into the CIA was '...*funneled through the lens of the U-2's aerial cameras*'. This information convinced President Dwight D. Eisenhower that Nikita Khrushchev was lying about the number of bombers and missiles being built by the Soviet Union.

In mid-August, Bissell assembled a group of advisors to begin work on solving the tracking problem. Under the title 'Project Rainbow' the CIA funded a research project aimed at reducing the radar cross section of the U-2 to reduce the chance that it would be detected and tracked by Soviet radars during its overflights of the USSR.

With the eventual failure of 'Project Rainbow', Bissell initiated

'Project Gusto' - and so preliminary work began inside Lockheed in late 1957 to develop a follow-on aircraft to overfly the Soviet Union and be 'stealthy' enough to avoid radar detection. They were also intended to be fast enough to avoid interception if they were located. The designs were nicknamed 'Archangel', after the U-2 programme, which had been known internally as 'Angel'. As the aircraft designs evolved and configuration changes occurred, the internal Lockheed designation changed from Archangel-1 to Archangel-2, and so on. These nicknames for the evolving designs soon simply became known as 'A-1', 'A-2', etc. The A-12 was Lockheed's 12th design in this development of the U-2. Many internal documents and references to individual aircraft designs used Johnson's preferred designation, using the prefix, 'the Article' for the specific examples. Thus on the A-'s first flight, the subject aircraft was identified as 'Article 121'.

In 1958 Allen Dulles appointed Bissell as the CIA's Deputy Director for Plans (DDP), replacing Frank Wisner, who had suffered a mental breakdown. Richard Helms stayed on as Bissell's deputy. The Directorate for Plans reportedly controlled over half the CIA's budget and was responsible for what became known as the CIA's Black Operations - the murky world of ultra-secret operations and projects. Although not part of this story , it is worth noting that the DDP oversaw plans to overthrow Jacobo Arbenz Guzmán, Patrice Lumumba, Rafael Leónidas Trujillo, Abd al-Karim Qasim, Ngo Dinh Diem, and others. Bissell's main target was Fidel Castro, which eventually surfaced with the Bay of Pigs operation. In September 1960 Bissell and Dulles initiated talks with two leading figures of the Mafia, Johnny Roselli and Sam Giancana. Later, other crime bosses such as Carlos Marcello, Santo Trafficante and Meyer Lansky became involved in this first plot against Castro. The Mafia were known to be angry with Castro for closing down their profitable brothels and casinos in Cuba. If the assassins were killed or captured the media would accept that the Mafia were working on their own. The Mafia played along in order to get protection from the FBI.

Meanwhile, back at The Ranch, in 1959 the CIA selected the A-12 over a Convair proposal. Then, on 26 January 1960, the CIA ordered 12 A-12s. After selection by the CIA, further design and production of the A-12 took place under the code-name 'Oxcart'.

After development and production at the Skunk Works, in Burbank, California, the first A-12 was transferred to Groom Lake test facility, where on 26 April 1962, Lockheed test pilot Lou Schalk took the A-12 on its shakedown flight. The first official flight occurred on 30 April. On its first supersonic flight, in early May 1962, the A-12 reached speeds of Mach 1.1.

The first five A-12s, in 1962, were initially flown with Pratt & Whitney J75 engines capable of 17,000 lb thrust each, enabling them to obtain speeds of approximately Mach 2.0. On 5 October 1962, with the newly developed J58 engines, the A-12 flew with one J75 engine, and one J58 engine. By early 1963, the A-12 was flying with J58 engines, and during 1963 these J58-equipped A-12s obtained speeds of Mach 3.2.

Trying to find any hard details about what happened is not easy - in the world of 'black' projects trying to get hold of facts is like trying to grab a hold of mist. It seems that the CIA thought its star was very much in the ascendancy with the success of the U-2 and the up-coming A-12/YF-12/RS-71 project. Politically it

These two views of the missile bays in the YF-12.

The missile bay doors, along with almost all of the airframe was made from titanium alloy.

These pictures give some impression of what the bomb-bay area of the RB-12 - a competitor to the B-70 - could have looked like. *(Lockheed)*

seemed a good move to advance its own status by latching onto the success of the Skunk Works. In the CIA's eyes, the CIA could do no wrong, and working 'in the black' appeared to be a cost-effective way to go. There is a good possibility that Bissell saw the proposed RSB-70 as a possible high-cost public threat to their own A-12/YF-12/RS-71 'black' project.

One person 'who was there' as it were, was Benjamin R 'Ben' Rich, who was Kelly Johnson's right hand man, and later headed up the Skunk Works from 1975 until his retirement in 1991. His biography *'Skunk Works'* appeared in 1994, just before he died in 1995. Rich was present at most of the meetings, but somehow describes them in a slightly different manner to almost every other source.

Certainly it is true that the A-12 design was modified into the long-range interceptor AF-12 by the Skunk Works engineering team, incorporating a fire control system integrated with a Hughes radar. A second seat in the original sensor system bay was added to accommodate a fire control system operator.

Concurrent to the activity on the AF-12, a bomber version of the A-12, referred to as the RB-12, also was being studied. A forward fuselage full-scale mock-up had been completed and on July 5 1960 along with the AF-12 mock-up, was reviewed by Generals Curtis LeMay and Thomas Power. The two found the mock-ups of considerable interest and asked if either configuration could be modified to carry a terminal radar or an air-to-ground missile.

Kelly Johnson responded by stating, '*...we could do this within the aerodynamic configuration of the A-12 and, for the job that they outlined to do, which was to place a missile within 200 feet of a target, one could not argue about the use of a guided missile rather than our simpler approach in the RB-12 report'.* This was a reference to the use of conventional free-fall bombs.

Left is Benjamin Robert 'Ben' Rich (18 June 1925 – 5 January 1995) along with his mentor Kelly Johnson. They are both posed in front of a new build U-2, after Kelly Johnson's retirement. *(Lockheed)*

The RB-12 study had resulted from the then recent development of small, high-yield nuclear warheads. Johnson, in an RB-12 proposal, had noted in his log that the aircraft could result in a '*...very powerful striking force...with little or no weight or space penalty...*' to the aircraft. Four hypothetical 400 pound bombs based on the new warheads, or a single Polaris-sized warhead could be accommodated in a fuselage bomb bay while retaining the same fuel load as the reconnaissance A-12. One design study showed the RB-12 fitted with a rotary bomb bay. No aerodynamic changes were required and the radar attenuating features of the aircraft could be retained. The latter, coupled with the aircraft's performance, almost certainly would make chances of detection close to non-existent. It seems that the RB-12 was intended as a 'clean-up' vehicle to be used after an initial ICBM strike, targeting command posts, air bases, missile sites, submarine pens and SAM sites.

Johnson noted in his daily log that, '*While Hughes was giving a presentation on a simplified air-to-ground weapon system, LeMay took me by the arm and we went to another office. He told me that he wasn't very sure that the RB-12 would become a model, but he felt sure 'we would get some fighters'. I asked him, 'what about reconnaissance airplanes like the A-12?' and he seemed surprised that the Air Force were not getting any. He made a note on a yellow paper pad and asked me how soon we would have to know about A-12s to continue our production. I told him within two to three months'.*

Ben Rich described things slightly differently: '*...LeMay suddenly raised his hand as a signal for Kelly to stop talking. Then he stood up, grabbed Kelly by the arm, and led him to the far corner of Kelly's huge office for a private, whispered conference that lasted nearly ten minutes, while the rest of us sat transfixed, watching these two titans of military aviation cooking up some sort of scheme or scenario.*

Kelly told us later that LeMay was enthusiastic about using the Blackbird as an interceptor but resisted the idea of using it as a bomber. The B-70 was still very much on his mind. 'Johnson, I want a promise out of you that you won't lobby any more against the B-70'.. Kelly agreed — a promise he would deeply regret in the years ahead. 'We'll buy your interceptors. I don't have a number yet but I'll get back to you soon'.

Kelly asked, 'What about the reconnaissance aircraft we built for the agency? Can't the Air Force use any?' LeMay looked dismayed. 'You mean, we haven't ordered any?' He wrote a note to himself and promised Kelly he would forward an Air Force contract for the two-seater version of the spy plane within a few weeks.

The RB-12 programme would not reach the hardware stage. This was not as a result of lack of capability, but rather because it was a threat to the on-going North American XB-70A Valkyrie - a programme that was seen to have considerable political clout and one on which the Air Force had hung its hat for a Boeing B-52 replacement. Surprisingly, as noted on 26 October 1961, Johnson discovered the Department of Defense found the RB-12 more interesting than the AF-12. He noted, however, *'The Air Force, from LeMay down, do want the AF-12.'* As John F. Kennedy was sworn in as the 35th President at noon on January 20, 1961 this is some nine months into the Kennedy Presidency.

Over the years, reported 'gossip' seems to indicate that President Kennedy asked Richard Bissell, who was listed as 'Secretary to the President' if Kelly Johnson could convert the A-12 into an intercontinental bomber - Bissell is supposed to have replied that this was exactly what Johnson intended to do. Bissell's answer to the President was supposedly yes, and this prompted Kennedy to ask - *'...Then why do we need the XB-70 program?'*

Ben Rich sheds more light on it, from a different perspective: *'But then Dick Bissell got into the act. Bissell briefed President Kennedy on the CIA Blackbird project and told him the spy version of the airplane would be operational in less than a year. When he learned how fast and how high it would fly the new president was astonished. He asked Bissell, 'Could Kelly Johnson convert your spy plane into a long-range bomber?'*

Bissell replied that Kelly aimed to do precisely that. 'Then why are we going ahead with the B-70 program?' Kennedy asked. Bissell shrugged. 'Sir' he replied, 'thats a question more properly addressed to General LeMay'.

The President nodded sheepishly. But Kelly was embarrassed by Bissell's

A head on shot if 'Habu' the nickname applied to the Lockheed SR-71.

A habu (pronounced 'hah-BOO') is a venomous snake found on Okinawa in southeast Asia where the SR-71 was based.
(Simon Peters Collection)

indiscretion. As he noted in his private journal, 'Bissell recounted his conversation about a bomber version of the Blackbird with the President. It was not right. The President asked for our proposal for the bomber before the Air Force had even seen one and I felt obligated to rush to Washington and present it as quickly as possible to our Air Force friends and showed the proposal to Gen. Thomas White. Lt. Gen. Bernard Shriever was there and they were all very upset, as was Gen. LeMay, about losing B-70s to our airplane. But at least they fully understood that was not my doing and they cannot control Dick Bissell's approach to the President'.

So despite the differing viewpoints, both suggest that Bissell had been manoeuvring both sides for the overall benefit of himself or The Company in order to score political points. If that was the case, then it was not Kelly Johnson and the Skunk Works that proposed the demise of the B-70, it was Bissell. Kelly Johnson always maintained that the final cancellation of the B-70 programme was not his idea but that of Richard Bissell.

In some respects it looks as if Bissell was using the Lockheed Skunk Works to build up a secret reconnaissance, fighter and bomber air force just for CIA use. However, Bissell soon afterwards found himself out of power because of his part in the ill-fated Bay of Pigs invasion of Cuba that happened 15-30 April 1961, so his conversation with the President over cancelling the XB-70 program must have occurred before Bissell fell from grace. Not much later, Kelly Johnson, feeling pressure from Robert McNamara, began to harbour some cancellation concerns of his own. Johnson was afraid that with Bissell out of power, McNamara - who was nicknamed by some as 'Mac the Knife' - would, in a cost-cutting frenzy, cancel the very expensive and very secret Oxcart programme.

A Soviet equivalent?

Over the years claims have been made that the Russians came up with their own version of the B-70 - the Sukhoi T-4, 'Aircraft 100', 'Project 100', or 'Sotka', whichever name you care to use.

The Sukhoi T-4 was a Soviet high speed reconnaissance, anti-ship and strategic bomber aircraft designed under the leadership of Pavel Sukhoi that did not proceed beyond the prototype stage. Despite design similarities, the Sukhoi T-4 was not intended as a Soviet equivalent of the North American B-70 Valkyrie, but was intended to take advantage of many of the XB-70's aeronautical innovations to develop a smaller reconnaissance and anti-carrier aircraft capable of reaching Mach 3. In a Soviet competition to develop such a bomber, it lost to the Myasishchev, and ultimately the Tupolev design which now exists as the Tupolev Tu-160 'Blackjack'.

The Sukhoi T-4. - a photograph that has almost certainly been retouched. *(Simon Peters Collection)*

As with the B-70, the T-4 was made largely from titanium and stainless steel, and featured a fly-by-wire control system but also employed a mechanical system as a backup. The aircraft's nose lowered to provide visibility during takeoff and landing. A periscope was used for forward viewing when the nose was raised, and could be employed at speeds of up to 600 km/h (373 mph). Braking parachutes were used in addition to conventional wheel brakes.

The first T-4, designated '101', first flew on 22 August 1972. The test pilot was Vladimir Ilyushin, son of famed aircraft designer, Sergei Ilyushin, who somewhat ironically, never seems to have served in his father's bureau, and navigator Nikolai Alfyorov.

Checking the accuracy of records in the former Soviet Union is not easy, but it appears that the T-4 only flew ten times for a total 10 hours and 20 minutes. It is believed to have reached at least Mach 1.3 using four Kolesov RD36-41 engines. These engines each produced 16,000 kgf (35,300 lb) thrust with afterburners. The aircraft was designed to achieve speeds of up to Mach 3.0, but the programme was

Comparative plan view artworks of the Sukhoi T-4 and XB-70A, demonstrating their relative sizes.

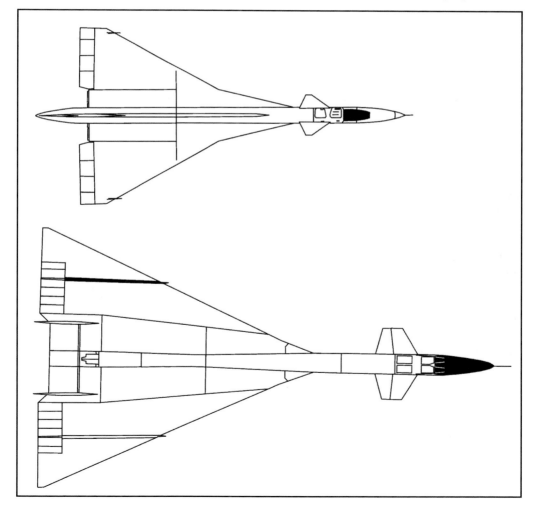

The Sukhoi T-4 on the ground and in the air. One example survives in Russia. *(Simon Peters Collection)*.

cancelled before the full performance of the aircraft could be reached.

Another reason of cancelling the project due to the VVS (Soviet Air Force) issuing the requirement of 250 T-4s. Meanwhile, some other high rank officers argued into gaining other more practical and supportive fighters instead of having such a huge flying titanium plate in the air. When Marshal Andrei Grechko was made the Minister of Defence, he seems he was told by a staff member, *'You could have your enormous MiG-23 order only if the T-4 would be abandoned'.*

One T-4 survives today. Aircraft '101' is on display at the Central Air Force Museum in Monino near Moscow. The serial numbers of the prototypes were '101' to '106'. Only '101' and '102' were built, other additional prototypes '103' and '104' were under construction, '105' and '106' only existed on draft charts. Only the '101' completed all the test flights and flew the last test flight before the project was canceled on January 22, 1974. The rest of prototypes were scrapped.

The XB-70A and the US SST

In the late 1950s, the United Kingdom, France, United States and Soviet Union were considering developing supersonic transport (SST). The British Bristol Aeroplane Company and the French Sud Aviation were both working on designs, called the Type 223 and Super-Caravelle, respectively. Both were largely funded by their respective governments. The British design was for a thin-winged delta shape - which owed much to work by Dietrich Küchemann - for a transatlantic-ranged aircraft for about 100 people, while the French were intending to build a medium-range aircraft.

The designs were both ready to start prototype construction in the early 1960s, but the cost was so great that the British government made it a requirement that BAC look for international co-operation. Approaches were made to a number of countries, but only France showed real interest. The development project was negotiated as an international treaty between the two countries rather than a commercial agreement between companies and included a clause, originally asked for by the UK, imposing heavy penalties for cancellation. A draft treaty was signed on 28 November 1962 and the two companies announced that a design called 'Concorde' would be built by a consortium. By this time, both companies had been merged into new ones; thus, the Concorde project was between the British Aircraft Corporation and Aérospatiale. The consortium secured orders for over 100 machines from the major airlines of the day: Pan Am, BOAC and Air France were the launch customers, with six Concordes each. Other airlines in the order book included Panair do Brasil, Continental Airlines, Japan Airlines, Lufthansa, American Airlines, United Airlines, Air India, Air Canada, Braniff, Singapore Airlines, Iran Air, Olympic Airways, Qantas, CAAC, Middle East Airlines and TWA.

In the USA, Boeing had worked on a number of small-scale SST studies since 1952. In 1958, it established a permanent research committee, which grew to a $1 million effort by 1960. The committee proposed a variety of alternative designs, all under their Model 733 name. Most featured a large delta wing, but in 1959

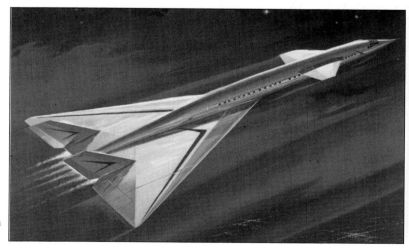

Artist's renditions are always thrilling - this design from North American's art department clearly has strong inspirations from the B-70. *(NAA)*

another design was offered as an offshoot of Boeing's efforts in the swing-wing TFX project. In 1960, an internal 'competition' was run on a baseline 150-seat aircraft for trans-Atlantic routes, and the swing-wing version won.

The 1961 study report

On 7 July 1961 North American released the results of a study into possible development plans for an early American SST. The internally-funded study had been conducted to aid the Federal Aviation Agency (FAA - it became an Administration later) in establishing the development plan for an eventual SST. The study assumed that the primary goal would be to develop a supersonic aircraft suitable for general airline passenger service and economically competitive with existing transport aircraft.

The North American study concentrated on the best way to develop the infrastructure necessary to support an SST, not necessarily on a definitive design for a production aircraft. The company realized that the development of an SST involved a broad spectrum of technical, economic, and practical problems. Many of these problems could be solved by incorporating the proper qualities and characteristics into the aircraft, but others required operational solutions - such as research into sonic booms, air traffic control, airports and terminal facilities, and operating policies, procedures, and regulations.

North American felt that the national investment in a commercial SST had already progressed considerably. They cited, as examples, the research necessary to produce supersonic fighters, and the development of the Convair B-58 Hustler medium bomber, which was the first long-range supersonic aircraft developed in the United States. The B-58's fuel consumption at supersonic speeds was considerably better than previous aircraft, but the basic design was '...*essentially a compromise between efficient subsonic and supersonic performance*'. An aircraft designed for an all-supersonic mission could do better. This was the same conclusion reached during the early WS-110A split-mission studies.

The concept of achieving efficient supersonic cruise by eliminating compromises for subsonic performance was first applied to the design of the XB-70A. Supersonic cruise efficiency was improved to the extent that the range of the aircraft at Mach 3 speeds was comparable to subsonic aircraft of similar gross weights. North American believed that the B-70 would provide a basis for a useful research aircraft, while admitting that it was a less than ideal configuration for any eventual production SST. After all, it was the only sustained Mach 3-capable aircraft in the free world.

They were quick to point out that the United States government had already invested over $500 million in technology to support the B-70 programme; an amount that could be quickly leveraged to develop an SST technology demonstrator.

North American wanted a cautious approach, recognizing that it would not result in an operational aircraft in the immediate future. '*This position pre-supposes that the primary objective is a profitable commercial transport, and that a plan is desired which balances urgency, risk, and cost to the extent that undue risk and excessive development costs are avoided. If any national objectives, such as prestige or military desirability, should shift the balance so that urgency became the dominant consideration, with cost and risk being minor factors, then obviously it would be possible to develop an SST somewhat earlier than the plans presented in this report."*

The report went on to describe three possible approaches of achieving the primary objective of a safe, profitable, supersonic transport for commercial airline service. The approaches were called: (1) production prototype, (2) experimental prototype, and (3) military or civil cargo prototype. Also described were two B-70 operational test vehicle programmes that could be implemented.

North American proposed to build two additional XB-70A airframes, modified for use as SST development aircraft. These machines could have flown, according to North American estimates, four years earlier than any purpose-designed SST prototype, allowing a great deal of time to evaluate areas of interest to the SST designers with modification and design changes 'fed back' to the purpose-built SST designs.

One of the modified XB-70s would be used to provide a flying testbed for new SST engines. Although the General Electric J93 turbojet used in the B-70 was one of the keys to its great performance, it would not be sufficiently reliable or economical for commercial service. Because of this, the government had begun financing the advanced Lightweight Gas Generator programme and had awarded contracts to both General Electric and Pratt & Whitney. The supersonic gas generator being developed could be adapted to several different engine cycles - turbofan, fan with duct burning, turboramjet, etc.

An American SST - North American style!

The plan and side views reveal a four-man flight crew, seating for 170 passengers, 3 rest rooms, a small galley but very little space for luggage or fuel! *(NAA)*

North American believed it was essential to gain flight experience with the new engine before the first prototype SST was completed - an excellent idea given the problems encountered with the JTD9 turbofan on the subsonic 747 a few years later. To accomplish this, they proposed modifying one of the additional XB-70A airframes to carry a single SST engine in place of two of the regular J93s. This would leave three J93s on one side and the outboard J93 on the other side, allowing the aircraft to fly under any conditions without the use of the SST engine. Modifications would be needed to the internal ducting to accommodate the

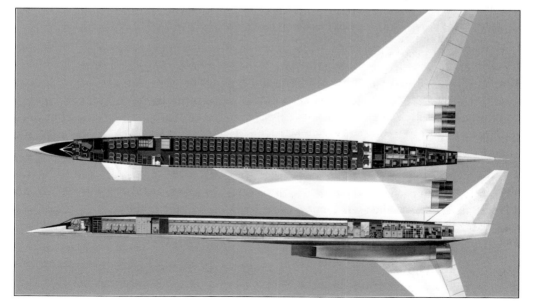

increased mass flow required by the new SST engine; minor modifications to the external mould line would also be necessary to accommodate the increased diameter expected of the new engine.

Alternatively, one of the SST engines could be mounted underneath the fuselage. This was essential if the final design required externally mounting the engines - much like the eventual Boeing SST design. In this case, flight testing the inlet configurations and nacelle shapes would be necessary. The engine would be mounted on a pylon that could be partially retracted into what had been designed as the weapons bay to minimize clearance problems during takeoff and landing. The engine would be equipped with a particular inlet design to evaluate engine performance at a particular design point speed. Alternate inlet designs could be tested, but not during a single flight.

The second XB-70A airframe would be modified to a limited passenger configuration by removing the military electronics and fuel from the upper fuselage and replacing it with a small passenger compartment. This version had a gross takeoff weight of 337,000 pounds and a range of 2,900 miles. With the second version 47,400 pounds of fuel was moved into the weapons bay (for a total of 185,000 pounds) and resulted in an aircraft weighing 384,500 pounds with a range of just over 4,000 miles.

A somewhat strange graphic, but considering this was the 1960s not surprising is this B-70 artwork that places the businessman racing to his next deal in the SST version. The chemist's beaker suggests that this artwork was done whilst thoughts of chemically augmented powerplants were still being considered - or our businessman was about to have a very large Martini! *(NAA)*

In March 1960 Lockheed were promoting their Mach 3 - Mach 3.5 airliner design that would weigh around 250,000lb and cost some $160 million to develop. *(The Aeroplane and Astronautics)*

Without changing the line of the upper fuselage, a total of 36 passengers could be accommodated in four-abreast seating. The internal diameter of the fuselage was only 100 inches - four feet narrower than the Boeing 707. A single restroom would be located at the extreme rear of the passenger compartment. A galley was not included, partly because of a lack of room, and partly because all flights were expected to be so short there was no need for one. Passenger entry and exit, as well as emergency evacuation, would be complicated by the height of the XB-70A fuselage above the ground.

Two other configurations were also proposed that slightly changed the outer mould line, but provided more realistic passenger counts. Both included the weapons bay fuel. The first extended the internal passenger compartment by 240 inches, resulting in seating for 48 passengers. This version had a gross takeoff weight of 427,000 pounds and could fly 3,850 miles while cruising at Mach 3. The other version increased the passenger compartment another 264 inches (for a total stretch of 504 inches) to seat 76 passengers. The gross takeoff weight increased to 461,000 pounds, but range was reduced to only 3,600 miles at Mach 3. Neither modification changed the overall length of the fuselage, but resulted in a more pronounced change in line of the rear part of the neck. The expected effect on stability was considered negligible.

North American's rationale for using an XB-70A as an precursor SST demonstrator was completely valid. The primary contribution was the early definition of problems associated with the operation of an SST, made possible by limited passenger flights as early as 1965. Since the FAA would not have certificated the aircraft, they would have been limited to military or government operations, but that did not create great problems The expected areas of concern included air traffic control, airport operations, maintenance, scheduling and possible noise complaints from sonic booms. Sufficient lead-time was available to resolve these problems in an efficient and orderly manner before large numbers of SSTs were produced. Regulations and systems could be developed to monitor and control the operations of supersonic aircraft by the time production aircraft were introduced into airline service. The FAA could use the early service experience to write new Federal Air Regulations covering the certification process and design criteria for supersonic transports.

By mid-1962, it was becoming clear that the tentative talks earlier that year between the United Kingdom and France on a merger of their SST projects were more serious than were first believed - and therefore much more of a threat to the American aviation

industry - than was originally thought. This set off something of a wave of panic, as it was widely believed that almost all future commercial aircraft would be supersonic, and it looked like the Europeans would start off with a huge lead.

The Concorde came as no surprise to American SST enthusiasts in the Federal Aviation Agency (FAA), which had been sponsoring SST research and feasibility studies since 1960. Ever since FAA administrator Najeeb Halaby had assumed office in early 1961 he immediately began lobbying for an American SST development project. He also rejected numerous European, especially British, overtures for a joint SST programme and never had any intention of becoming partners with the British or the French. As he testified on Capital Hill in April 1961, *'We want to be there ahead of our competitors'*. This American posture helped drive the British and French into each other's arms.

The creation of the Concorde programme provided Halaby with a formidable promotional weapon. By November 1962 the danger posed by the Anglo-French project was his main lobbying theme. In a report to President Kennedy, Halaby portrayed a successful Concorde as forcing the United States to *'...relinquish world civil transport leadership'* that would cost over 50,000 US jobs and potentially leading to U.S. dependence on foreign suppliers for supersonic military aircraft. Halaby clinched his appeal by jingoistically warning that conceivably an American president would someday be forced to fly in a foreign aircraft.

The Concorde announcement was a crucial factor in mobilizing support within the administration for an American SST program. As Halaby recalled years later, *'When de Gaulle embraced the joint [Anglo-French] Concorde project, it seemed to trigger competitiveness in JFK. In fact, I think JFK associated the Concorde most with de Gaulle; on more than one occasion, he said, 'We'll beat that bastard de Gaulle.' Every time I saw the President, from the day de Gaulle made his announcement, he would press me on how our studies were going—and how the British and French were doing'.*

Clearly the B-70 could be used as a serious research tool and provided a foundation already in place that the Americans could use - and that starting point was Mach 3 speeds. Going through all the US material, one forms the distinct impression that the Americans were being 'driven' by the Concorde - to better it

Clearly this artwork is to demonstrate the transition from B-70 to SST. However, there are also the first inkling of a further NAA Rockwell product, the B-1 with the engine nacelles. *(NAA)*

in both speed and size and therefore win the commercial battle. They were determined that what had happened a decade or so earlier when the de Havilland Comet had given all the American manufacturers a bloody nose by soundly beating them to the commercial jet market was not going to occur again.

In November 1962 the NASA Research Center initiated a programme called SCAT - Supersonic Commercial Air Transport - in order to evolve a configuration that could cater for unique requirements for a commercial SST over the entire spectrum from take-off to landing. Their studies came down to two approaches - SCAT-4, a was a fixed-wing proposal that integrated wing, fuselage, engines and tail into a highly swept, cambered and twisted aircraft design aimed at minimising wave drag due to lift, and the variable-sweep SCAT-15. By early 1963, two other geometries were also being pursued: the SCAT-16 variable-sweep proposal that had evolved from -15, and SCAT-17, a fixed delta-wing layout with a forward canard surface - in other words, a modified B-70 design.

In an even more direct way the Concorde was a major factor forcing the President to announce an American SST programme. During the spring of 1963 Pan American Airlines - the 'flagship' of American airlines, flying many international routes, including the crucial transatlantic run, and who traditionally led the way in ordering new aircraft - made sure that the FAA and the White House knew that the airline was considering ordering a number of Concordes, although it really wanted to purchase a fleet of larger and faster American Mach 3 SSTs. Juan Trippe, president of Pan American, informed high-level US officials, including Halaby, Civil Aeronautics Board Chairman Alan Boyd, and Secretary of the Treasury C Douglas Dillion, and that he intended to place a 'protective order' for six Concordes.

Trippe's actions had the desired effect. Vice-President Lyndon B Johnson, who was chairing a cabinet-level SST review committee at that time and who had already recommended an SST go-ahead to President Kennedy, became extremely worried over the impact of the Pan American Concorde decision. Armed with Johnson's recommendation and the knowledge of Trippe's move to order

The big white bird taxis at Edwards AFB sometime during service with NASA *(USAF)*

'Cecil the sea-sick sea serphent' banks away from the camera during one of the sonic boom tests. *(USAF)*

Concordes, Kennedy quickly decided to establish an SST program. But to Kennedy's great anger and Halaby's shock. Pan American announced its order for six Concordes on 4 June 1963, one day before Kennedy's SST declaration.

On 5 June 1963, in a speech before the graduating class of the United States Air Force Academy, President John F. Kennedy committed the United States to *'develop at the earliest practical date the prototype of a commercially successful supersonic transport superior to that being built in any other country in the world....'*

In the summer of 1963 Halaby was at the peak of his power. He had achieved his long-sought goal: an SST programme under FAA direction. However, he soon suffered a dramatic decline in authority from which he would never recover. His fall from grace was partially due to the change in administrations that occurred as a result of the assassination of John F Kennedy on November 22, 1963. Halaby, a Kennedy appointee, was never close to Lyndon Johnson and did not particularly get along with him. Although a SST supporter, Johnson also wanted to put his own stamp on what had been a Kennedy programme.

Just as important in promoting a power shift were complaints from the manufacturers - they objected to President Kennedy's original cost-sharing requirements. In August 1963 Kennedy asked Eugene Black, former head of the World Bank, to review the SST financing issue. Black brought in a fellow industrialist and financier, Stanley de J. Osborne - their report was submitted to President Johnson in December 1963 and quickened Halaby's decline. Black and Osborne sided with industry in deciding that the 75-25 cost-sharing ratio was too much and recommended that 90% of the development cost be assumed by the government and 10% by the manufacturers. Black and Osborne went beyond their charter and offered proposals that were the opposite of what Halaby advocated. They recommended that the SST programme be taken from the FAA and be made an independent 'Authority', reflecting a growing opinion by informed persons in the government and industry that the FAA lacked the managerial skills and experience to run a complex effort like the SST programme. They also saw no necessity for a crash programme, noting that the British and French were already encountering major problems of their own.

The Black-Osborne report triggered a series of internal administration reviews of the whole SST effort in early 1964 that finally led to the formation of the President's Advisory Committee on Supersonic Transport (PAC-SST) in April 1964. This was chaired by probably the most powerful and influential official in the government at that time, next to the president, Secretary of Defense Robert S McNamara, and was made up of cabinet-level officials, including the secretaries of treasury and commerce, the Boom director, the administrators of NASA and the FAA, and Black and Osborne. A massive power shift had taken place. McNamara was now the most important decision maker in the SST programme and major policy decisions were now made in the PAC-SST rather than the FAA.

By definition, a Chairman is selected to preside over meetings, and lead a committee to consensus from the disparate points of view of its members. The chairman is expected to be impartial, fair, a good listener, and a good communicator. Nothing could be further from the truth with Robert McNamara. He, and his team of Whizz Kids had killed off the B-70 - now he set about killing off the American SST. In his own words:

'Right at the beginning I thought the project was not justified, because you couldn't fly a large enough payload over a long enough nonstop distance at a low enough cost to make it pay. I'm not an aeronautical engineer or a technical expert or an airline specialist or an aircraft manufacturer but I knew that I could make the calculation on the back of an envelope.

So I approached the SST with that bias. President Johnson was in favor of it. As chairman of the committee I was very skeptical from the beginning. The question, in a sense, was how to kill it. I conceived an approach that said: maybe you're right, maybe there is a commercial market, maybe what we should do is to take it with government funds up to the point where the manufacturers and the airlines can determine the economic viability of the aircraft. We'll draw up a program on that basis'.

Testing the bangs

The need to evaluate the effects on sonic booms on the general population led to the running of a series of sonic booms being 'dropped' over Oklahoma City, Oklahoma over a period of six months in 1964.

The experiment, which ran from 3 February through 29 July 1964 inclusive, intended to quantify the effects of transcontinental SSTs on a city. The programme was managed by the FAA, which enlisted the aid of NASA and the USAF. Public opinion measurement was subcontracted to the National Opinion Research Center (NORC) of the University of Chicago.

It was not the first experiment of this nature, as tests had been done at Wallops Island, Virginia in 1958 and 1960, at Nellis Air Force Base, Nevada in 1960 and 1961, and in St. Louis, Missouri in 1961 and 1962. However, none of these tests examined sociological and economic factors in any detail. The Oklahoma City experiments were much larger in scope, seeking to measure the boom's effect on structures and public attitude, and to develop standards for boom prediction and insurance data.

Oklahoma City was chosen, as the region's population was perceived to be relatively tolerant for such an experiment. The city had an economic dependency on

the nearby FAA's Mike Monroney Aeronautical Center and Tinker Air Force Base.

Starting on 3 February 1964, the first sonic booms began, eight booms per day that began at 07:00 and ended in the afternoon. The noise was limited to 1.0 to 1.5 pound-force per square foot for the first twelve weeks, then increased to 1.5 to 2.0 psf for the final fourteen weeks. This range was about equal to that expected from an SST. Though eight booms per day were harsh, the peak overpressures of 2.0 psf were an order of magnitude lower than that needed to shatter glass, and were considered marginally irritating according to published standards.

Oklahomans initially took the tests in their stride, as the booms were predictable and coming at specific times. An FAA-hired camera crew, filming a group of construction workers, were surprised to find that one of the booms signalled their lunch break.

However, in the first fourteen weeks, 147 windows in the city's two tallest buildings, the First National Bank and Liberty National Bank, were broken. By late spring, organized civic groups were springing into action, but were rebuffed by city politicians, who asked them to show legislators their support. An attempt to lodge an injunction against the tests was denied by district court Judge Stephen Chandler, who said that the plaintiffs could not establish that they suffered any mental or physical harm and that the tests were a vital national need. A restraining order was then sought, which brought a pause to the tests on May 13 until it was decided that the court had exceeded its authority.

Pressure mounted from within. The Federal Bureau of the Budget lambasted the FAA about poor experiment design, while complaints flooded into Oklahoma Senator A S Mike Monroney's office. Finally, East Coast newspapers began to pick up the issue, turning on the national spotlight. On 6 June the *Saturday Review* published an article titled *The Era of Supersonic Morality*, which criticized the manner in which the FAA had targeted a city without consulting local government. By July, the *Washington Post* reported on the turmoil at local and state level in Oklahoma. Oklahoma City council members were finally beginning to respond to citizen complaints and to put pressure on Washington.

This pressure put a premature end to the tests. The results of the experiment,

A truly stunning picture of 20001 seen up close and personal from one of the chase aircraft. The wing tips are in the fully down position. *(USAF)*

reported by NORC, were released beginning in February, 1965. The FAA was displeased by the overly academic style of the report, but stressed the positive findings, saying '...*the overwhelming majority felt they could learn to live with the numbers and kinds of booms experienced'*. Indeed, the NORC reported that 73% of subjects in the study said that they could live indefinitely with eight sonic booms per day, while 25% said that they could not. About 3% of the population telephoned, sued, or wrote protest letters, but Oklahoma City surgeons and hospitals filed no complaints.

However, with the city population at 500,000, that 3% figure represented 15,000 upset individuals. At least 15,452 complaints and 4,901 claims were lodged against the US government, most for cracked glass and plaster. The FAA rejected 94% of all the claims it received, fueling a rising tide of anger that soared even after the experiment's conclusion.

The Oklahoma City experiments were partly to blame for weakening the FAA's authority in sonic boom issues. After the tests, President Lyndon B. Johnson's presidential advisory committee transferred matters of policy from the FAA to the National Academy of Science. Secretary of the Interior Stewart Udall complained that the NAS did not include one environmental preservationist, and pointed out that although the Oklahoma City tests were stacked in favor of the SST, they were still extremely negative. Indeed by 1966, national grassroots campaigns against sonic booms were beginning to affect public policy.

The FAA's poor handling of claims and its payout of only $123,000 led to a class action lawsuit against the U.S. government.

SST design and devlopment work

North American submitted the NAC-60 design, which was essentially a scaled-up B-70 with a less tapered fuselage and new compound-delta wing. The design retained the high-mounted canard and box-like engine area under the fuselage. The Lockheed CL-823 was essentially a scaled-up Concorde with a compound-delta wing (as opposed to the smoothed ogee of the Concorde), with individually podded engines.

The American designs, the Boeing 2707 and the Lockheed L-2000 were to have been larger, with seating for up to 300 people. Running a few years behind Concorde, the winning Boeing 2707 was later redesigned to a cropped delta layout.

It was obvious that supersonic flight had to provide a shirtsleeve environment for passengers - it would be totally impracticable to fit hundreds of people with temperature-resistant pressure suits before launching them across the sky at speeds in excess of Mach 2. Lots of designers had lots of theories as to how this would be possible, but some realised that the XB-70A programme was attempting to supply some hard, real-time solutions. It was almost if the aircraft had been ready made to answer some of the questions. As always, the XB-70A programme was having financial problems because of arguments between Congress and McNamara's DoD. NASA was happy to climb aboard and fund the testing with the idea that it might be a good way to bolster the SST programme, for there were many problems to be solved before an American SST could be built.

In 1965, the United States had not yet come up with accurate wind tunnel models, so it had difficulty estimating the base drag of a multi-engine aircraft. The

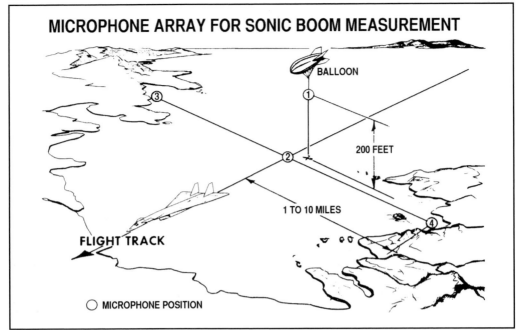

MICROPHONE ARRAY FOR SONIC BOOM MEASUREMENT

BALLOON

200 FEET

1 TO 10 MILES

FLIGHT TRACK

○ **MICROPHONE POSITION**

XB-70A was able to run these tests live, during regular flight. Tests called for cameras to be placed on the fuselage so in-flight photographs could be taken to resolve boundary layer transition pattern issues. Later on, a wing glove would be installed, permitting the study of the effects of roughness on airflow, especially during the subsonic-transonic-supersonic transition.

A chart showing how a series of four microphones were arrayed for the sonic boom tests. *(AFMCHO)*

The instrumentation was designed, manufactured, and installed - mainly on Air Vehicle Two - with data gathering, reduction, and analysis performed on a non-interference basis during the XB-70A development program. As North American Aviation stated in its final report: *'The SST flight research data was obtained in various areas as designated by the eight tasks. All of the tasks indicated were sponsored by NASA except for acoustic loads which was sponsored by FAA'.*

Prior to the loss of AV 2, the aircraft had become a surrogate for the proposed Boeing SST. The government and private researchers embarked on a major sonic boom test programme at Edwards in an effort to accurately forecast psychological reaction and structural damage associated with overpressures from supersonic transports. The National Sonic Boom programme (NSBP) was set up by the President's Office of Science and Technology, and consisted of three principal participants - the Air Force, NASA, and Stanford Research Institute.

The XB-70A was used to perform the tests because it most closely resembled the size of the proposed Boeing SST. The Valkyrie was the only aircraft capable of simulating the SST primarily because weight and size had a marked affect on sonic boom signatures. Although overpressures of equal peak magnitudes could have been obtained by using F-104s and B-58s, the duration of the boom itself varied with each aircraft as to the shape of the shock waves themselves and the forces involved.

The NSBP began on 6 June 1966 when AV 2 performed the initial sonic boom test, reaching Mach 3.05 at 72,000 feet. The second NSBP test was conducted two days later but it was followed by the mid-air collision that destroyed the aircraft.

Both the Air Force and NASA were unsure that AV 1, with its Mach 2.5 speed limitation, could continue the research since the Boeing SST was planned as a Mach 2.7 aircraft. AV 1 had not flown since 9 May because the original test programme was scheduled to end in early June. Nevertheless, given that AV 1 was the only large supersonic aircraft available, NASA thought that it had no choice other than to install a duplicate set of test equipment in AV 1. During this period AV 1 was also equipped with improved escape capsules and an automated AICS, thereby eliminating its troublesome manual air induction control system.

Subsequent to the XB-70A flight test development program, two flight research programmes were initiated on the remaining XB-70A. The first programme was for Sonic Boom Measurements and was sponsored jointly by NASA and USAF.

The XB-70A was fitted with two sets of 'passenger windows' while with NASA, in order to visually demonstrate the American SST. They were, in reality, just stickers. *(USAF)*

The first of these flights occurred on 11 March 1966 and the programme was completed on 1 January 1967. The primary purpose was to determine the proper method of combining the theoretical sonic boom intensity due to lift and due to volume for the far field case. Pressure signatures of several aircraft, but principally the XB-70A, were measured on the ground at various distances

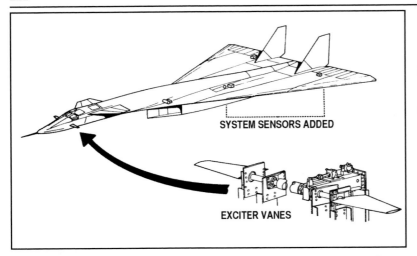

SYSTEM SENSORS ADDED

EXCITER VANES

The ILAF system of exciter vanes and associated sensors installed by NASA on board AV 1 for the 73rd and subsequent flights. NASA hoped this system would serve as a prototype for advanced systems that would be installed on SSTs, enabling them to fly with increased smoothness and reduced the fatigue on both passengers and airframe. The first ILAF flight was on 11 June 1968; from then until the end of the programme in 1969 AV 1 acquired much information applicable to not only the design of future SSTs but also large, supersonic military aircraft. *(NASA)*

from the ground track of the air vehicle. Atmospheric effects on the sonic boom intensity were also investigated.

A follow-on programme was sponsored by NASA and was an investigation into the control of structural dynamics. The first flight was on 25 April 1967 and the programme was completed on 4 February 1969 when the #1 XB-70A was ferried to Wright-Patterson AFB for the USAF Museum.

To conduct the structure dynamics investigation, the air vehicle was modified for the installation of an Exciter Vane System in the nose section and an elevon control system titled Identically Located Acceleration and Force (ILAF).

The Exciter Vane System comprised of two small vanes protruding from both sides of the nose section, tied together through the fuselage and hydraulically driven. The system was controllable from the cockpit for both frequency and amplitude which provided controlled dynamics to the air vehicle structure. The ILAF system tied into the XB-70A Flight Augmentation Control System which provided elevon control for structural dynamic dampening. This concept was based on locating the input accelerometers near the elevons (for system stability), mixing this input signal with CG signals which cancelled normal flight accelerations and provided a structural dynamics frequency spectrum.

Meanwhile, behind the scenes, the initial concern caused by the Concorde had faded by 1964 and the Concorde programme was not the center of American SST policy-making attention. As in the past almost all significant American-European SST exchanges were limited to purely technical SST information. In fact, the Concorde seemed to be in deep political and technical trouble. In late 1964 the newly elected Labour government called for a thorough review of British participation in the programme. The CIA reported in October that the Labour Party's stance would have serious repercussions for the Concorde, and McNamara was even warned in November 1964 that Great Britain might withdraw completely. However, McNamara's key SST aide, Joseph Califano, believed that the British would probably continue to participate, though the British reappraisal had clearly weakened the Concorde. *'Whatever the outcome...'* Califano told McNamara, *'...the introduction of so much strain and uncertainty into the Concorde program because of the political factors makes it*

TASKS	A/V #1	A/V #2
1. Aerodynamics (Panel Response)	X	X
2. Structures (Landing Loads)	X	
3. Structures (Gust Loads)		X
4. Structures (Acoustic Loads)		X
5. Aerodynamics (Skin Friction Drag)		X
6. Aerodynamics (Base Drag)		X
7. Thermal Environment (Cabin & Structures)		X
8. Thermal Environment (Fuel System)		X

The instrumentation installed in the XB-70's for the SST flight research program is summarized as follows: (See Exhibit 15, page II-25.)

Panel Response	-	A NASA tape recorder and two microphones in the cockpit area.
Landing Loads	-	Rate of sink trailing arms, landing gear cameras, and NASA VGH recorder.
Gust Loads	-	A gust probe boom, accelerometers, pressure transducers, and yaw and pitch angle instrumentation.
Acoustic Loads	-	Microphones and pressure tape to measure the properties of a turbulent boundary layer.
Skin Friction Drag	-	Wing pressure rakes, static pressure lines, thermo couple wires, and fuselage pressure rakes.
Base Drag	-	Boattail and pressure tapes around engines 4, 5, and 6.
Thermal Environment	-	Thermo couples on cabin windshield and structure, flight control components, landing gear, and fuel system.
Additional Data	-	The VGH recorder was also utilized to obtain fatigue data. The XB-70 development instrumentation, such as aerodynamic and stability and control transducers, were used for program correlation.

From North American's own files come this list of additional equipment installed in the XB-70A for supersonic transport tests.

Interestingly there are very few references in the entire B-70 Study Report to the airframe 'growing' due to thermal expansion caused by frictional heating. *(NAA)*

doubtful whether the degree of cooperation that has thus prevailed between the British and French can be maintained'.

Design revisions had also set the Concorde programme back as much as two years and development costs were spiraling (estimated at $400 million for the British share in November 1964). A NASA analysis of the Concorde optimistically estimated that Concorde direct operating costs would be 1.4 cents per seat-mile - compared with 1.0 to 1.1 cents per seat-mile for the subsonic Boeing 707. Califano also indicated that Concorde's performance would probably further deteriorate.

At the end of 1964 only the strongest SST proponents, including Halaby and potential SST contractors like Lockheed, even bothered stressing the danger of Concorde success. Both SST proponents and sceptics in the United States also continued their long-standing aversion to joint SST development with the Europeans. In 1965 the Americans squashed a new feeler by the British and French for co-operation and, according to the French, for 'dividing the world SST market' between the United States and the Europeans.

The generally disdainful American view of the Concorde effort was expressed at the 30 March 1965 PAC meeting when CIA director John McCone, in presenting the current intelligence on the Concorde - paying careful attention to noting that the CIA had not used '...*clandestine sources*' because of the '...*risk of offending one of the host countries*' and minimized Concorde accomplishments -

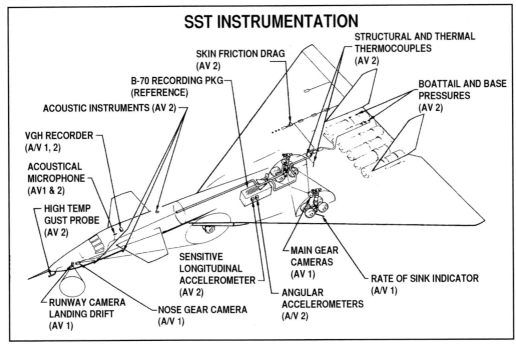

SST INSTRUMENTATION

STRUCTURAL AND THERMAL
THERMOCOUPLES
(AV 2)

SKIN FRICTION DRAG
(AV 2)

B-70 RECORDING PKG
(REFERENCE)

BOATTAIL AND BASE
PRESSURES
(AV 2)

ACOUSTIC INSTRUMENTS (AV 2)

VGH RECORDER
(A/V 1, 2)

ACOUSTICAL
MICROPHONE
(AV1 & 2)

HIGH TEMP
GUST PROBE
(AV 2)

SENSITIVE
LONGITUDINAL
ACCELEROMETER
(AV 2)

MAIN GEAR
CAMERAS
(AV 1)

RATE OF SINK INDICATOR
(A/V 1)

RUNWAY CAMERA
LANDING DRIFT
(AV 1)

NOSE GEAR CAMERA
(A/V 1)

ANGULAR
ACCELEROMETERS
(A/V 2)

Also from North American comes this diagram showing where the dedicated instrumentation was installed in the XB-70A airframe. *(NAA)*

interestingly, he never bothered to state which country he was not concerned about offending! He reported that little European work seemed to have been done on the sonic boom problem and that extensive design modifications and economic uncertainties would surely cause further delays. This in itself is remarkably surprising, for the British aviation magazines alone contain many reports on noise studies and associated work done from as early as 1959. McCone went on to remind the PAC members that as one moved gradually upward from the Mach-1.5 to the Mach-2 range unexpected technical problems were bound to arise, and these would take time to correct. He was not at all worried about the Concorde's alleged two-to-three-year lead, and suggested at any rate that Anglo-French forecasts be taken 'with a grain of salt...quite a large one'. Halaby, of course, disagreed. He noted that the Concorde had already won significant airline commitment - in addition to BOAC and Air France, a total of forty-eight delivery positions had been reserved by other airlines.

McNamara strongly backed McCone, calling his review '...*a very interesting report, the best we have had so far.*' McNamara argued that the American SST should be a profitable commercial venture and that the pace of Concorde work should not dictate American SST development. He felt that the United States would ultimately build a better SST; there was therefore no need to worry about Concorde's lead.

McNamara was also receiving economic evaluations that supported his scepticism about the Concorde from an SST economics task force that he had established in the Pentagon in early 1965, headed by Stephen Enke, a respected economist. The estimates of the task force gave the Concorde only a minor market niche, and Enke was convinced that the Concorde would have a hard time keeping up with the American competition. Anglo-French dates for commercial

North American proposed a number of different versions of the B-70 that could be used as a SST.

The first was this operational test vehicle that had the compartment aft of the cockpit converted into a 100-inch wide four abreast seating area.

While not cleared for commercial airline use, this B-70 could be involved in a number of tasks ahead of a commercial SST design.

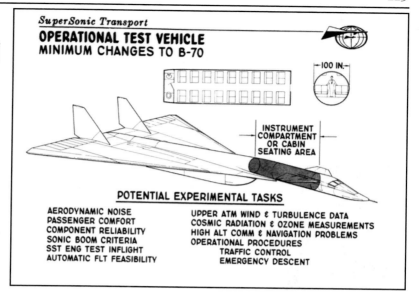

SuperSonic Transport
OPERATIONAL TEST VEHICLE
MINIMUM CHANGES TO B-70

├─100 IN.─┤

INSTRUMENT
COMPARTMENT
OR CABIN
SEATING AREA

POTENTIAL EXPERIMENTAL TASKS

AERODYNAMIC NOISE
PASSENGER COMFORT
COMPONENT RELIABILITY
SONIC BOOM CRITERIA
SST ENG TEST INFLIGHT
AUTOMATIC FLT FEASIBILITY

UPPER ATM WIND & TURBULENCE DATA
COSMIC RADIATION & OZONE MEASUREMENTS
HIGH ALT COMM & NAVIGATION PROBLEMS
OPERATIONAL PROCEDURES
TRAFFIC CONTROL
EMERGENCY DESCENT

Concorde operation were termed '*...patently unrealistic*'. The British and French were inexperienced at sustaining Mach 2.0 speeds. One task force member noted, '*The American SST has great growth potential, the Concorde almost none*'.

By their May 5, 1965 meeting, the PAC members, including a defeated Halaby - who would shortly leave the government to work for Pan American - , appeared even less troubled than before by Concorde and more confident of the American SST's ultimate success. McNamara flatly predicted that the American SST would be '*...far more successfully commercially than the Concorde*' and that the United States need not feel the pressure of a 'crash' Concorde effort.

American unease over the European SST refused to go away, and renewed

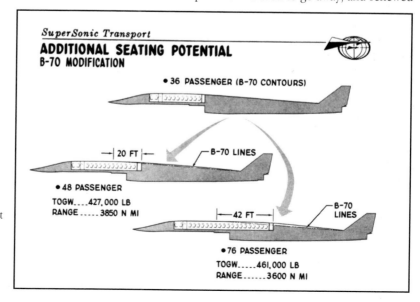

SuperSonic Transport
ADDITIONAL SEATING POTENTIAL
B-70 MODIFICATION

● 36 PASSENGER (B-70 CONTOURS)

├─ 20 FT ─┤   ┌─ B-70 LINES

● 48 PASSENGER

TOGW.....427,000 LB
RANGE.....3850 N MI

├── 42 FT ──┤   ┌─ B-70
                    LINES

● 76 PASSENGER

TOGW.....461,000 LB
RANGE......3600 N MI

North American also proposed a number of other modifications that would allow up to 76 passengers to be carried by 'stretching' the fuselage somewhat. *(both NAA)*

concern began to grow during the latter half of 1965. This development was due to a genuine worry about Concorde as a threat to American aviation interests and to a reinvigorated FAA lobbying effort to influence PAC-SST members that was directed by two air force generals, William McKee, the new FAA administrator, and Jewell Maxwell, the new director of the SST programme.

In August 1965 Enke's task force produced an important study which concluded that Concorde would displace approximately 23% of the 100-odd American SSTs expected to be sold by 1985 under a sonic boom-induced restricted route condition. The study concluded that Concorde's lower plane-mile costs —in contrast to the Concorde's higher seat-mile costs - would make the Concorde more suitable for low-density routes and hours. Cheaper subsonic airfares would hurt the larger capacity American SST more than the Concorde, as would route restrictions, given the resulting limited demand for SST air travel. British and French production techniques tended to be less capital intensive than American ones. It went on to say: *'The US SST needs a relatively large supersonic market - which probably means only moderately restricted routes for Concorde competition to be unimportant'.*

The FAA was employing a well-planned and effective lobbying campaign that emphasized the Concorde threat. The agency told the PAC-SST in early October 1965 that the gap between time of announced Concorde commercial introduction (1971-1972) and estimated American SST commercial availability (mid-1975) was sufficient to assure an adequate market for the Concorde given a reasonably economic design.

The United States must assume that Concorde will be a successful programme, declared the FAA. The notion that Concorde might be a real future competitor assumed new credence at the 9 October PAC-SST meeting where Osborne and Boeing - via Secretary of Commerce John Connor - reported that the Concorde would actually meet its announced schedule. Media reports helped the FAA.

Enke immediately attempted to block the FAA resurgence. In January 1966 Enke flew to Paris and London to meet with high-level French and British officials, ostensibly to deal with various economic and sonic boom research problems, but really to discuss 'time phasing' - proportionately slowing down both the Anglo-French and American programmes.

Enke sent back less than favourable assessments of Concorde: economic prospects were pessimistic and the airlines were not enthusiastic about the aircraft. Significantly, Enke reported that the British and French had different performance and political goals; Concorde was a matter of pride and national prestige to the French, while the British tended to view it as the price they had to pay to avoid a French veto of British membership in the Common Market. *'Great Britain...'*, Enke wrote, *'...was the reluctant partner, with the British mood being one of 'fatalistic hopelessness that combined an awareness of financial losses ahead with a belief that little could be done about it'.* Enke concluded that the time was ripe to explore time phasing and design differentiation with the British and French. Then, to the FAA's great dismay, Enke's discussions and views were leaked to the British press.

The FAA quickly counter-attacked, emphasizing the positive aspects of Concorde's development. It received additional favourable Concorde reviews from TWA, Lockheed, and Boeing and began to systematically organize and assess Concorde information.

Concorde's image again began to decline in the eyes of key American decision makers. The CIA reported in late March 1966 of Concorde's engine difficulties. At the 6 May 1966 PAC-SST meeting McNamara stated that this negative information demonstrated that although *'...not a failure, the Concorde did have a few problems'.* He added that lack of supersonic experience had led the British and French to underestimate the Concorde's technical difficulties. Both McCone and McNamara once more explicitly warned against letting Concorde influence American SST development.

The information on Concorde that the Americans received - from public and private sources - was contradictory. Some of the data indicated that the Concorde was proceeding smoothly and on schedule, and the FAA particularly was more than willing to believe Concorde claims. The FAA was assisted in early July 1966 by Juan Trippe of Pan American, who told the PAC that the Concorde's timetable

A full scale mock-up of the swing-wing Boeing SST. *(Aeroplane and Astronatics).*

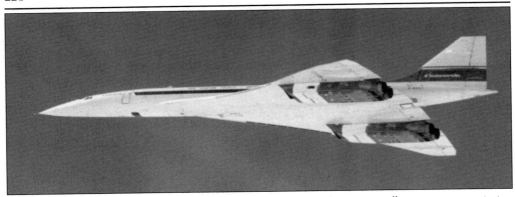

was realistic and that its performance characteristics had improved. He pointedly added, '*Any place that we* [Pan American] *don't have such a ship* [the Concorde] *covered, as more or less a loss leader for advertising purposes and so forth, we think we would be in trouble during the period after Concorde delivery*'.

Concordes were built in both the United Kingdom and France and entered commercial service in 1976 - 27 years later they were retired. *(BAC)*

Again the lack of American confidence in the Concorde programme came to the fore. US sources throughout the rest of 1966 stressed the Concorde's long-term problems, such as substantial cost increases, and making claims regarding the Europeans neglect of the sonic boom issue, and the likelihood of a substantial delay.

This was brought about by a US disregard not only of the Concorde but also that the Americans generally disparaged the entire European aviation industry. Juan Trippe spoke of the '*...miserable performance in Europe compared to what we have done in this country*' and admitted that Pan American's Concorde orders were nothing but '*...a sort of an insurance program*' to cover Pan American if an American SST was delayed.

Supporting American poor opinion of European commercial aviation, a number of CIA reports emphasized Concorde's major technical and non-technical problems, and, though acknowledging that Concorde was currently on schedule, warned of serious future delays in the Concorde's production phase. The search for solutions to technical problems, according to the CIA, could delay the programme for up to two years. In the non-technical area, the CIA reports dwelled on potentially fatal disagreements; the French, worried about the proposed American SST and unsure of their British partners, wanted to enter production quickly, and rejected a British proposal to increase Concorde passenger capacity to 167; the British, on the other hand, already doubting the Concorde's economic strength, felt that a larger vehicle was needed to compete with the Americans on transatlantic routes, which would require more development time. No one seemed to question the accuracy of any of these reports, which, if they were based on 1966-era data, were seriously inaccurate and out of date. Enke and his group naturally continued to minimise the seriousness of the Concorde challenge, arguing that even a year's slippage in the American effort would have little impact on American SST sales.

At the 9 October 1966 PAC-SST meeting presidential science adviser Donald Hornig added that the Concorde developers had '*...sort of shut their eyes to the sonic boom problem and resigned themselves to at least having the overseas market*'. Even Maxwell at the FAA admitted to the PAC-SST that no solutions had been found for the Concorde's problems; development costs and the sales price were increasing; but so were airline orders.

As the CIA also acknowledged in October 1966, the Concorde did exist and was apparently on schedule. Concorde orders had increased from fifty-four to a tentative sixty-four since August, and the project had assumed a high order of diplomatic political importance. The CIA observed that *'General de Gaulle continues to view the Concorde as an important step in demonstrating the technical competence required of a major power. He sees the project as a means, also, to enhance French prestige, particularly vis-a-vis the US and has taken a personal interest in it. The French government's determination that the project be completed, despite growing British disenchantment because of mounting costs also stems from Gaullist assertions that France's 'independent foreign policy has not harmed its friendship with its allies'*. As another high French official put it, *'For technological, commercial, and also political reasons, our European countries cannot allow themselves to sink to the level of mere subcontractors'*.

TWA president Charles Tillinghast was even more bullish. He told the PAC on 7 December 1966 that the Concorde could indeed be a real threat, although the

Two of a series of pictures taken during engine ground runs. The raw power of the six-pack can clearly be seen. *(USAF)*

Concorde had lousy seat-mile economics and that TWA would love to skip the Concorde, he maintained that if the American SST fell further behind, TWA would have no choice but to opt for the Anglo-French aircraft. Tillinghast estimated that TWA could afford at the most an eighteen-month lag. Tillinghast warned the PAC *'The British and French are in. They may have been silly to have done it. They are in. They are going ahead. I think anyone who has a tendency to write off the Concorde as a lot of flop is being very unrealistic. Its economics are considerably less than sensational but it will fly, it will fly well.'*

The PAC's fourth and final interim report to the president, emphasized the technical and economic superiority of the American SST, and observed that many aircraft development problems typically do not become apparent until the prototype stage. The PAC expected significant delays with Concorde, and predicted little performance improvement, given the aircraft's small engine thrust and resulting limited range. The committee also claimed that Concorde's estimated direct and total operating costs were, respectively, 25 percent and 15 percent higher than those of the American SST and were increasing rapidly,

In 1967, with the selection of the Boeing-General Electric swing-wing model as the American SST's design at the very end of 1966, the whole US decision-making structure for the SST programme began to change.

American designs begin to take shape.
A slimming down of the proposed models resulted in the NAC-60 and Curtiss-Wright efforts being dropped from the programme, with both Boeing and Lockheed asked to offer SST models meeting the more demanding FAA requirements and able to use either of the remaining engine designs. In November, another design review was held, and by this time Boeing had scaled

Air Vehicle Two demonstrates very graphically Bernoulli's principle whereby condensation becomes visible over the upper surface of a wing caused by a pressure drop due to air acceleration over the upper surface as it comes in to land at Edwards AFB. It sounds highly technical, but looks absolutely amazing! *(USAF)*

One more landing at Edwards by AV 1, with three braking 'chutes streaming. *(USAF)*

up the original design into a 250-seat model, the Model 733-290. Due to concerns about jet blast, the four engines were moved to a position underneath an enlarged tailplane. When the wings were in their swept-back position, they merged with the tailplane to give a delta-wing planform.

Both companies were now asked for considerably more detailed proposals, to be presented for final selection in 1966. When this occurred, Boeing's design was now the 300-seat Model 733-390. Both the Boeing and Lockheed L-2000 designs were presented in September 1966 along with full-scale mock-ups. A lengthy review followed, and on December 31, 1966, Boeing was announced as the winner. The design would be powered by the General Electric GE4/J5 engines. Lockheed's L-2000 was judged simpler to produce and less risky, but its performance was slightly lower and its noise levels slightly higher.

The SST mock-up included both overhead storage for smaller items with restraining nets, as well as large drop-in bins between sections of the aircraft. In the main 247-seat tourist-class cabin, the entertainment system consisted of retractable televisions placed between every sixth row in the overhead storage. In the 30-seat first-class area, every pair of seats included smaller televisions in a console between the seats. Windows were only six inches due to the high altitudes the aircraft flew at maximizing the pressure on them, but the internal pane was twelve inches to give an illusion of size.

Boeing predicted that if the go-ahead were given, construction of the SST prototypes would begin in early 1967 and the first flight could be made in early 1970. Production aircraft could start being built in early 1969, with the flight testing in late 1972 and certification by mid-1974.

The PAC did not formally meet again after December 1966. SST decisions now became more programmatic, centering on relations with contractors and on technical problems - especially on the fact that the winning swing-wing design was not economic and on the two-year reassessment by Boeing resulting in the firm selecting a new fixed-wing SST design in 1969. High level and wide-ranging policy discussions on such issues as overall design selection, the sonic boom, economic performance, and project financing were infrequent. In the same vein American officials began to view the Concorde more passively, and discussions about the Concorde threat diminished considerably. The FAA continued to monitor the Concorde's development, but the intelligence effort became less focused and more irregular and the CIA's role diminished. In addition, the

Taken from one of the chase aircraft, 62-0001 with the wingtips in the mid-way position banks away from the camera. The picture was from the days in service with NASA. *(USAF)*

usefulness of the raw intelligence on foreign SST programs from the CIA and the State Department was questionable, since this data usually added little to what was already know publicly.

The first Concorde prototype was unveiled on 11 December 1967 at Toulouse, France. In the US, the FAA and its SST contractors worked strenuously to counter the resulting publicity from the unveiling. Boeing contacted twenty media people in Washington, DC - including representatives from the Washington dailies, the three major television networks. *Time, Newsweek,* and the *Wall Street Journal* - to supply them with background information and a picture of the newly designed American SST.

The SST project continued, but the negative publicity associated with the tests and spiralling costs brought the cancellation of the Boeing 2707 project and led to the United States' complete withdrawal from SST design.

In March 1971, despite the project's strong support by the administration of President Richard Nixon, the US Senate rejected further funding. A counter-attack was organized under the banner of the 'National Committee for an American SST', which urged supporters to send in $1 to keep the programme alive. Afterward, letters of support from aviation buffs, containing nearly $1 million worth of contributions, poured in. Labor unions also supported the SST project, worried that the winding down of both the Vietnam War and Project Apollo would lead to mass unemployment in the aviation sector. The President of the American Federation of Labor and Congress of Industrial Organizations, George Meany suggested that the race to develop a first-generation SST was already lost, but the US should '*...enter the competition for the second generation —the SSTs of the 1980s and 1990s*'.

In spite of this new found support, Congress also voted to end SST funding on 20 May 1971.

The XB-70 had played an important part in doing a lot of the groundwork for the American SST - but politics and back-stabbing ensured that it really was a Mach-number too far.

RETIREMENT

The final B-70 flight, NASA Flight 23, was scheduled for an 08:00 departure on 22 January 1969. This was delayed until 4 February for work on exciter vane and its associated sensors.

Then at 10:57 on 4 February, the last surviving B-70 rotated and climbed up and away from what had been its home for four years and five months, Edwards AFB. Its destination was the U.S. Air Force Museum at Wright-Patterson AFB near Dayton, Ohio.

Two of its seven pilots, Fitz Fulton and Ted Sturmthal, commanded it on its last flight. Even on that final flight, the XB-70A recorded flight research data; shaker/exciter vane and ILAF data was recorded during the three hour and 18 minute flight. The 1,880-statute mile trip was flown at .91 Mach subsonic cruise at 33,000 feet. No supersonic dash occurred. Prior to its final landing it made a farewell pass low over the field. At 14:15 it touched down, popped its drag chutes, rolled out its momentum, and stopped. It then taxied behind a follow-me vehicle to where instructed and shut down.

In the ceremony that followed, pilot Fulton turned over its logbook to the museum's curator. Then he and copilot Sturmthal walked toward the awaiting crew van. If either sneaked a look back, they never told anyone.

Valkyrie Number One had carried on boldly since its sister ship had perished. This was its 83rd flight and its logbook showed a total flight time of 160 hours and 18 minutes. Considering the total cost of the B-70 programme to industry and the Air Force - $1.7 billion - it cost about $13.1 million per flight—that is, considering two XB-70A air vehicles, flying 129 times.

It was this staggering cost that may have prompted Ted Sturmthal to say: *'I'd*

'Fitz' Fulton leads Ted Sturmthal climbing the ladder and into the cockpit of 62-0001 for the last time. The exciter vane installed for the last flight is clearly visible. *(NAA Rockwell)*

The arrival at Wright-Patterson AFB from Edwards on 4 February 1969. After handing over the log-book, the crew walked away. Little did anyone realise that the aircraft would remain outside in the harsh Ohio climate for nineteen years. *(NAA Rockwell)*

do anything to keep the B-70 in the air—except pay for it myself.

The aircraft was placed on outdoor display at Wright-Patterson's Area C, where the U.S. Air Force Museum was then located, adjacent to the city of Fairborn. It soon became a major attraction, drawing visitors from far and wide.

The XB-70 did not remain in place for very long, for in June 1970, construction of a new facility for the museum began at a site about five miles away, on one of Wright Field's now unused runways. In October and November of 1970, well before the new building was completed, the XB-70 and thirty-seven of the museum's other aircraft were towed off the base from the old museum at Patterson Field, along local and state roads and freeways, to the new museum at Wright Field. The route covered some eight miles, crossing over load-limited bridges, under height-limiting power lines, and between span-limiting poles and other obstacles.

Moving the XB-70 over this route presented the greatest challenge of all. The Valkyrie's length needed to be considered, but its 105-foot wingspan was of great concern. The aircraft's height also had to be factored into the move, but this was helped by the removal of the twin verticals. Weight was the most serious problem

The move from Wright-Patterson AFB to Wright Field was fraught with problems. Signs and wires had to be moved and the aircraft weight reduced by almost half to allow it to go over Route 444 Bridge near Mad River. The problems here were compounded by only an eight-inch clearance between curb and main wheels!
(both USAF Museum)

– the XB-70 had an empty weight of 262,000 pounds, well above the allowable load for the freeway bridge it had to be towed across to reach the new museum site. Removal of the six engines, the air conditioning system, and practically everything else that could be taken out reduced the Valkyrie's weight to around 147,000 pounds, which was within the design limits of the bridge.

Eventually, the aircraft reached its new parking area and was proudly on display when the newly completed US Air Force Museum facility was dedicated in September 1971.

The XB-70 was destined to remain there on outdoor display for another seventeen years. Over time the machine took on the role of US Air Force Museum logo, parked as it was facing the museum's access road. On two occasions it was repainted and each time inspections by the museum's restoration division staff noted some degree of deterioration and delamination.

Air Vehicle 1 gets close to the new Air Force Museum site - Route 444 does not often see traffic like this! *(USAF Museum)*

Moves, bubbles, blisters and dings

The most notable deterioration was where certain areas on the fuselage and underside showed evidence of spot delamination of the stainless steel honeycomb skin panels.

This delamination has been characterized by bubble-like 'blisters' on the fuselage around the wing apex and similar blisters on the bottom of the main centre section. Certainly it is true that the delamination process did not begin with the XB-70 s retirement to the US Air Force Museum, for as we have already seen, some delamination occurred during the flight testing programme. However, given that the aircraft was parked outside in an environment that has an annual temperature gradient of -20° F to well over 100° F for nineteen years, it is not surprising that the deterioration was gradual, but progressive.

This deterioration was not helped by the fact that even after the aircraft was

62-0001 is towed along Ohio Route 444 past the historic Huffman Dam. *(USAF Museum)*

XB-70A valkyrie 62-0001 poses nose-to-nose with the Rockwell B-1A *(USAF Museum)*

supposedly permanently installed in the Museum's second major exhibits building - dubbed the Modern Flight Hangar - it was still subject to a series of moves over the years and as anyone involved in aircraft preservation knows - aircraft moves increases the likelihood of hangar rash!

Whenever the aircraft was stripped and repainted it had to be taken off display and moved to another area where the work could be done in safety away from the public. When the job was complete, the XB-70 was towed to a special area for update photography, then back to the display area - a round trip of about two miles. Shortly after the museum acquired the Rockwell B-1A it was again towed to the photography area and posed nose-to-nose with the B-l before being moved back again to the display position in front of the museum.

Also, the year-to-year reposition of outdoor display aircraft forced other moves of the XB-70. Each time that the aircraft was moved, extreme care and a large, heavy-duty tug were required and the landing gear had to be positioned on steel plates to prevent the wheels from sinking into the tarmac. During one such move, a tyre on a main gear wheel caught the edge of one of the steel plates and blew out. Fortunately, no one was hurt.

Before the Modern Flight Hangar could be opened to the public, a great deal of preparation and shuffling of aircraft took place. Before the XB-70 went into the Modern Flight Hangar, it was towed to the restoration hangar for some routine maintenance. As the aircraft entered the restoration hangar, the movement crew heard a loud bang, followed by the frightening sight of numerous metal shards falling from the nose gear well. After giving the area an inspection, the crew concluded that a metal conduit support had fractured but posed no structural integrity problem.

The Valkyrie was towed into the north end of the display hangar nose first. On the first attempt it was discovered that her twin tails were about two inches too tall to clear the hangar door opening. Rather than resort to the removal of the vertical tails, the restoration crew doing the moving found a simpler solution: deflate the main gear struts and fully inflate the nose gear strut. That pushed up the nose and lowered the tail, which allowed more than an inch of tail clearance to tow the airplane into display position.

Over the next few years, the XB-70 was temporarily moved outdoors several times so that additional aircraft could be pulled into the Modern Flight Hangar. Always, it was returned to its prominent display area in the north end of the hangar. Interestingly enough, after the airplane was safely installed in the Modern

Flight Hangar, several groups of XB-70 buffs suddenly became interested in the aircraft's state of preservation and began to express to the museum their concerns regarding the delamination problem, much to the Museum's annoyance.

The standard answer given out over the years by Museum staff, and reiterated in Joe Ventolo Jnr and Jeanette Remak's 1998 book *XB-70 Valkyrie The Ride to Valhalla* is that the honeycomb construction is extremely strong and a few flaws would not be significant. Besides, the AV 1 had only the first in a series of refinements of the honeycomb construction processes. No, the Valkyrie was absolutely not going to come apart despite a few popped lamination bonds.

This I would seriously question, for a number of reasons. Firstly, the XB-70 was not known as 'Cecil the sea-sick sea serpent' for nothing. Look at any video of the aircraft moving and you can clearly see the nose of the aircraft bouncing up and down at exactly the same time as the aircraft nose wheels cross over joints in the concrete taxiways. Not only does it move at the same time, the movement is magnified by the lever-arm moment of the entire structure above and ahead of the nose wheel, which is acting as a fulcrum. The further away from the pivot-point (the nose wheel) the greater the movement.

This is just simple high school physics of fulcrums. A fulcrum, or pivot point, is the area around which a lever turns. For it to work, there are two distances - 'levers'- away from the pivot point - one long, one short. A lever is a length - or distance used to put out force or maintain weight at one end, while pressure is exerted on its second end. Think of a crowbar used to move a large rock - move the end of the crowbar the furthest away from the rock and it moves a long way compared to the end touching the rock, but in reducing the amount of movement, the force applied is magnified.

A line of delamination blisters just below horizontal of the fuselage cross section of 62-0001 in the National Museum of the USAF at Dayton Ohio in 2001.

The area shown in the photograph is about fifteen feet long, spread either side of the front fuselage join - each blister scales to an area about twelve inches square - somewhat more than *'a few popped lamination bonds'* I think!
(author)

Clearly North American expected problems with delamination of the stainless steel honeycomb, for this is just one of the approved 'repairs' to the stainless steel honeycomb panels using doublers, a plug and welded pins. *(North American Rockwell)*

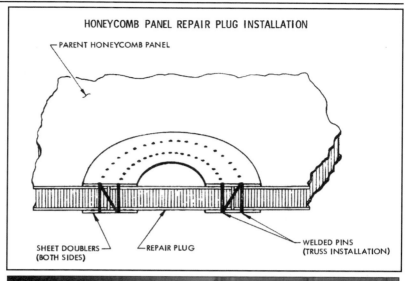

HONEYCOMB PANEL REPAIR PLUG INSTALLATION

PARENT HONEYCOMB PANEL

SHEET DOUBLERS
(BOTH SIDES)

REPAIR PLUG

WELDED PINS
(TRUSS INSTALLATION)

Another view of the same delaminated area, this time looking up from underneath, which gives a better idea as to how 'high' each blister is.

In recent years aviation museums in Great Britain - in particular the de Havilland Heritage Centre - have undertaken a programme of ultrasonically testing their laminated and/or composite aircraft structures to better determine 'what is going on' inside them. The DH Heritage Centre were surprised at their discoveries - I do not know if the XB-70 has been so tested, but if so, I would love to see the results! *(author)*

The same applies to the unsupported end of the nose of the XB-70. Move the nose-tip a great distance by bumping the aircraft over hangar door sills, drain covers, over joints in concrete slabs, and a smaller movement but greatly magnified force is applied to the other end - in this case the area around and above the centre-section at the apex of the wing-box. Any force applied to what is basically a fixed structure - even if the aircraft is at rest - is translated into 'stress' - and stress will always seek out the weakest point of any given structure.

The area of the fuselage in the vicinity of the apex of the wing-box is basically circular in cross-section. This means that the unsupported nose is 'hanging off' this area - therefore the top of the cross-section in this zone is under tension, and the bottom under compression. The forces feeding back from the nose will tend to want to 'push out' the structure at the horizontal part of the structure, which is exactly where a long line of delamination blisters can be seen.

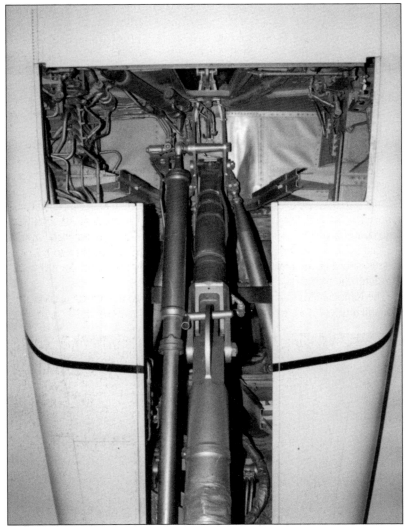

During a September 1992 visit to the Museum I was 'tipped off' that there had been problems discovered in the nose wheel bay.

Surreptitiously I took this photograph by flash looking 'straight up' into the nose wheel bay. I still cannot see any damage, but I have been assured it is there!

(author)

Another problem generated by years of outdoor display and miles of towing for one reason or another caused a great deal of wear and tear on the Valkyrie's tyres. Not long after the XB-70 moved indoors, all ten tyres were replaced with a set of spares received with the aircraft. Each was filled with a urethane rubber compound to eliminate the need to service them regularly with high-pressure air. This process also completely eliminated the risk of any tyre having a high pressure blow-out.

The next problem to strike the aircraft occurred in 1992, when the US Air Force Museum was to receive a temporary but very large exhibit of former Soviet space hardware and required more than the 20,000 square feet occupied by the XB-70. It was planned that the XB-70 would be moved from the Modern Flight Hangar and put back outdoors again for the six or eight months the Soviet Space Exhibit would be in place. Just prior to moving the XB-70 out of the hangar, however, the nose gear well area where the supposedly fractured conduit support had been noted several years earlier was given a further inspection. Far from being a broken conduit support, what had actually fractured was the nose gear drag brace support bracket. Aircraft structures engineers who looked at the damage believed that any further movement whatsoever of the XB-70 could result in collapse of the nose gear. It was a miracle that the gear had not collapsed during one of the earlier moves of while the aircraft was on display. Immediately, a jack pad was affixed to the fuselage jack point forward of the wing apex, and a large hydraulic jack stand was put in place. Other aircraft made way for the Soviet Space Exhibit, but the Valkyrie could not be moved again until repairs were made.

The repairs took nearly a year. Meanwhile, the jack under the XB-70 s forward fuselage was turned into a display item with the addition of a mannequin clad in a North American maintenance technicians coveralls. The broken bracket was removed, measured, and replaced. The new bracket was check fitted, then heat treated, and finally reinstalled. Although the new bracket was not airworthy, it was said by its replicators to be stronger than the original and able to take the stresses of towing. Interestingly enough, the Valkyrie was not moved for nearly five years after the repair.

The National Museum of the US Air Force still move the aircraft around, the nose still unsupported. Whenever I get over to see it, I'm never quite sure where

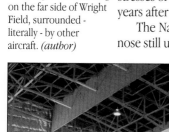

62-0001 inside the R&D/Flight Test building on the far side of Wright Field, surrounded - literally - by other aircraft. *(author)*

to look. At the time of writing, 'Cecil' is in the Research & Development/Flight Test Gallery away from the main museum, located on the controlled-access portion of Wright-Patterson Air Force Base, accessible using the shuttle bus service from the main museum complex.

Nose seeking out the sun and air - XB-70 62-0001 looks out of the R&D Hangar at Wright Field.
(author)

The North American XB-70A Valkyrie was and is a legend. It is a priceless piece of aeronautical engineering and a work of art.

As a manned bomber, the B-70 died in infancy without the opportunity to prove its worth, overtaken by the progress for which the B-70 itself had become a symbol. The B-70 was a watershed project covering many years of major development, tens of millions of man hours, and nearly two billion dollars.

It was, more than anything, killed off by one man - Robert Strange McNamara. He killed the B-70, just as he was the main instigator in killing off the American supersonic transport project. Mack the Knife is gone now yet the last unique, futuristic B-70 can be found sitting in that R&D hangar at Wright Field, looking longingly towards the sunlight.

'Cecil the sea-sick sea serpent' still looks like it's going supersonic!

XB-70A FLIGHT TEST LOG

Flt No.	A/C Flt.No.	Date	Time Flt	Total	Altitude (feet)	Flight Crew (1P/2P)	Max Speed Mach No.	Supersonic Flt	Total	Mach 2+ Flt	Total	Mach 3 Flt	Total	Remarks
1	1-01	21-9-64	1:07	1:07	16,000	White/Cotton	0.50	-	-	-	-	-	-	1st flt of AV/1 Start of Phase 1.
2	1-02	5-10-64	0:55	2:02	28,000	White/Cotton	0.85	-	-	-	-	-	-	Emergency landing on Rogers Dry Lake.
3	1-03	12-10-64	1:35	3:37	35,400	White/Cotton	1.11	0:15	0:15	-	-	-	-	1st Mach 1 flight.
4	1-04	24-10-64	1:25	5:02	46,300	White/Cotton	1.42	0:40	0:55	-	-	-	-	Ret.to Palmdale for static tests. End of Phase 1.
5	1-05	16-2-65	1:10	6:12	45,000	White/Cotton	1.60	0:40	1:35	-	-	-	-	AV 1 began Phase 2. A/C landed at Edwards AFB.
6	1-06	25-2-65	0:53	7:05	35,000	White/Fulton	0.97	-	1:35	-	-	-	-	Fulton's 1st flt.
7	1-07	4-3-65	1:37	8:42	50,200	White/Fulton	1.85	1:00	2:35	-	-	-	-	Env. expansion.
8	1-08	24-3-65	1:40	10:22	56,100	White/Shepard	2.14	1:14	3:49	0:40	0:40	-	-	Shepard's 1st flt. 1st double-sonic flt.
9	1-09	2-4-65	0:54	11:16	34,500	White/Cotton	0.95	-	3:49	-	0:40	-	-	Abbreviated flt.
10	1-10	20-4-65	1:42	12:58	58,500	White/Cotton	2.30	1:14	5:03	0:50	1:30	-	-	Env. expansion.
11	1-11	28-4-65	1:43	14:41	64,300	White/Shepard	2.45	1:16	6:19	0:57	2:27	-	-	Cont.env. expansion
12	1-12	7-5-65	1:25	16:06	65,000	White/Fulton	2.60	0:58	7:17	0:33	3:00	-	-	Cont. env. expansion.
13	1-13	16-6-65	1:37	17:43	65,000	White/Cotton	2.60	1:15	8:32	0:50	3:50	-	-	Cont.env. expansion.
14	1-14	1-7-65	1:44	19:27	68.000	White/Shepard	2.85	1:19	9:51	0:50	4:40	-	-	Env.expansion to near tri-sonic speed to meet M3 design speed.
15	2-1	17-7-65	1:13	1:13	42,000	White/Cotton	1.41	0:21	0:21	-	-	-	-	1st flt of AV2. Start of Phase 1.
16	1-15	27-7-65	1:43	21:10	66,000	White/Fulton	2.82	1:05	10:56	0:43	5:23	-	-	Preparation for M3 flt.
17	2-2	10-8-65	1:27	2:40	41,000	Cotton/White	1.45	0:31	0:52	-	-	-	-	Cotton's first flight as 1st pilot.
18	2-3	18-8-65	1:58	4:38	46,000	Shepard/White	1.45	0:44	1:36	-	-	-	-	Shepard's first flight as 1st pilot.
19	2-4	20-8-65	2:04	6:42	42,000	Fulton/White	1.44	0:41	2:17	-	-	-	-	Fulton''s first flight as 1st pilot.
20	2-5	17-9-65	1:55	8:37	50,500	White/Fulton	1.83	1:00	3:17	-	-	-	-	Env. expansion
21	1-16	22-9-65	1:57	23:07	67,000	White/Cotton	2.83	1:17	12:13	0:56	6:19	-	-	Final rehearsal for M3 flt.
22	2-6	29-9-65	1:44	10:21	54,000	White/Shepard	2.23	0:32	3:49	0:05	0:05	-	-	first double-sonic flt for AV 2
23	2-7	5-10-65	1:40	12:01	55,000	White/Shepard	2.30	0:31	4:20	0:09	0:14	-	-	Env. expansion
24	2-8	11-10-65	1:55	13:56	57,500	White/Shepard	2.34	1:18	5:38	0:53	1:07	-	-	Env. expansion
25	1-17	14-10-65	1:47	24:54	70,000	White/Cotton	3+	1:10	13:23	0:46	7:05	0:02	0:02	Design goal of AV 1, M3 at 70,000 ft.
26	2-9	16-10-65	1:43	15:39	59,500	White/Fulton	2.43	1:12	6:50	0:47	1:54	-	-	Env. expansion
27	2-10	20-10-65	2:07	17:45	59,000	White/Fulton	2.46	1:11	8:01	0:43	2:37	-	-	Env. expansion
28	2-11	2-11-65	1:54	19:40	59,000	White/Cotton	2.45	1:20	9:21	0:46	3:23	-	-	Env. expansion
29	1-18	4-11-65	2:04	26:58	46,000	Fulton/White	1.86	1:17	14:40	-	7:05	-	0:02	System evaluations
30	1-19	8-11-65	2:23	29:21	45,500	Cotton/White	1.89	0:46	15:26	-	7:05	-	0:02	System evaluations
31	1-20	12-11-65	2:25	31:46	46,000	Shepard/White	1.84	0:36	16:02	-	7:05	-	0:02	Increased endurance.
32	1-21	18-11-65	2:02	33:48	47,000	Cotton/Shepard	1.88	0:50	16:52	-	7:05	-	0:02	First flt without White.

Flt No.	A/C Flt.No.	Date	Time Flt	Time Total	Altitude (feet)	Flight Crew (1P/2P)	Max Speed Mach No.	Supersonic Flt	Supersonic Total	Mach 2+ Flt	Mach 2+ Total	Mach 3 Flt	Mach 3 Total	Remarks
33	2-12	29-11-65	2:19	21:59	15,200	White/Fulton	0.53	-	9:21	-	3:23	-	-	Low speed tests with landing gear down.
34	1-22	30-11-65	1:59	35:47	56,000	Fulton/White	2.34	1:12	8:04	0:53	7:58	-	0:02	Systems evaluations.
35	2-13	1-12-65	2:02	24:01	64,000	White/Fulton	2.67	1:24	10:45	0:59	4:22	-	-	Env. expansion
36	1-23	2-12-65	1:51	37:38	60,000	Cotton/White	2.46	1:22	19:26	0:34	8:32	-	0:02	Systems evaluations
37	2-14	3-12-65	1:55	25:56	69,000	White/Cotton	2.87	1:14	11:59	0:51	5:13	-	-	Prep for M3 flt.
38	1-24	7-12-65	2:26	40:04	62,000	Shepard/Fulton	2.45	0:40	20:06	0:22	8:54	-	0:02	Systems evaluations
39	1-25	10-12-65	2:18	42:22	50,700	Fulton/Shepard	1.82	0:55	21:01	-	8:54	-	0:02	Systems evaluations
40	2-15	11-12-65	2:03	27:59	70,600	White/Shepard	2.94	1:16	13:15	0:53	6:06	-	-	Pre-M3 attempt.
41	1-26	14-12-65	2:10	44:32	20,000	Shepard/Fulton	0.95	-	21:01	-	0:54	-	0:02	Low speed handling characteristics test.
42	1-27	20-12-65	1:58	46:30	42,000	Cotton/White	1.78	1:11	22:12	-	8:54	-	0:02	Climb schedule test.
43	2-16	21-12-65	1:49	29:48	72,000	White/Cotton	2.95	1:20	14:35	1:02	7:08	-	-	Pre-M3 attempt.
44	1-28	22-12-65	2:35	49:05	34,000	Shepard/Cotton	1.42	0:14	22:26	-	8:54	-	0:02	Systems evaluations.
45	2-17	3-1-66	1:52	31:40	72,000	White/Cotton	3.05	1:22	15:57	1:06	8:14	0:03	0:03	Design goals of AV/2, M3 at 70,000 ft
46	1-29	3-1-66	2:41	51:46	26,000	Fulton/Shepard	0.94	-	22:26	-	8:54	-	0:02	Stability and control.
47	1-30	6-1-66	3:40	55:26	33,000	Shepard/Fulton	0.94	-	22:26	-	8:54	-	0:02	Subsonic cruise and environmental tests.
48	1-31	11-1-66	1:35	57:01	46,000	Fulton/Shepard	1.85	0:46	3:12	-	8:54	-	0:02	Performance and propulsion tests.
49	1-32	11-1-66	0:58	57:59	27,000	Cotton/White	0.95	-	23:12	-	8:54	-	0:02	Hydraulic pressure lost during flight.
50	2-18	12-1-66	1:46	33:28	72,000	White/Cotton	3.06	1:24	17:21	1:03	9:17	0:04	0:07	M3 perf at 70,000 ft and AICS tests.
51	1-33	15-1-66	1:27	59:26	47,000	Fulton/White	1.85	0:50	24:02	-	8:54	-	0:02	Propulsion, stability and control tests.
52	2-19	7-2-66	2:11	35:39	42,000	Shepard/Cotton	1.44	1:03	18:24	-	9:17	-	0:07	Propulsion, stability and control tests.
53	2-20	9-2-66	1:49	37:28	70,800	White/Cotton	3.04	1:09	19:33	0:48	10:05	0:05	0:12	Duct unstart, restart at M3.
54	2-21	16-2-66	3:06	40:34	32,000	White/Cotton	1.10	0:02	9:35	-	10:05	-	0:12	Airspeed calibration and other tests.
55	2-22	17-2-66	1:47	42:21	73,000	White/Cotton	3.04	1:23	20:58	1:05	11:10	0:15	0:27	M3 at 70,000 ft: landed with No. 4 engine shut down.
56	1-34	26-2-66	2:22	61:48	20,000	Shepard/Fulton	0.92	-	24:02	-	8:54	-	0:02	Propulsion, stability and control tests.
57	1-35	3-3-66	2:42	64:30	15,000	Fulton/Shepard	0.55	-	24:02	-	8:54	-	0:02	Tuft survey, stability and control tests.
58	1-36	4-3-66	2:27	66:57	56,000	Fulton/Shepard	2.02	0:48	24:50	0:12	9:06	-	0:02	AICS, stability and control tests.
59	1-37	7-3-66	2:19	69:16	67,000	Shepard/Cotton	2.22	1:02	25:52	0:16	9:22	-	0:02	U1 and U2 hydraulic failure; emergency landing.
60	2-23	10-3-66	1:56	44:17	67,000	White/Fulton	2.76	1:25	22:23	0:54	12:04	-	0:27	High-perf duct evaluation at M2.7.
61	2-24	15-3-66	1:59	46:16	69,500	White/Fulton	2.85	1:33	23:56	1:11	13:15	-	0:27	37 minutes at M2.8
62	2-25	17-3-66	1:52	48:08	70,350	Fulton/White	2.85	1:27	25:23	1:09	14:24	-	0:27	AICS, stability and control tests.
63	2-26	19-3-66	1:57	50:05	74,000	White/Shepard	2.93	1:30	26:53	1:10	5:34	-	0:27	33 minutes at M2.9; highest altitude flt.
64	1-38	22-3-66	2:11	71:27	32,000	Cotton/Shepard	0.97	-	25.52	-	9:22	-	0:02	Perf, stability and control tests.
65	2-27	24-3-66	1:32	51.37	64,000	Fulton/White	2.71	0:47	27:40	0:29	16:03	-	0:27	Perf and ferry flight

Flt No.	A/C Flt.No.	Date	Time Flt	Time Total	Altitude (feet)	Flight Crew (1P/2P)	Max Speed Mach No.	Supersonic Flt	Supersonic Total	Mach 2+ Flt	Mach 2+ Total	Mach 3 Flt	Mach 3 Total	Remarks
66	1-39	24-3-66	2:00	73:27	60,000	Shepard/Cotton	2.42	1:06	27:58	0:21	9:43	-	0:02	to Carswell AFB, Texas. Encapsulated descent test, AICS tests.
67	2-28	36-3-66	3:09	54:46	36,000	Cotton/White	0.94	-	27:40	-	16:03	-	0:27	Return to Edwards from Carswell AFB.
68	1-40	28-3-66	1:41	75:08	65,000	Shepard/Cotton	2.43	1:21	28:19	0:32	10:15	-	0:02	AICS, propulsion tests.
69	2-29	29-3-66	1:51	56:37	48,000	Shepard/White	1.65	1:25	29:05	-	16:03		0:27	Perf. tests.
70	2-30	31-3-66	2:10	58:47	72,000	Shepard/White	2.95	1:20	30:25	1:02	17:05	-	0:27	32 minutes at M2.9.
71	1-41	1-4-66	2:09	77:17	58,800	White/Fulton	2.45	1:15	29:34	0:20	10:35	-	0:02	Perf. tests.
72	2-31	4-4-66	1:57	60:44	73,000	Cotton/White	2.95	1:30	31:55	1:09	18:14	-	0:27	31 minutes at M2.9 and above.
73	1-42	5-4-66	2:01	79:18	61,000	Fulton/Shepard	2.43	1:12	30:46	0:48	11:23	-	0:02	Perf. tests.
74	2-32	8-4-66	2:05	62:49	73,000	Fulton/White	3.07	1:09	33:04	0:50	19:04	0:16	0:43	16 minutes at M3.0
75	2-33	12-4-66	1:49	64:38	72,800	White/Cotton	3.08	1:17	34:21	0:53	19:57	0:20	1:03	Highest speed attained, 20 minutes at M3.0.
76	1-43	13-4-66	2:03	81:21	62,500	Shepard/Cotton	2.60	1:05	31:51	0:47	12:10	-	0:02	Perf. tests.
77	2-34	16-4-66	2:01	66:39	71,000	White/Cotton	3.03	1:03	35:24	0:43	20:40	0:01	1:04	Tuft survey; Perf. tests.
78	1-44	19-4-66	2:12	83:33	17,000	Shepard/Fulton	0.58	-	31:51	-	12:10	-	0:02	low speed perf. tests.
79	1-45	21-4-66	2:02	85:35	61,000	Shepard/Fulton	2.42	1:20	33:11	0:59	13:09	-	0:02	Perf. tests.
80	2-35	23-4-66	2:01	68:40	66,000	White/Cotton	2.73	1:22	36:46	1:01	21:41	-	1:04	AICS unstart tests.
81	1-46	25-4-66	2:07	87:42	63,000	Fulton/Shepard	2.55	1:12	34:23	0:52	14:01	-	0:02	Perf. tests.
82	2-36	426-4-66	2:05	70:45	65,500	Fulton/Cotton	2.65	1:17	38:03	0:50	22:31	-	1:04	Perf. tests.
83	1-47	27-4-66	2:41	90:23	31,000	White/Fulton	1.50	0:08	34:31	-	14:01	-	0:02	Perf. tests.
84	2-37	30-4-66	2:16	73:01	16,000	White/Cotton	0.55	-	38:03	-	22:31	-	1:04	Nose gear jammed into door during retraction, gear re-extended using paper clip: emergency landing.
85	1-48	3-5-66	1:22	91:45	23,000	White/Fulton	0.55	-	34:31	-	14:01	-	0.02	landing gear failed to retract due to U2 leak.
86	1-49	9-5-66	2:16	94:01	15,000	White/Fulton	0.50	-	34:31	-	14:01	-	0:02	AICS and landling quality tests: landing gear extended on emergency electrical system.
87	2-38	16-5-66	2:09	75:10	65,000	White/Cotton	2.73	1:11	39:14	0:46	23:17	-	1:04	Perf. tests.
88	2-39	19-5-66	1:59	77:09	72,500	White/Cotton	3.06	1:31	40:45	1:13	24:30	0:33	1:37	Sustained M3 for 32 minutes.
89	2-40	22-5-66	2:22	79:31	36,500	Fulton/Cotton	1.51	0:25	41:10	-	24:30	-	0:37	Perf. tests.
90	2-41	25-5-66	2:23	81:54	42,000	Shepard/Cotton	1.63	0:49	41:59	-	24:30	-	0:37	Perf. tests.
91	2-42	27-5-66	2:08	84:02	62,000	Shepard/Cotton	2.53	1:17	42:16	:39	25:09	-	0:37	Perf. tests.
92	2-43	31-5-66	2:02	86:04	57,000	Shepard/Fulton	2.25	1:12	43:28	0:22	25:31	-	0:37	Perf. tests.
93	2-44	4-6-66	2:05	88:09	70,000	Shepard/Cotton	2.93	1:20	44:48	0:54	26:25	-	0:37	Perf. tests at M2.9.
94	2-45	6-6-66	2:00	90:00	72,000	Shepard/Cotton	3.05	1:15	-	0:53	27:18	0:09	0:46	M3 perf. tests.
95	2-46	8-6-66	2:13	92:22	32.000	White/Cross	1.41	0:14	47:17	-	27:18	-	1.46	F-104 and AV/2 midair collsion.
96	1-50	3-11-66	2:00	6:01	61,000	Cotton/Fulton	2.10	0:35	35:06	0:12	14:13	-	0:02	NSBT
97	1-51	10-11-66	1:39	97:40	60,000	Fulton/Cotton	2.50	1:12	36:18	0:32	14:45	-	0:02	NSBT
98	1-52	23-11-66	1:38	99:18	61,000	Shepard/Cotton	2.51	1:06	37:24	0:22	15:07	-	0:02	NSBT
99	1-53	12-12-66	1:57	101:15	60,000	Fulton/Shepard	2.52	1:01	38:25	0:32	15:39	-	0:02	NSBT
100	1-54	16-12-66	1:54	103:09	60,300	Shepard/Fulton	2.55	1:01	39:26	0:27	16:06	-	0:02	NSBT

Flt No.	A/C Flt.No.	Date	Time Flt	Time Total	Altitude (feet)	Flight Crew (1P/2P)	Max Speed Mach No.	Supersonic Flt	Supersonic Total	Mach 2+ Flt	Mach 2+ Total	Mach 3 Flt	Mach 3 Total	Remarks
101	1-55	20-12-66	1:45	104:54	60,800	Cotton/Shepard	2.53	1:00	40:26	0:32	16:38	-	0:02	NSBT
102	1-56	4-1-67	1:44	106:38	60,400	Fulton/Shepard	2.53	0:57	41:23	0:35	17:13	-	0:02	NSBT
103	1-57	13-1-67	1:46	108:24	61,000	Cotton/Fulton	2.57	1:00	42:23	0:38	17:51	-	0:02	NSBT
104	1-58	17-1-67	1:44	110:08	60,200	Cotton/Shepard	2.54	1:01	43:24	0:38	18:29	-	0:02	NSBT
105	1-59	25-1-67	1:32	111:40	35,000	Fulton/Shepard	1.41	0:51	44:15	-	18:29	-	0:02	NSBT
106	1-60	31-1-67	1:32	113:12	37,000	Fulton/Cotton	1.40	:49	45:04	-	18:29	-	0:02	NSBT
107	1-61	25-4-67	1:07	114:19	17,000	Cotton/Fulton	-	-	45:04	-	18:29	-	0:02	First NASA flight
108	1-62	12-5-67	2:18	116:37	6,500	Fulton/Cotton	-	-	45:04	-	18:29	-	0:02	NASA tests
109	1-63	2-6-67	2:23	119:00	42,000	Cotton/Shepard	1.43	0:42	45:46	-	18:29	-	0:02	NASA tests.
110	1-64	22-6-67	1:54	120:54	54,000	Fulton/Mallick	1.83	0:57	46:43	-	18:29	-	0:02	Mallick's first flight.
111	1-65	10-8-67	2:29	123:23	15,500	Cotton/Sturmthall	0.92	-	46:43	-	18:29	-	0:02	Sturmthall's first flight
112	1-66	24-8-67	1:52	125:17	58,000	Fulton/Mallick	2.27	0:56	47:39	0:23	18:52	-	0:02	NASA tests.
113	1-67	8-9-67	1:55	127:10	59,700	Cotton/Sturmthall	2.30	1:15	48:54	0:51	19:43	-	0:02	NASA tests.
114	1-68	11-10-67	1:39	128:49	58,000	Fulton/Mallick	2.43	1:11	50:05	0:47	20:30	-	0:02	NASA tests.
115	1-69	2-11-67	1:56	130:45	64,000	Cotton/Sturmthall	2.55	1:14	51:19	0:47	21:17	-	0:02	NASA tests.
116	1-70	12-1-68	1:54	132:39	67,000	Fulton/Mallick	2.55	1:01	52:20	0:42	21:59	-	0:02	NASA tests.
117	1-71	13-2-68	2:43	135:22	41,000	Mallick/Cotton Mallick as pilot.	1.18	0:16	52:36	-	21:59	-	0:02	First flight for
118	1-72	28-2-68	1:51	137:13	18,500	Fulton/Sturmthall	-	-	52:36	-	21:59	-	0:02	NASA tests.
119	1-73	21-3-68	2:32	139:45	15,500	Cotton/Fulton	-	-	52:36	-	21:59	-	0:02	NASA tests.
120	1-74	11-6-68	1:11	140:56	9,500	Mallick/Fulton	-	-	52:36	-	21:59	-	0:02	NASA
121	1-75	28-6-68	2:39	143:35	39,400	Sturmthall/Cotton	1.23	0:18	52:54	-	21:59	-	0:02	First flight for Sturmthall as pilot.
122	1-76	19-7-68	1:55	145:30	42,000	Mallick/Fulton	1.62	0:48	53:42	-	21:59	-	0:02	NASA
123	1-77	16-8-68	1:55	147:25	63,000	Fulton/Sturmthall	2.47	0:55	54:37	0:34	22:33	-	0:02	NASA
124	1-78	10-9-68	1:48	149:13	63,000	Mallick/Fulton	2.54	1:04	55:41	0:35	23:08	-	0:02	NASA
125	1-79	18-10-68	1:56	151:09	52,000	Fulton/Sturmthall	2.18	0:54	56:35	0:13	23:21	-	0:02	NASA
126	1-80	1-11-68	2:08	153:17	41,000	Sturmthall/Fulton	1.62	0:48	57:23	-	23:21	-	0:02	NASA
127	1-81	3-12-68	1:58	155:15	39,400	Mallick/Fulton	1.64	0:56	58:19	-	23:21	-	0:02	NASA
128	1-82	17-12-68	1:45	157:00	63,500	Fulton/Sturmthall	2.53	1:12	59:31	0:55	24:16	-	0:02	NASA
129	1-83	4-2-69	3:16	160:16	29,000	Fulton/Sturmthall	0.92	-	59:31	-	24:16	-	0:02	Final flight of AV/1, landed at Wright-Patterson AFB.

Flight Log Statistics

XB-70 pilots in chronological order and number of flights as pilot and co-pilot:

Alvin White, NAA, 49 as pilot, 18 as co-pilot

Joseph Cotton, USAF, 19 as pilot, 43 as co-pilot

Van Shepard, NAA, 23 as pilot, 23 as co-pilot

Fitzhugh Fulton, USAF and NASA, 31 as pilot, 32 as co-pilot

Carl Cross, USAF, 1 as co-pilot

Donald Mallick, NASA, 4 as pilot, 5 as co-pilot

Emil Sturmthal, USAF, 3 as pilot, 7 as co-pilot

The fastest MPH flight was on 12 January 1966; the speed was 2,020 mph with White and Cotton as crew.

The fastest Mach flight was on 12 April 1966; it achieved Mach 3.08 with White and Cotton as crew.

The highest flight was on 19 March 1966; it attained 74,000 feet with White and Shepard as crew.

The total flight time was 252 hr and 38 min. The breakdown of flight time was:

Subsonic, 145 hr and 28 min.   Mach 1-2, 55 hr and 50 min.   Mach 2-3, 49 hr and 32 min.   Mach 3, 1 hr and 48 min.

ABBREVIATIONS

ADS	Accessory Drive System.
AMC	Air Materiel Command.
ACTS	Air Corps Tactical School.
AEDC	Arnold Engineering Development Center.
AICS	Air Inlet Control System .
ALBM	Air-Launched Ballistic Missiles.
ARDC	Air Research and Development Command.
AWPD	Air War Plans Division.
AFFTC	Air Force Flight Test Center.
AMPSS	Advanced Manned Penetrating Strategic System.
BLC	Boundary Layer Control.
BTU	British Thermal Unit.
CAF	Continental Air Force.
CBO	Combined Bomber Offensive.
CIA	Central Intelligence Agency.
CPB	Chemically Powered Bomber .
DEI	Development Engineering Inspection.
DoD	Department of Defense.
FY	Fiscal Year.
FOD	Foriegn Object Damage.
GHQ	General Headquarters.
GOR	General Operational Requirement.
HEF	High Energy Fuel.
IBM	International Business Machines.
IFF	Identification Friend or Foe.
ICBM	Intercontinental Ballistic Missile.
IOC	Initial Operational Capability.
JP	Jet Petroleum.
JCS	Joint Chiefs of Staff .
L/D	Lift/Drag.
LRL	Lawrence Radiation Laboratory.
M&TC	Mission and Traffic Control.

MAD	Mutually Assured Destruction
MBA	Masters of Business Administration
MPB	Missile Platform Bomber
NAA	North American Aircraft
NACA	National Advisory Committee on Aeronautics
NASA	National Aeronautics and Space Administration.
NORC	National Opinions Research Center.
NSBP	National Sonic Boom Program.
OP	Operational Plan.
OSS	Office of Strategic Services.
PPBS	Planning, Programming, and Budgeting System.
RAM	Radar Absorbant Material.
RBS	Recoverable Boost System.
RCS	Radar Cross-Section.
RFA	Request For Alterations.
RTD&E	Research, Test, Development and Evaluation.
SR	Study Requirement.
ST	Solution Treated.
SAC	Strategic Air Command.
SST	Supersonic Transport.
STA	Solution Treated and Aged.
SLAB	Subsonic Low Altitude Bomber.
TF-X	Tactical Fighter 'X'.
USAAC	United States Army Air Corps.
USAAF	United Sates Army Air Force.
USAF	United States Air Force.
VG	Variable Geometry.
VGH	Velocity - Gravity - Height (data recorder)
VSS	Soviet Air Force.
WS	Weapon System
WSPO	Weapon System Project Office

BIBLIOGRAPHY

A Thousand Days: John F. Kennedy in the White House. Arthur Scheslinger; Riverside Press/Houghton-Mifflin Co., 1965.

Aeroplane and Astronautics, magazine, London - 1958-1965

Aeroplane and Commerical Aviation; magazine, London 1965-1967

Aircraft Prototype and Technology Demonstration Symposium: XB-70 Technology Advancements North American Aviation Operations, , J. W Ross, and D. B. Rogerson. American Institute of Aeronautics and Astronautics, March 23-24, 1983.

Air Force Headquarters Air Research and Development, Vol III. Washington, D.C.: Office of Air Force History, Jan. 1, 1959.

Air Force Magazine. Air Force Association, Arlington, VA.

Air Transport Policy and National Security. J Thayer; University of North Carolina Press 1965.

America Is in Danger. Gen. Curtis E. LeMay, and Maj. Gen. Dale O. Smith. Funk & Wagnalls, 1968.

Analysis of Aircraft Structure Bruce K Donaldson; McGraw-Hill, 1990.

Assignment of High Priority to the Soviet Titanium Industry. Economic Intelligence Report Directorate of Intelligence, Central Intelligence Agency April 1964.

Astrophile Supplement, NASA Flight Research Center, XB-70 Research Aircraft, Flight Test Chronology, 1970.

Aviation Week & Space Technology. McGraw-Hill Companies, New York, NY.

Aviation Week and Space Technology magazine, McGraw-Hill, New York, N.Y.

B-70 Aircraft Study Final Report Volume I Space Division, North American Rockwell 4 April 1972.

B-70 Aircraft Study Final Report Volume II Space Division, North American Rockwell 4 April 1972.

B-70 Aircraft Study Final Report Volume III Space Division, North American Rockwell 4 April 1972.

B-70 Aircraft Study Final Report Volume IV Space Division, North American Rockwell 4 April 1972.

B-70 Program Status Report, USAF/SC, November 2, 1961.

B-70: State-of-the-Art Improver Part I." Iain Pike; Flight International, June 25, 1964.

B-70 Strategic Bomber Prototype Configuration, North American Aviation, Los Angeles, CA, January 11, 1960.

Balance of Terror (Nuclear Weapons and the Illusion of Security, 1945-1985). Edgar Bottom; Brown Press, 1986.

Blundering into Disaster: Surviving the first century of the Nuclear Age. Robert S. McNamara; Pantheon Books, 1986.

Bombers of the West. Bill Gunston; Charles Scribner's Sons 1973.

Clipped Wings: the American SST Conflict. Mel Horwitch; MIT Press, 1982.

Coming: The B-70 Jet; It's Half Plane, Half Spaceship. Jack Anderson, Parade Magazine, July 1958.

Danger and Survival—Choices about the Bomb in the First 50 Years. McGeorge Bundy; Random House, 1988.

Dark Eagles: A History of Top Secret U.S. Aircraft Programs. Curtis Peebles; Presidio Press, 1995.

Deep Black. William E Burrows; Berkeley Books, 1986.

Developmental Program Manual, XB-70A (Propulsion System), USAF, July 30, 1966.

Development of Airborne Armament, 1910-1961, (Historical Study) Historical Division, Office of Information, Aeronautical Systems Division (Air Force Systems Command), Wright-Patterson AFB, OH, October 1961.

Development of the XB-70 Propulsion System. Edward Freschel Jr. and Elbert S. Steel; North American Aviation, Los Angeles, CA, November 1965.

From Huffman Prairie to the Moon: The History of Wright-Patterson Air Force Base. Lois E Walker and Shelby E. Wickam; Hq. Wright- Patterson AFB, OH: Air Force Logistics Command, 1985.

Ground Support Equipment, North American Aviation, Los Angeles, CA, 1960.

In Retrospect: The Tragedy and Lessons of Vietnam, Robert S. McNamara with Brian VanDeMark.; Times Books, 1995.

Investigation of the B-70 Preparedness Program. Committee On Armed Services, U.S. Senate; 86th Congress,

2nd Session. U.S. Government Printing Office, Washington, D.C., 1960.

Iron Destinies/ Lost Opportunities: The Arms Race Between the USA and the USSR 1945-1987. Charles Morris; Harper Row, 1988.

Iron Eagle: The Turbulent Life of General Curtis LeMay. Thomas M Coffey; Crown Publishers, 1986.

JFK and Vietnam. John M Newman; Warner Books, 1996.

Jane's All the World's Aircraft, Mcgraw-Hill, New York, N.Y., 1966.

Lessons from the XB-70 as Applied to the Supersonic Transport. Fitzhugh Fulton Jr.; NASA Flight Research Center, Edwards AFB, October 1968.

Lockheed Aircraft Since 1913. René J.Francillon; Naval Institute Press, 1987.

Lockheed Martin's Skunk Works. Jay Miller; Midland Publishing, 1995.

Mayday: Eisenhower and the U-2 Affair. Michael R Beschloss.Harper Row, 1986.

Mission with LeMay: My Story. Gen. Curtis E. LeMay, with MacKinlay Kantor. Doubleday & Company, 1965.

New Evidence of the Soviet Supersonic Transport Intelligence Memorandum, Directorate of Intelligence, Central Intelligence Agency May 1967.

New Weapons-Old Politics: America's Procurement Muddle. Thomas L McNaughton; Brookings Institution, 1989.

North American Aviation, Inc. B-70 Research Program Objectives: TFD-65-575, 1965.

North American Aviation, Inc. The Recon-Strike B-70 Weapon System 'GO' Plan.1961.

North American XB-70: Half Airplane-Half Spacecraft. Parts One and Two, Thomas G Foxworth; Historical Aviation Album, Volume 7, 1969 and Volume 8, 1970.

Promise and Power: The Life and Times of Robert McNamara. Deborah Shapely; Little, Brown and Company, 1993.

Public Papers of the Presidents—John F. Kennedy, 1961-1963. U.S. Government Printing Office, 1963.

Safe, Secure, and Soaring—A History of the Federal Civil Aviation Administration Policy— 1967-1972, Richard Kent Jr. U.S. Department of Transportation, 1980.

Seven Decades of Progress: A Heritage of Aircraft Turbine Technology. Leonard A Dalquest, Eric R. Falk, et al./ ed. Aero Publishers, 1979.

Shield of Faith. B. Bruce Briggs; Simon and Schuster, 1988.

Skunk Works: A Personal Memoir of My Years at Lockheed. Ben R Rich and Leo Janos; Little, Brown and Company, 1994.

Soviet SST: The Techno-politics of the Tupolev-144. Howard Moon; Orion Books, 1989.

Structural Design of the XB-70. Richard L. Schleicher; North American Aviation, Inc., 1967.

The Air Force Museum. Dayton, OH: Nick P. Apple and Gene Gurney. The Central Printing Company, 1991.

The B-70 Valkyrie Story. Douglas L. Emmons; The United States Air Force Museum, 1980.

The Central Intelligence Agency and Overhead Reconnaissance - the U-2 and Oxcart Programs 1954-1974 Gregory W Pedlow and Donald E Welzenbach, Central Intelligence Agency

The CIA and the U-2 Program 1954-1974 Gregory W Pedlow and Donald E Welzenbach, Central Intelligence Agency 1998.

The collection of papers in the Air Force Flight Test Center History Office, Edwards AFB

The collection of papers in the NASA Dryden Flight Research Centre.

The collection of papers in the President John F Kennedy Library.

The collection of papers in the President Lyndon B Johnson Library.

The daily White House diary of President John F Kennedy.

The daily White House diary of President Lyndon B Johnson

The Development of Ballistic Missiles in the United States Air Force, 1945- 1960. Jacob Neufeld; Washington, D.C.: Office of Air Force History, 1990.

The Essence of Security: Reflections in Office. Robert S. McNamara; Harper and Row, 1968.

The Full Story of the 28 Seconds That Killed the XB-70. Keith Wheeler; Life Magazine, November 1966.

The Great White Bird. Steven Pace; Air Classics Quarterly Review, Challenge Publications Volume 4, Number 3; Fall 1977.

The Manned Missile: The Story of the B-70. Ed Rees; Sloan and Pearce, 1960.

The National Security Act: A Blueprint for the Congressional Role in Weapons Development." (A Case Study of the B-70 Bomber Program.) Dennis Sherman; University of Wisconsin, 1978.

The Office of the Secretary of the Air Force, 1947-1965. George M Watson; Center for Air Force History, 1993.

The Supersonic Transport Race: the European Side. Special Report, Weekly Review, Directorate of Intelligence, Central Intelligence Agency, March 1967.

The Thump of Disaster: Test Pilot Recalls 1966 Crash of the B-70 Bomber. Marvin Miles;The Los Angeles Times, 1966.

The U-2 Affair. David Wise and Thomas B. Ross; Random House, 1962.

The United States Air Force: A Turbulent History. Herbert Molloy Mason Jr. Mason/Carter, 1976.

The United States Air Force: Basic Documents on Roles and Missions. (Air Staff Historical Study.) Richard I Wolf; Office of Air Force History, 1987.

The War Profiteers. Richard Kaufman; Bobbs Merril Press, 1970.

The Whiz Kids: Ten founding fathers of American business—and the legacy They left us. John A Byrne; Doubleday, 1993.

Titanium Fabrication Technique for the XB-70 and Beyond North American Aviation. Wayne A Reinsch; Society of Automotive Engineers, Aeronautics Space Engineering and Manufacturing Meeting, Los Angeles, CA, October 3-7, 1966.

To Win a Nuclear War: The Pentagon's Secret War Plans. Michio Kaku and David Axelrod; South End Press, 1987.

Triplesonic Twosome. Steve Pace; Wings, Sentry Books, Granada Hills, California; Volume 16, Number 1; February 1986.

US Air Force ROTC Air University. Fundamentals of Aerospace Weapon Systems. U.S. Government Printing Office, 1961.

US Bombers: 1928 to 1980s. Lloyd S Jones; Aero Publishers, Inc., Fallbrook, California, Second Edition, 1980.

USAF Accident/Incident Report, USAF Mishap Report, and Accident Board Proceedings concerning loss of XB-70 #20207 and F-104 #813, 8 June 1966, with multiple attachments (181 pages).

United States Military Aircraft Since 1909, Gordon Swanborough and Peter M. Bowers; Smithsonian Institution Press, Washington, D.C., 1989.

United States Air Force History: An Annotated Bibliography. Mary Ann Cresswell and Carl Berger; Office of Air Force History, 1971.

War and Peace in the Nuclear Age. John Newhouse; Knopf Press, 1984.

*War by Other Means.*Jeffery Herf; Free Press/MacMillian Press, 1991.

World Mythology. Arthur Cotterell; Oxford Press, 1986.

XB-70: Greatest of Them All? Dave Nolan; World's Great Aircraft, 1972.

XB-70 Investigation, Memorandum for the Secretary of Defense. Department of the Air Force, Washington, D.C., August 12, 1966.

XB-70 Pilots Describe the World of Mach 3. Richard Slawsky; Airline Management and Marketing Magazine, Parts One and Two, March and April 1967.

XRS-70 Program: North American Aviation, Inc. 62-3-3. November 1, 1961.

XB-70 Program Engineering Effort to be Accomplished on Contract AF33(600)-42058 (31 July 1962 through 30 June 1964), North American Aviation, Inc. September 8,1962.

XB-70 Program Study (WS110A), Air Force Logistics Command Office of History, Wright-Patterson AFB,OH , February 3, 1964.

XB-70A Interim Flight Manual; USAF 1965

XB-70A Mach 3 Design and Operating Experience. W.A Spivak; Society of Automotive Engineers, Inc., New York, N.Y, 1966.

XB-70A Number One and Two Flight Hours Log and Flight Summary, Prepared by Engineering Flight Test, North American Aviation, Inc., July 1, 1966.

Air Vehicle Two banks hard to port over part of Edwards Air Force Base. *(USAF)*

62-0001 in it's proper environment -at high altitude. *(USAF)*

INFERNO...CONTROLLED

B-70's high speeds and tremendous cooling loads pose the most demanding environment control problems ever encountered

At 2,000 mph, skin temperatures of the USAF/North American B-70 will soar as high as 600°F. Yet the crew and avionic gear will function in ideal temperatures—from sea level to 70,000 feet.

To solve the plane's extraordinary operational requirements, Hamilton Standard is developing the most advanced and comprehensive environment conditioning system ever planned for an aircraft. It will provide completely automatic . . .

- cooling and pressurization of avionic gear and crew compartments
- emergency ram-air cooling and pressurization
- temperature control for drag-chute and landing-gear compartments
- moisture removal
- air-contaminant control

MAIN COOLING for crew and avionic compartments is provided by a closed vapor-cycle/air recirculation system and several closed-loop transport systems.

THE B-70 PROGRAM is an excellent example of Hamilton Standard's unmatched systems capability in environment conditioning and control. It incorporates skills and experience the company has amassed in creating systems for such advanced aircraft as the F-104, F-105, B-58, 880 Jet-Liner and over 40 other leading military and commercial planes.

HAMILTON STANDARD TODAY is a leading designer and manufacturer of aerospace equipment. Among current products at Hamilton Standard are advanced aircraft propellers, electronic equipment, engine and flight controls, and ground support equipment.

FURTHER INFORMATION on current Hamilton Standard programs and services is available. Your inquiry is invited.

UNITED AIRCRAFT EXPORT CORPORATION

East Hartford 8, Connecticut, U.S.A.